Guide to Damages

Guide to Damages

Simon Allen
Solicitor

Ivan Bowley
Barrister

Hugh Davies
Barrister

Published by Jordan Publishing Limited
21 St Thomas Street
Bristol BS1 6JS

British Library Cataloguing-in-Publication Data

A catalogue record for this book is available from the British Library.

ISBN 978 1 84661 051 6

Typeset by Letterpart, Reigate, Surrey

Printed in Great Britain by Antony Rowe Ltd, Chippenham, Wiltshire

The authors would like to dedicate this book to their families.

CONTENTS

FOREWORD TO THE FIRST EDITION

At a time when more and more of our energy seems to be spent arguing about legal costs, this new guide is a very welcome reminder of what it is really all about – properly compensating our clients for the consequences of injury.

This books is a practical guide, gathering together authoritative guidance on the principles of damages in one place for the busy practitioner. Most works on damages tend to concentrate on the case-by-case awards for general damages and/or on arcane methods of calculation of future loss awards for the catastrophic claim. But in this book the authors have admirably balanced their treatment of the subject so that it is a concise, user-friendly and, above all, practical one-stop shop for all claims.

I warmly welcome this book and whole-heartedly recommend it to personal injury practitioners.

David Marshall
(Former President APIL)

APIL is the UK's leading association of claimant personal injury lawyers, dedicated to protecting the rights of injured people.

Formed in 1990, APIL now represents over 5,000 solicitors, barristers, academics and students in the UK, Republic of Ireland and overseas.

APIL's objectives are:

- To promote full and just compensation for all types of personal injury;
- To promote and develop expertise in the practice of personal injury law;
- To promote wider redress for personal injury in the legal system;
- To campaign for improvements in personal injury law;
- To promote safety and alert the public to hazards;
- To provide a communication network for members.

APIL is a growing and influential forum pushing for law reform, and improvements, which will benefit victims of personal injury.

APIL has been running CPD training events, accredited by the Solicitors Regulation Authority and Bar Standards Board, for well over fifteen years and has a wealth of experience in developing the most practical up-to-date courses, delivered by eminent leading speakers, either publicly or in-house.

APIL training now runs almost 200 personal injury training events nationally each year, plus up to a further 100 meetings of our regional and special interest groups. Topics cover a wide range of subjects and are geared towards giving personal injury lawyers a thorough grounding in the core areas of personal injury law, whilst keeping lawyers thoroughly up-to-date in all subjects.

APIL is also an authoritative information source for personal injury lawyers, providing up-to-the minute PI bulletins, regular newsletters and publications, information databases and online services.

For further information contact:

APIL
11 Castle Quay
Nottingham
NG7 1FW

DX 716208 Nottingham 42

Tel: 0115 9580585
Email: mail@apil.org.uk
Website: www.apil.org.uk

ACKNOWLEDGEMENTS

The authors and publishers are grateful to Stephen Grime QC of Deans Court Chambers, Manchester, for kind permission to reproduce material which has been incorporated into the table in chapter 1 which illustrates the uplift in general damages for pain, suffering and loss of amenity following Heil v Rankin.

Crown Copyright material is reproduced with kind permission of the Controller of Her Majesty's Stationery Office.

TABLE OF CASES

References are to paragraph numbers.

TABLE OF STATUTES

References are to paragraph numbers.

TABLE OF STATUTORY INSTRUMENTS

References are to paragraph numbers.

CHAPTER 1

PAIN, SUFFERING AND LOSS OF AMENITY (GENERAL DAMAGES)

1.1 HEAD OF CLAIM

In the foreword to the first edition of the Judicial Studies Board Guidelines, Lord Donaldson stated that the assessment of general damages for pain, suffering and loss of amenity is 'one of the most difficult' tasks a judge in a civil court has to perform. There is no process of calculation for this head of damage. How is the level of damages assessed for someone who, for instance, loses a finger, or is blinded as the result of an accident? The courts have looked for a pragmatic solution[1] and have sought to arrive at 'a conventional figure derived from experience and from awards in comparable cases'.[2]

This head of damage consists of two elements: (1) pain and suffering (subjective) and, separately, (2) loss of amenity (objective). They are combined into a single head and it is inappropriate to separate them in making an award. It incorporates both physical and psychiatric injury, in respect of past, present and future loss.

1.2 PRINCIPLES OF ASSESSMENT

1.2.1 Pain and suffering

Damages are awarded for pain which the claimant feels consequent to an injury, both in the past and into the future. The level of damages will depend upon the duration and intensity of the pain and suffering. For example, where a claimant suffered third degree burns and died 10 days following the accident, as a direct consequence of the injuries, he received a sum of £2,500 for the pain and suffering aspect of the claim. If the claimant is unconscious or killed instantly as the result of an accident, there will be no damages under this head, although they may be recoverable for loss of amenity (ie for persistent vegetative state). The assessment is subjective and it is for the claimant to give evidence of the

---

[1]   Diplock LJ in *Every v Miles* (unreported) 1964, CA.
[2]   Lord Diplock in *Wright v British Railways Board* [1983] 2 AC 773.

effects of the injuries. This is made at the date of trial in order to provide the court with as full a picture as possible resulting in an award of damages in the money of the day.

Suffering is treated as distinct to pain. But the term 'suffering' is meant to cover the mental element of the injury, including the claimant's anxiety, fear, worry, distress and embarrassment caused by the injuries suffered in the accident.

1.2.2   Loss of amenity

Damages are awarded for the reduction in the ability of the claimant to perform everyday tasks and enjoy life, and it does not matter whether the claimant is conscious or not of the affect upon his life. It can include interference with hobbies and pastimes, loss of a skill or craft, a reduction in marriage prospects[3] and loss of enjoyment of a holiday,[4] or interference with the claimant's sex life.[5]

1.3   EVIDENCE

1.3.1   The claimant's statement

As with all heads of damages, but perhaps more importantly with damages for pain, suffering and loss of amenity, it is imperative that the claimant's statement describes life before the accident and life afterwards. The contrast between his capability and enjoyment of life before, and the limitations and restrictions endured and which he may continue to endure following the accident, is critical in providing the judge with a true picture of the impact of the injuries on the claimant.

The statement should record the past and future medical treatment, the operations he may have undergone, visits to hospital (eg physiotherapy) and, importantly, the mental anguish suffered by the claimant should be described. The claimant is under an obligation to outline how he feels about the injuries and their continuing residual effects. If he fails to do so, damages for the pain and suffering element of this head of damage will not truly reflect the loss he has suffered.

1.3.2   Statements from friends and family

Statements from friends and family can bolster the claimant's evidence in terms of the effect on his lifestyle and the suffering that he has undergone and continues to endure. Some claimants may be reluctant to reveal, in their witness statement or to members of the medical profession, the way

---

[3]   *Moriarty v McCarthy* [1978] 1 WLR 155.
[4]   *Ichard v Frangoulis* [1977] 2 All ER 461.
[5]   *Cook v JL Kier & Co Ltd* [1970] 1 WLR 774.

in which injuries affect them. Their partners/spouses may well be able to give a truer picture of the mental anguish that the claimant suffers.

1.3.3 Medical evidence

The report of the medical expert should include the following:

(1) The age of the claimant.

(2) Accurate details of the accident.

(3) A full history of the injuries suffered, the treatment provided, present condition and a prognosis for the future.

(4) Description of the limitation that the accident places on the claimant's working and social life.

(5) Indication whether there is a mental element to the claimant's symptoms, which depending on its severity can be investigated by separate psychiatric evidence.

(6) Confirmation that there is no past medical history of relevance in relation to the diagnosis and prognosis.

(7) Where there was a pre-existing injury, the likely future course of those symptoms but for the accident.

(8) Documents which the expert has read, including x-rays, scans, etc.

1.3.4 Photographs

In all cases where there is a noticeable physical deformity or scarring, photographs of the claimant pre- and post-accident should be produced. In cases of serious scarring, hospital photographs will be of good quality and will provide an excellent contemporaneous account of the nature of the injuries. Photographs taken soon after the accident are beneficial, not only to show the level of scarring or deformity, but also to support the claimant's claim for the distress suffered.

1.3.5 Hospital records

Hospital records may provide contemporaneous accounts of the claimant's pain and suffering, which may have receded by the time the claimant seeks legal advice. It will, of course, depend upon the quality of the notes.

1.3.6 Certificates

When claiming for loss of amenity on the basis of an interference with hobbies and pastimes, etc, proof of achievements in this field pre-accident will support the claim.

1.4 QUANTIFICATION

1.4.1 General

It is the job of the trial judge to make the assessment and to quantify damages. Reliance upon previous awards resulted in damages that increased gradually over time. However, there was a general recognition that awards for pain, suffering and loss of amenity were too low, and in 1996 the Law Commission recommended the following:

- awards to be increased by a factor of at least 1.5;

- but no more than 2 in respect of injuries for which the current award was not more than £3,000;

- tapered increases of less than 1.5 were recommended for damages between £2,000 and £3,000.

This was the background to the case of *Heil v Rankin*[6] in which the Court of Appeal considered a series of cases. In brief, the findings were as follows:

(1) For all cases in which general damages are assessed at less than £10,000 there was to be a nil increase;

(2) The maximum damages of £150,000 are to be increased by 33.33%, ie to £200,000;

(3) All cases between the two extremes outlined above were to be subject to a tapered increase in the award;

(4) The decision was to remain good law for some time;

(5) Thereafter, trial judges were to apply only inflation increases to the awards through the retail prices index;

(6) The Judicial Studies Board was to amend their guidelines by the introduction of a fifth edition to their book;

---

[6]   *Heil v Rankin* [2000] 2 WLR 1173, [2000] 3 All ER 138.

(7) It was right that the Court of Appeal consider the level of damages under this head and it was not a matter for Parliament.

The Court of Appeal provided a graph which illustrated approximately the necessary adjustment. However, it is difficult to define in terms which are not a multiple of £5,000. It is perhaps more clearly represented in table form, reproduced below:

Conventional award	Uplift
£10,000	0.0%
£20,000	2.4%
£30,000	4.8%
£40,000	7.1%
£50,000	9.5%
£60,000	11.9%
£70,000	14.3%
£80,000	16.7%
£90,000	19.0%
£100,000	21.4%
£110,000	23.8%
£120,000	26.2%
£130,000	28.6%
£140,000	30.9%
£150,000	33.3%

The practical effect of this is that for most fast track cases there will be no increase at all. For those that manage to reach the fast track upper limit of £15,000, an increase of 1.2% is applied, ie £179. The uplift increases by almost ¼% for each £1,000 of the conventional award so that for a mesothelioma sufferer damages are increased from £50,000 to £54,761. Finally, in cases involving moderate brain damage, where an award of £110,000 would previously have been awarded, the increase is 21.4% to £121,426.

It is important to note that post *Heil v Rankin* awards should continue to be increased in line with inflation.

1.4.2 Multiple injury claims/quantification

The claimant will often suffer injuries to more than one part of his body. Assessment of damages is calculated by looking at the individual injuries, ascertaining their individual value, adding them up and then discounting by a factor. It is largely impressionistic. Assistance may be gained from looking at other awards for multiple injuries and then standing back and comparing them with the claimant's overall disabilities. By way of simple example, if the claimant suffers a straightforward broken wrist, the loss of his index finger and a torn cartilage in his knee, the individual awards might be approximately £3,750, £9,500 and £10,000, the total damages being £23,000, where an award of no higher than £20,000 would be appropriate.

However, note that the court may not always apply a discount.[7] The claimant suffered head injuries and a de-gloving injury to the left foot together with damage to his hearing in the form of tinnitus. The general damages were assessed at £35,000 for brain injury, £20,000 for the foot injury and £4,000 for the hearing damage. The court simply aggregated those elements together to create the total damages figure with no discount as each injury was distinct and did not overlap.

1.4.3 Asymptomatic

Pleural plaques are localised areas of fibrous tissue on the lining of the lung. In 99 percent of cases they are asymptomatic. They are caused through asbestos exposure. In the past, these claims were usually resolved by a settlement of £5,000 on a provisional damages basis with a right to return in the event of a contraction of one of the more sinister asbestos illnesses. There are considerably more pleural plaques cases than any other asbestos condition. Pleural plaques occur in approximately 50% of persons with heavy and prolonged exposure to asbestos.[8]

In 2006[9] the Court of Appeal overturned a decision from Holland J who found that pleural plaques cases are actionable. The claimants' argument in the eleven test cases heard in the Manchester High Court was that the aggregation of the asymptomatic plaques, in combination with the risk of developing one of the more serious long term diseases and the anxiety such a prospect understandably creates, amounted to an injury which was actionable in damages. The Court of Appeal, with Lord Phillips giving the lead decision on behalf of Longmore LJJ and himself, found that despite pleural plaques 'blighting the lives' of some of the sufferers, as a matter of policy there was no legal precedent for aggregating three heads of claim which individually could not found a cause of action.

On appeal in June of this year, the House of Lords unanimously found against the appellants.[10] According to Lord Hoffmann, in order to recover damages the claimant has to be 'worse off'. Lord Scott astutely dismissed the aggregation point by stating that 'nought plus nought plus nought equals nought'.

---

[7] *George v Stagecoach SE London* [2003] EWHC 2042, [2003] All ER (D) 522 (Jul).

[8] Asbestos related lung disease O'Reilly, McLaughlen, Beckett & Sime. Vol 75 No 5 American Family Physician 3/07.

[9] *Rothwell v Chemical and Insulating Co Ltd* [2006] EWCA Civ 27.

[10] *Johnston v NEI International Combustion Ltd* [2007] UKHL 39.

In practical terms asymptomatic pleural plaques are not actionable. However, Lord Hoffman stated 'the rare victim whose plaques are causing symptoms is worse off on that account' and therefore can presumably succeed in damages.

In respect of asymptomatic pleural thickening and asbestosis claims, Lord Rodger (paragraph 88) stated that the mere possibility of future injury does not assist a claimant. Medical evidence will have to establish that there is a real risk of some deterioration and not a modest risk with the likelihood of the claimant remaining asymptomatic. Therefore, practitioners must ensure that their medical evidence addresses the issue with some precision and that the factors outlined in *Cartledge* are addressed.

Finally, Lord Scott made the observation that there may be an opportunity for a claimant to pursue a claim arising out of a breach of contract rather than in negligence. The difference being that damage need not result. One suspects that whilst, unlike the Court of Appeal, the House of Lords did not address policy considerations to defeat these cases they would look to introduce policy to defeat breach of contract cases.

An additional difficulty for claimants is that limitation will become a more pressing issue. A claim for breach of contract has to be pursued within a six-year period arising from the time of the breach. All claimants will necessarily be out of time and an attempt to rely upon sections 11 and 14 of the Limitation Act 1980 would result in a need to satisfy the criterion that the injury must be 'significant'. The House of Lords has already decided that pleural plaques are not significant.

The advice at the present time must be that when pursuing an asymptomatic diffuse pleural thickening or asbestosis case it should perhaps be amended to include a breach of contract claim.

1.5 CONCLUSION

There have been few reported cases since *Heil*. The Court of Appeal has avoided having to deal with appeals on quantum through its findings in *Heil*, combined with the growing importance of the Judicial Studies Board (JSB) Guidelines, which Smith LJ in the foreword to the seventh edition refers to as 'a vital part of the judge's and practitioner's kit'. Despite the fact that Lord Justice Staughton stated in *Arafa v Potter*,[11] that the guidelines are, 'not in themselves law and the law is to be found elsewhere in rather greater detail', they are presented in a convenient, logical and coherent form to assist judges in the assessment of general

---

[11] *Arafa v Potter* [1994] PIQR Q73, [1995] IRLR 316.

damages. Unfortunately, Lord Woolf's suggestion that they are merely 'a starting off point, rather than the last word' is often lost.

There have been few reported cases since *Heil*. The Court of Appeal has avoided having to deal with appeals on quantum through its finding in *Heil* and the growing importance and use of the Judicial Studies Board (JSB) Guidelines. These guidelines, which Smith LJ in the foreword to the 7th Edition refers to as '*a vital part of the judges' and practitioners' kit*', have developed an importance far beyond the expectation of Lord Justice Staughton who in *Arafa v Potter*[12] took the view that the Guidelines are 'not in themselves law and the law is to be found elsewhere in rather greater detail'. It is, however, because the Guidelines are presented in a convenient, logical and coherent form to assist judges in the assessment of general damages that Owen J in the introduction to the latest 8th Edition states 'in fact, it is now only in rare cases that courts make awards outside the margins reproduced in the Guidelines'. Lord Woolf's suggestion that they are merely 'the starting off point rather than the last word' is often forgotten.

---

[12] *Arafa v Potter* [2004] PIQR Q73, [1995] IRLR 316.

CHAPTER 2

DAMAGES FOR LOSS OF EARNINGS

2.1 HEAD OF CLAIM

Apart from maximum severity cases, which involve high care costs, loss of earnings is often the largest head of damage in a personal injury claim.

The objective of the award is to put the claimant in the position he would have been in if he had not sustained the injury.[1] In a simple case this should be a relatively straightforward exercise. The assessment becomes more complex with losses running into the future or where the number of uncertainties or 'imponderables' mean that a straightforward calculation is not possible.

For a claimant the most important consideration is to ensure that his evidence is sufficient to support each aspect of his claim. Losses claimed in the Schedule may disappear at trial due to lack of attention to small details that can have a significant impact on the value of the claim.

2.2 PAST LOSS

2.2.1 Basic principles

Where a claimant was in regular employment at the date of the accident or onset of disabling symptoms the calculation of loss of earnings up to the date of calculation or trial should be relatively simple.

In a straightforward injury case earnings loss is usually based upon an average of the claimant's net earnings for a period immediately preceding the injury. A period of 13 weeks is frequently used. The claimant should be able to produce his wage slips or evidence of income from bank statements. Alternatively this information may be provided by the employer.

---

[1]   *Hodgson v Trapp* [1989] AC 807.

If the claimant's income varies significantly over time, a longer period, say 6 to 12 months, may have to be looked at in order to calculate an average income.

Any irregular variations in income, such as bonus payments, should also be taken into account in calculating the likely earnings. Claimants should obtain some evidence that such irregular payments would have continued after the accident, either from the employer or by using a comparator.

2.2.2   Gross or net

Loss of earnings is always calculated net of tax and national insurance contributions.[2] If gross figures only are available a reasonably accurate net figure can be derived from the tables set out in the most recent edition of the PNBA publication *Facts & Figures*.[3]

2.2.3   Failure to declare earnings for tax/national insurance

The issue here is whether the claimant's source of income was itself illegal. If the income came from an illegal source the claimant cannot recover for any loss from this source during a period of injury or ill-health. See for example *Hunter v Butler*,[4] in which the deceased had been working while at the same time claiming State benefits and *Burns v Edman*,[5] in which the claimant was illegally moonlighting.[6]

Conversely if the income was earned legally, the claimant's failure to declare his earnings for the purposes of tax and national insurance is not of itself a bar to a claim.[7] The object is to compensate the claimant for his loss rather than permit the defendant to benefit, but in assessing the claimant's loss the court will deduct the tax and national insurance that the claimant *should* have been paying on his earnings.

2.3   PAST LOSS: COMPLEX CASES

2.3.1   Longer periods off work

Any increases in salary between the accident and trial must be reflected in the claim. These can usually be established from the employer, or, if

---

[2]   *British Transport Commission v Gourley* [1956] AC 185.

[3]   *PNBA Facts & Figures* (Sweet & Maxwell).

[4]   [1996] RTR 396.

[5]   [1970] 2 QB 541.

[6]   See also *Hewison v Meridian Shipping PTE* [2002] EWCA Civ 1821, in which the CA disallowed a claim by a merchant seaman for loss of earnings/loss of congenial employment which depended upon his continued deliberate concealment of his epilepsy.

[7]   See *Duller v South East Lancs Engineers* [1981] CLY 585 and *Newman v Folkes & Dunlop Tyres Ltd* (unreported) 2001, unreported at First Instance. Although the case went to the Court of Appeal the First Instance decision on this point was not appealed.

necessary, a comparator. Where the evidence is not available at the time of drafting a schedule, annual estimated salary increases may be based upon earnings related indices.

2.3.2 Short-term contracts

Many employees are now employed on short-term contracts, often for periods of no more than a few months. In such cases the claimant's employment history will have to be looked at in more detail and over a much longer period. It may be necessary to go back over several years to ascertain the proportion of each year that a claimant was in work and his income during each period of employment in order to establish some kind of pattern.

Evidence should also be obtained from the claimant's employer or potential employers about the availability and likely duration of future contracts.

In the most uncertain cases it may be necessary to look at local and regional labour conditions. In the absence of direct evidence a report from an employment consultant may be justified.

2.3.3 Self-employed

For the self employed, proof of post accident income may be more complex. The claim should include both loss of income (salary) and loss of business profit. Usually the claimant will have to produce accounts and/or tax returns for a number of years (at least three years if possible) to establish a pattern of income. A claimant who contends his business was becoming more successful than historical accounts suggest should produce evidence in the form of recent invoices or contracts. His statement must address the good will of the business and work in the pipeline.

A claimant may have been able to return to work but his business declines due to the ongoing effects of his injury/disease. The claimant's evidence must allow the court to distinguish between the genuine effects of injury and a downturn in work that would have occurred in any event. Evidence from business partners, other similar businesses, trade associations or forensic accountants may assist in this regard.

2.3.4 Partnership

Loss of profits will be based upon the claimant's share of the partnership. It is the claimant's contribution to the partnership that forms the basis of his claim.

In *Ward v Newalls Insulation Co*[8] the partnership was divided equally between the two working partners (one of whom was the claimant) and their respective spouses who were not working. This was a perfectly legal arrangement for tax purposes. The defendant argued that the claimant's loss was therefore only one-quarter of the partnership profits. The court rejected this and held that it should look instead at the reality of the partnership and the relative contributions from each partner. As the spouses contributed nothing to the partnership in real terms, they were left out of account in determining the claimant's loss, which was therefore half of the partnership profits.

2.3.5   Overtime

Overtime payments are usually structured as a multiple of the basic wage. Frequently, however, the availability of overtime fluctuates significantly and a claim based upon pre-accident earnings may not be representative of the situation during the period of loss.

Information about the amount of overtime available will have to be obtained from the employer. In some circumstances it may be necessary to use a comparator but the amount of overtime undertaken pre-accident should be sufficiently similar to justify the particular comparator relied upon. The claimant should also be asked whether there were any special circumstances that might have led to an increase in overtime, ie financial demands due to the birth of a child, college fees or to pay for a holiday.

2.4   FUTURE LOSS

The assessment of future loss is complicated by the fact that the court is required to evaluate a number of uncertainties. As the number of uncertainties increases so the court's ability to assess loss with anything approaching accuracy diminishes.

The conventional method of assessment involves the use of a multiplier/multiplicand, representing an annual loss sustained over a given number of years. Where the assessment of earnings is less straightforward, a more sophisticated use of the multiplier/ multiplicand approach may be required. In the most uncertain of cases the court will have to do the best it can to award a lump sum to reflect the claimant's loss (see para 2.4.1).

2.4.1   Multipliers

Multipliers are used to calculate future loss of earnings in all but the most speculative claims. Although multipliers are used to calculate future loss for a number of different heads (earnings, care, medical expenses, services,

---

[8]   [1998] 1 WLR 1722.

housing, transport etc) here they are dealt with specifically in relation to the calculation of lump sum awards for earnings loss.

The object of the multiplier is to provide the claimant with a lump sum that will as nearly as possible match the future loss, so that when the lump sum is invested both capital and interest will be used up at the end of the period in question. Ideally there should be no excess from which the claimant profits and no shortfall resulting in under-compensation. This is achieved by discounting the number of years' loss to reflect the fact that all of the damages will be received at the date of assessment.

Save for the most exceptional cases the discount rate for the vast majority of claims is currently 2.5%.[9]

The Ogden tables (reproduced at Appendix 3), appropriate for the gender of the claimant and the period of loss in question, should be used to determine the appropriate multiplier for the claimant's age *at the date of trial* and read from the 2.5% column.

2.4.2 Contingencies

The resulting multiplier is adjusted to take account of contingencies other than mortality. In previous editions of the Ogden tables the recommended discounts for contingencies have taken account separately of such factors as the prevailing level of economic activity and employment, geographical location and the nature of the claimant's job.

The current edition[10] of the Ogden tables reflects the results of two recent studies directed at the effect of contingencies on working life. This research suggests that both able bodied and disabled men and women of working age spend longer periods out of work than had previously been thought to be the case. A factor which appears to impact significantly on the time spent out of work is the level of educational qualification achieved by the particular claimant. Also relevant are whether the claimant was in work at the outset and whether the claimant is disabled. Differences in qualifications, disability and employment are reflected in the tables. Economic activity, geographical location and occupation have been shown to be less important and no longer feature.

The probable effect of the new tables is that awards for loss of earnings will fall.

---

[9] *Wells v Wells* [1998] 3 WLR 329; cf the rate prescribed by the Lord Chancellor under s 1(1) of the Damages Act 1996. Note that although the courts have the power to use a different rate (s 1(2)) the circumstances when this will be appropriate will be limited – see *Biesheuvel v Birrell* [1999] PIQR Q40.

[10] Ogden Tables (6th Edn).

The tables do not give figures for the appropriate deduction for ages above 54. In any event, and particularly for claimants aged over 54, the court should assess the appropriate multiplier according to the facts of the individual case, the tables being expressed to be a useful starting point and the appropriate multiplier ultimately being matter for judicial discretion based upon the evidence adduced at trial.

Example

An able bodied man aged 40. Employed as a teacher with a degree, intending to retire at age 65.

(i)   Multiplier to age 65 (Ogden 6th Edn. table 9): 18.01

(ii)   Discount for contingencies other than mortality (Ogden 6th Edn. Section B, Table A): 0.88

(iii) Appropriate multiplier: 0.88 × 18.01 = 15.85

The research suggests also that disabled men/women are likely to work for much shorter periods. Accordingly, for the example given above, assuming that the teacher was left with a permanent disability as a result of the accident, the multiplier for his residual earning capacity would be as follows:

(i)   Multiplier to age 65: 18.01

(ii)   Discount for contingencies other than mortality (Ogden 6th Edn. Section B, Table B): 0.57

(iii) Appropriate multiplier: 0.57 x 18.01 = 10.27

Note that this approach takes into account the claimant's residual disability after the accident, in which case there should be no need for an additional award under *Smith v Manchester*. However, it may be more appropriate, depending on the facts of the case, to seek a *Smith v Manchester* award instead.

2.4.3   Split multipliers

Not all claims allow the use of a single multiplier for the whole period of loss. A claimant may have a reasonable prospect of promotion at some identifiable point in the future or may intend to stop full time work at a particular age and carry on with some part time work for several years. In such cases the multiplier for the full period of loss should be derived as set out above but this should then be split between the various periods in question. There are a number of ways in which this can be achieved but splitting the multiplier simply according to the number of years in each period may produce an unjust result.

Example

A professional man with a degree aged 45 and earning £20,000 p a intends to work full time to age 55, thereafter he intends to work part time to age 65 earning about £5,000 pa. The working life multiplier for a male aged 45 to retirement at age 65 (Ogden 6th Edn. table 9) is 15.19. Discounts for contingencies other than mortality (say 0.86) may reduce this to about 13.06. If the multiplier is split equally for each 10-year period the total future loss would be as follows:

$$(6.5 \times £20,000) + (6.5 \times £5,000) = £162,500$$

However, as the loss in the first 10 years is more predictable a more accurate split should weight the respective periods. The multiplier for a 45-year-old to age 55 (Ogden 6th Edn. table 5) is 8.73. The current edition of the Ogden tables suggests using the same discount regardless of the retirement age – this may produce an unjust result but for present purposes, applying the same discount of 0.86 for contingencies gives a multiplier of 7.5. The balance of the multiplier of 15.19 less 8.73 is 6.46. Applying the same discount of 0.86 for the later period of 10 years gives a multiplier for this period of 5.55. The total future loss then becomes:

$$(7.5 \times £20,000) + (5.55 \times £5,000) = £177,750$$

The use of the same discount for both periods, while having the attraction of simplicity, does not reflect the fact that losses in the more distant future are less certain. It is therefore reasonable to expect judges to continue to apply a greater discount for contingencies other than mortality to more distant future losses.

2.4.4 Early retirement

Some cases involve injuries that can lead to retirement earlier than planned. The appropriate multiplier can be extracted from the relevant table (2.5% discount column) in the Ogden tables. For example, if, as a result of his injuries, the man aged 45 will have to retire at 55 instead of 65, the multiplier for the period of loss taken from the example given above will be 5.55.

2.4.5 Multiplicand

The multiplicand is based upon the claimant's annual loss. For an individual in regular full time employment up to the date of injury, but unable to continue working in any capacity because of his injury, the starting point will be his annual pre-accident net earnings as described above. If the claimant is able to continue working in some less well paid employment the multiplicand will usually be the difference between the earnings lost and the earnings now received and likely to be received into the future.

As the multiplicand for future loss is taken at the date of trial any historic salary increases should be reflected in the multiplicand.

In a simple case, therefore, the loss of future earnings will be based upon the multiplier for the number of years over which the claimant is likely to suffer a reduction in his earnings as a result of his injury and the difference between his pre-accident earnings and his likely future earnings.

2.5   ISSUES AFFECTING FUTURE LOSS OF EARNINGS

There are many issues affecting loss of earnings and these will obviously vary from case to case. Those that commonly arise in practice are set out in paras 2.5.1–2.5.5.

2.5.1   Employment history

Inevitably, the claimant with a consistent track record of employment is more likely to be able to convince the court that he would have remained in full time employment for the foreseeable future.

The claimant with a poor track record may overcome the potential difficulty in establishing his claim for future loss but the evidence required will have to be more convincing. The claimant's statement should account for any lengthy periods away from work as there may often be a simple explanation. The claimant may have taken time off because of a medical condition that has since been treated; he may have taken time off for retraining or to care for a disabled or sick parent or spouse. In each case, periods of apparent inactivity should not be assumed to reflect a poor track record of employment.

Similarly, a claimant who frequently changed jobs may also be able to provide a plausible explanation. He may simply have been seeking better-paid work or work with better promotion prospects.

A claimant may also have 'turned the corner' in his search for more secure employment. Evidence from an existing or prospective employer that long-term employment has now been secured can substantially increase the value of a claim.

A poor employment history or uncertainty about future employment will usually be reflected by a reduced multiplier.

2.5.2   Retirement age

Conventionally this has been 65 for men and 60 for women, coincident with entitlement to State Pension. The nature of the claimant's job often has a significant impact upon retirement age. Men involved in heavy manual work tend to stop work earlier than those in less strenuous occupations. Men in the forces or services usually serve fixed terms or face upper age limits. Conversely, there are now many occupations in which workers continue after 60/65. For many people, like the self-employed, there is a choice.

Factors other than the nature of the work are likely to influence retirement age. Recent falls in the stock-markets and pension funds have forced many people to reconsider their intended retirement age, sometimes necessitating working beyond 60/65.

Some do not stop work altogether. A claimant may have intended to stop full-time work but continue to work in some part time employment for several years.

In collating the evidence used to justify a particular retirement age, care should be taken to make use of all potentially relevant information. A claimant may have bought his house relatively late in life and still have many years of mortgage repayments ahead of him. The increased cost of further education, which is often born by the parents, obliges more people to work beyond 60/65.

2.5.3   Prospect of future promotion/future employment

A claimant in work with a real chance of promotion or re-deployment would be under-compensated if his loss of earnings did not reflect this chance. Inevitably future promotion is speculative but the court should do the best it can on the evidence to assess this chance.

The evidence required to support a claim that includes an increase in income due to promotion/re-deployment needs particular attention. A useful starting point may be statistical information on the proportion of workers in a particular occupation or workplace who go on to obtain promotion, and when such promotion usually takes place (ie average ages for promotion in the armed forces and/or police). If available, a claimant's personnel records should always be reviewed. Thereafter, the particular characteristics of the claimant must be taken into account in determining his chances of promotion and when this might have arisen.

In *Herring v MOD*[11] the CA stated that it was necessary in most cases to adopt a likely 'career model' for the claimant which fairly reflected his earning capacity. Where, as in that case, the trial judge had determined that the claimant would almost certainly have applied for and obtained particular employment, it was not necessary to make any discount for the risk that these eventualities might not have occurred. The chance that he would take up that employment or the risks that he might retire early would usually be irrelevant, provided that the career model chosen was a reasonable one, on the basis that the claimant would have found alternative employment of a similar nature.

A claimant does not necessarily have to prove on the balance of probabilities that he would have been promoted or obtained a better paid post, only that there is a 'real' or 'substantial' chance that this event will occur.

In *Doyle v Wallace*,[12] the claimant adduced evidence that he would have completed training and gone on to find employment as a teacher. The trial judge assessed the claimant's prospects of achieving this goal and obtaining a commensurately higher wage as not less than 50%. He accordingly assessed the loss of earnings as the mid point between the earnings as a teacher and earnings in clerical work. The Court of Appeal approved this approach, indicating that the claimant need not show that the chance of promotion was more than 50%.[13] However, this separate assessment of the chance of a career change need only be undertaken if the proposed career change is one that would significantly alter the claimant's earning capacity one way or another.[14]

Example

A man aged 45 expected to remain in his current job for the next 10 years, earning about £20,000 per annum (as at the date of trial). He intended to apply for promotion at about age 55 to a job which at the date of trial would have paid £28,000 per annum. The evidence indicates he had a 25% chance of securing that promotion. He intended to retire at age 65. The multipliers, as given above, are 7.5 and 5.55 respectively.

The multiplicand for the period from age 55 to 65 is:

$$£28,000 - £20,000 = £8,000$$

$$£8,000 \times 25\% = £2,000$$

---

[11]   [2003] EWCA Civ 528, [2004] 1 All ER 44. See also *Brown v Ministry of Defence* [2006] EWCA Civ 546, in which the effect of *Herring v Ministry of Defence* is explained.

[12]   [1998] PIQR Q146.

[13]   See also *Langford v Hebran* [2001] All ER (D) 169 (Mar).

[14]   *Brown v Ministry of Defence* [2006] EWCA Civ 546.

$$£20,000 + £2,000 = £22,000.$$

His total loss of earnings claims is therefore:

$$(7.5 \times £20,000) + (5.55 \times £22,000) = £272,100$$

2.5.4   Variation of future income

The court may be able to estimate with reasonable accuracy the likely level of earnings over particular periods. For the claimant who intends to reduce his working hours or take up part time work the working life multiplier will have to be split as set out above for the different multiplicands.

2.5.5   More speculative claims

The court should use the multiplier/multiplicand approach where it can, but ultimately it may be impossible to assess future loss with anything approaching accuracy. In such cases the court will have to determine the value of a lump sum for the loss of a chance of future earnings. This was the approach used by the trial judge in *Blamire v South Cumbria Health Authority*.[15] The Court of Appeal approved his broad brush approach to quantifying a lump sum award for future loss of earnings where there were so many imponderables that the multiplier/multiplicand approach was deemed to be inappropriate.

Such an award should not be confused with an award under *Smith v Manchester* for disadvantage on the labour market. The former is an award for continuing future loss of earnings, but in respect of which there are too many imponderables to be able to use the multiplier/multiplicand approach, the latter is an award for a contingent future loss: *Ronan v Sainsbury's Supermarkets Ltd.*[16]

2.6   MITIGATION OF LOSS

A defendant is only liable for such part of the claimant's loss as is properly to be regarded as caused by the defendant's breach. This has significant implications for loss of earnings claims.

A claimant will not recover damages for losses caused by his own 'unreasonable' actions (ie refusing to return to work when he is fit to do so). However, the burden is on the defendant to show that the claimant has acted 'unreasonably' in failing to mitigate his loss.[17] What is reasonable will obviously depend upon the particular circumstances of

---

[15]   *Blamire v South Cumbria Health Authority* [1993] PIQR Q1.
[16]   *Ronan v Sainsbury's Supermarkets Ltd* [2006] EWCA Civ 1074, (2006) 150 SJLB 921.
[17]   *Geest plc v Lansiquot* [2003] 1 All ER 383.

the case. A single man with no dependants and no ties to a particular geographical area may be expected to look further afield for suitable employment than a married man with children in local schools.

The evidence relevant to residual earning capacity may come from a variety of sources but the starting point is usually the medical evidence. The medical expert should identify as precisely as possible the kind of work that the claimant will be able to undertake.

Future employment may require retraining in which case account should be taken of the delay while retraining takes place. Note should be taken of when and where retraining is available. A six-month course does not necessarily start on the day that the claimant is fit to start retraining. There may also be an excessive demand for places on the appropriate course. All this should be investigated. In the final analysis, the complexity of the issues may necessitate expert evidence from an employment consultant who can deal with labour market conditions and the availability of work, likely periods of job search and retraining.

The cost of employment experts may not be recoverable on grounds of proportionality. In such circumstances, a claimant's advisers should obtain the necessary statistical information from the Employment Service.

2.7   AGE AT DATE OF ASSESSMENT

It will usually be relatively simple to calculate the loss of earnings for an adult claimant in full time work. At the other end of the scale the loss to an infant claimant sustaining catastrophic or permanent injury will be particularly difficult to evaluate.

2.7.1   Infancy

In the absence of any useful guide to the claimant's abilities or propensities the court will usually look to the parents and/or the wider family of the claimant and in particular their social, economic, educational and employment histories. A number of important questions need to be answered: what sort of education was and is the claimant likely to have, would he have gone on to further education, what was he physically capable of doing and what is he now capable of doing, and what qualifications is he likely to be able to obtain with his injuries.

In the absence of other information, courts tend to assume that the claimant would probably have followed a similar career path to his parents or siblings. However, even with the most detailed evidence it will usually only be possible to provide an approximate guide to earning potential. In *Cassel v Hammersmith and Fulham Health Authority*,[18] the

---

[18]   *Cassel v Hammersmith and Fulham Health Authority* [1992] PIQR Q1.

infant claimant aged eight years at the date of trial was rendered incapable of work by cerebral palsy. The trial judge heard a substantial amount of evidence about the claimant's family and background and described the claimant's family as 'well to do'. The claimant's paternal uncle, grandfather and great-grandfather all became QCs, and on his mother's side the family were all, in one way or another, distinguished. His parents intended to send him to Eton and the judge accepted that he was likely to go from there to university and thereafter to enjoy substantial earnings. From this information the trial judge concluded that the claimant would probably have earned in the region of 2½ times the national average earnings or equivalent to a partner in a medium-sized city firm of solicitors or accountants.

2.7.2   School age

Once the child has attained school age and particularly after a number of years at school it is usually possible to assess the academic abilities and personality of the child more accurately. The first and most important source of information will be the child's educational records but the headmaster/mistress and form teacher should also be asked to provide statements in addition to the claimant's parents. In some cases the instruction of an educational psychologist is justified.

An adolescent claimant may make a partial or complete recovery only to find that he has fallen too far behind his peer group to catch up. Where a child has fallen back to a lower year group damages should be claimed for the delay in commencing employment.

Cases of particular difficulty are those in which the injury/delayed recovery resulted in lower exam grades. A wide range of evidence will be required to substantiate the claim, ranging from the school reports, statements from class or subject teachers and even the intended university or college.

2.8   COLLATERAL BENEFITS

Care should be taken to claim for all additional earnings related benefits: company car, domestic or mobile telephone bills, fuel and health benefits.

2.9   PROCEDURE

CPR, r 16.4(1)(e) and PD16, para 4.2 require a claimant to serve a schedule of any past and future losses. Proceedings frequently have to be issued before the full extent of the loss can be ascertained or before all the evidence has been collated. This should not usually present a problem as long as the defendant is put on notice of each head of damage likely to be claimed and the basis upon which damages are sought.

CPR, r 16.3 requires the claimant to state the likely value of the claim. Where it is not possible to state the likely value, the claimant should say as much in the claim form (CPR, r 16.3(3)(c)).

2.10 DEDUCTIONS

Strictly, a claimant should give credit for any expenses usually incurred in obtaining his earnings which are not incurred during the period of loss. In a simple case, where a claimant paid for his travel to and from work his loss of earnings claim should be net of such costs.

CHAPTER 3

LOSS OF EARNING CAPACITY (*SMITH V MANCHESTER AWARDS*)

3.1 HEADS OF CLAIM

3.1.1 Development of head of claim

This head of damage compensates for an injured person's disadvantage in seeking employment in the labour market caused by the residual disability resulting from an accident. This is known as 'loss of earning capacity'.

The head of damage is often referred to as the 'Smith and Manchester' award after the Court of Appeal decision in the case of that name.[1] The case itself did not lay down a new principle of law but certainly marked the beginning of an increase in the claim for damages under this head of claim.

The eponymous Mrs Smith's loss resulting from the permanent limitation of movement in her right arm was identified by Scarman LJ:

> 'There was a real risk that sometime between now and the end of her working life, the plaintiff would find herself having to compete, disabled as she is, in the open labour market.'

Damages are awarded under this head as part of general damages. Lord Denning underlined the contrast between a continuing loss of earnings and loss of earning capacity in *Farley v John Thompson (Design and Contracting Division Ltd)*:[2]

> 'It is important to realize that there is a difference between an award for loss of earnings as distinct from compensation for loss of earning capacity. Compensation for loss of future earnings is awarded for real assessable loss proved by evidence. Compensation for diminution in earning capacity is awarded as part of general damages.'

Hughes LJ gave a helpful definition of what a Smith and Manchester award involves[3] when he stated 'a Smith v Manchester award is

---

[1]   *Smith v Manchester Corpn* [1974] KIR 17.
[2]   *Farley v John Thompson (Design and Contracting Division Ltd)* [1973] 2 Lloyd's Rep 40.
[3]   *Johnson v Warren* [2007] EWCA Civ 595.

appropriate when there is a real risk that at some time in the future the claimant will be out of work or in some cases, in poorer paid employment, when, but for the residual effects of the accident, she would be in work or in better paid employment'.

In *Woolley v Essex County Council*[4] the claimant failed to achieve an award under this head of damage because the court found that there was no shortage of work for men of the claimant's skills and there was nothing to suggest that his current employment was at risk; this is despite the fact that he was a man of 34 years of age.

3.1.2   *Smith v Manchester Corporation*

The case involved a 49 year old lady who slipped on a substance deposited on a floor surface at her place of work. In doing so she sustained injury to her right elbow and developed a frozen shoulder. Movement of her right arm was permanently impaired. At trial the employers gave an undertaking that they would keep Mrs Smith in their employment as long as they could properly do so. The trial judge awarded £300 for loss of earning capacity on the basis that, should she find herself looking for other work, her prospects would be considerably weakened as a result of her disability. The following factors were important in assessing the disadvantages, namely:

(1)   That she found that the work she was employed to do was, for a variety of reasons, no longer congenial to her.

(2)   The care home in which she worked may be closed down.

(3)   One must be realistic and accept the possibility that, despite the employer's best endeavours and undertakings, they may be unable to retain her services for a variety of reasons.

(4)   Because of her disability she is 'anchored' to that particular job.

The Court of Appeal increased her damages from £300 to £1,000.

3.2   PRINCIPLES OF ASSESSMENT

The question which has created complexity and uncertainty in respect of this head of damages is 'how do you value loss of earning capacity?'.

---

4   *Woolley v Essex County Council* [2006] EWCA Civ 753.

3.2.1   *Moeliker v A Reyolle and Co Ltd*[5]

A good starting point was identified in the case of *Moeliker*. Mr Moeliker, the claimant, was a 45 year old man who suffered a partial amputation of his left thumb and left index finger. He was employed as a central lathe turner and had worked for the defendants throughout his working life. He was a skilled man and a valued employee, earning £15,000 a year. The medical evidence showed that there was little pinch grip between what was left of his thumb and forefinger. He had difficulty in grinding small tools and using a micrometer. The defendants stated that it was very unlikely that he would lose his job with them, and if he did he could easily be diverted into another trade.

Browne LJ gave guidance on the questions that had to be answered in assessing the injured person's loss of earning capacity.

The two questions were:

(1)   What is the risk that the claimant will, at some time before the end of his working life, lose his job and be thrown onto the open labour market?

(2)   What is the value of the risk in financial terms should the claimant lose his employment (ie will he get other employment at a similar level)?

Having looked at the factors outlined and applied them to the claimant's situation the court assesses whether the risks are 'real' or 'substantial' as opposed to 'fanciful'. These terms are not necessarily easy to define and the courts have been reluctant to do so.

In *Moeliker*, Brown LJ stated that unless the risk of losing his employment was 'real' or 'substantial' then the claimant should receive no award. Stephenson LJ stated that if the risk in (1) or (2) was 'real' or 'substantial' but neither was serious the award should not be a token or derisory award but should generally be in the hundreds of pounds (in 1976!). A 'real' risk can be something less than a probability.[6]

Moeliker was followed by *Drummond v J Hewitt & Son (Fenton) Ltd.*[7] The court accepted that the claimant could also choose to leave his current employment rather than simply being forced onto the labour market by the employer making the decision for him.

The fact that a claimant is self-employed does not preclude an award under this head.

---

5   [1977] 1 All ER 9, [1977] 1 WLR 132.
6   *Robson v Liverpool City Council* [1993] PIQR Q78.
7   [1979] CLY 66.

3.3 EVIDENCE IN SUPPORT OF A CLAIM

While a lack of evidence to support the main claim is not fatal, the claimant risks a diminution in damages if he fails to provide the court with sufficient evidence on which to base an award. Lord Justice Laws stated:

> 'the absence of any particular reason to suppose that the respondent might be thrown onto the market means in my judgement that the award of £30,000 is much too high. The Judge was estimating the prospects of a contingency arising as to which there was no specific evidence'.[8]

To an extent, assessment of this head of damage is speculative but the foundation for a claim needs to be constructed. As most cases in which a 'Smith' award will be made will be of multi-track value, it is proportionate to devote time to attempting to collate this evidence.

The following evidence should be considered:

(1) The claimant should include evidence in relation to this head of damage in his statement or supplementary statement. A question-naire can identify the information required.

(2) Evidence on the business prospects of the current employer. A trade union/staff association representative may well be able to assist by providing a statement.

(3) Evidence from a witness(es) as to the restrictions placed on the claimant in performing his 'normal' duties in the workplace.

(4) Evidence from the claimant's doctor confirming the limitations placed on the claimant in the labour market.

(5) An Inland Revenue work history. This will outline how frequently the claimant has changed employment in his pre-accident life and provide an indication as to whether he is likely to find himself looking for other work in the future.

(6) Evidence from the Employment Service on the percentage of unemployed people in the claimant's travel to work area and, in particular, in relation to the job sector in which he qualified.

The evidence adduced by the claimant must show that any loss of mobility on the labour market is not 'inconsequential in terms of financial loss'.[9] The claimant received award for her disability on the open labour market following a road traffic accident in which she suffered a

---

[8]   *Evans v Tarmac Central Ltd* [2005] EWCA Civ 1820.
[9]   Per Sedley LJ in *Johnson v Warren* [2007] EWCA Civ 595.

fracture of the breast bone with subsequent PTSD. She no longer felt comfortable driving or being driven in a motor vehicle and physically was limited in attempting occupations involving strenuous activity, in particular bending, heavy lifting or carrying. However, she failed to achieve an award for two main reasons, namely:

1) Her employment history was largely clerical including work as a typist and telephonist, shop assistant and auxiliary nurse.

2) She lived in Greater Manchester which is well-connected by public transport and had a good range of clerical or equivalent work.

3.4 QUANTIFYING THE CLAIM

Providing guidance on placing a value on the claimant's disadvantage in the labour market has proved beyond the Court of Appeal in the past 30 years.

In *Smith v Manchester* Scarman LJ stated: 'There is nothing notional about the damages awarded for this item of loss'.

In assessing Mrs Smith's award of £1,000 in comparison to her annual income of £858, Scarman LJ said that the Court should look at things 'in the round'.

In *Moeliker*, Browne LJ stated that there is no standard or formula to be used in assessing damages and discounted the multiplier/multiplicand approach. Nevertheless, this approach, multiplying the annual net income of the claimant by a multiplier (historically up to five times the claimant's net income), has been adopted in a number of cases.[10]

There have been various comments throughout the years culminating in Taylor LJs observation in *Forey v London Buses*,[11] that:

> 'The exercise of finding the appropriate figure in a case as uncertain as this must necessarily be imprecise. It must involve weighing up all the circumstances as best one can and taking a stab at what is an appropriate figure.'

However, in recent years the multiplier/multiplicand approach appears to have been more commonly adopted. In broad terms, judges usually use a multiplicand of one year's net income and multiply this by a multiplier from a fraction of a year up to five years. There are lists of 'Smith' awards in *Kemp & Kemp*, vol 1. The *Herbert* decision of £50,000, which by today's valuation would be over £100,000, remains the highest. The great majority fall in the bracket which, by today's value, would be £5,000–£20,000.

---

[10] *Herbert v Ward* (unreported) 1982.
[11] [1991] 1 WLR 327, [1991] 2 All ER 936, [1992] PIQR P48.

On occasion, because of the number of imponderables that surround the assessment of a claimant's future loss of earnings, the court will abandon the conventional multiplier/multiplicand approach in favour of a lump sum.[12] The Court of Appeal in upholding the trial judge's award of the lump sum found that in trying to assess the two principle issues in that case, concerning the future earnings of a female nurse, assessment of the likely pattern of her earnings had she not been injured together with the likely pattern of her earnings given the fact that she had been injured was met with great uncertainty and factors such as having more children and doing part time work together with the reducing burden of her mortgage meant that the uncertainties were 'very great'. The judge was therefore entitled to award a lump sum as there was no perfect arithmetical way of calculating the compensation.

The distinction between a Blamire award and a Smith and Manchester award was set out in clear terms by Lord Justice Hughes[13] when he states:

> 'a Blamire award and a Smith and Manchester award may be combined but they are quite distinctive. The former is appropriate where the evidence shows that there is a continuing loss of earnings, but there are too many uncertainties to adopt the conventional multiplier and multiplicand approach to its quantification. It is an award for a contingent future loss, in the event of the claimant losing his current job where, as a result of the accident, he would then be at a handicap on the labour market at which he would not have been but for the accident.'

Proof of the rather arbitrary approach that can be adopted in assessing the Smith award was recently demonstrated in *Brown v Ministry of Defence*.[14] The Court of Appeal interfered with the trial judge's award of a year's loss of earnings for a physiotherapist who suffered an ankle injury, with a future risk of osteoarthritis which would require her to accept a more sedentary type of employment, by substituting the award with one of four months' earnings which, according to Moore-Bick LJ, was 'all that is appropriate in this case where the degree of disadvantage is unlikely to be very great'. The award was reduced to £5,000.

Most recently the amendments made to the calculation of future loss of earnings in the 6th edition of the Ogden Tables has created the opportunity for the judiciary to apply a strict mathematical approach to the calculation of the claimant's disadvantage on the labour market. The tables factor in the effect of disability and educational achievement to produce separate multipliers for both the pre-accident and residual earning capacity. Applying such an approach can create substantial awards under this head of damage which are far higher than any previously awarded.

---

[12] *Blamire v South Cumbria Health Authority* (1993) PIQR Q1.
[13] *Ronan v Sainsbury's Supermarkets Ltd* [2006] EWCA Civ 1074.
[14] [2006] EWCA Civ 546.

Example

Claimant's Details:

Male

Net Earnings £25,000 per annum.

Educational Attainment: Below GCSE grade C or CSE Grade 1 Passes.

Age at date of Trial: 45

Normal Retirement Age: 65

At the time of the accident, he was employed and not disabled. At the time of the trial he is still employed, but permanently disabled.

1.   Look up the base multiplier to retirement age (Table 9, at 2.5%) is 15.19

2.   Look up the deduction for an employed male who is not disabled (Table A). The figure is 0.86, so the reduced multiplier is 0.86 x 15.19 = 13.06

3.   Look up the deduction for an employed male who is disabled (Table B). The figure is 0.39, so the reduced multiplier is 0.39 x 15.19 = 5.92

4.   Calculate the reduction in the multiplier for disablement, 13.06 − 5.92 = 7.14

5.   Smith & Manchester Claim = 7.14 x £25,000 = £178,500

3.5   DISABILITY DISCRIMINATION ACT 1995

The Disability Discrimination Act 1995 should have diminished the need for damages under this head of claim. However, there are three main reasons why this head of claim continues to be important. First, the Act is rather toothless and disability continues to limit the opportunities for an injured person in the open labour market. Secondly, it is also true that that if a person is not capable of performing a role by virtue of their disability then the prospective employer will not have acted unlawfully. Thirdly, the provisions of the Act only apply to organisations with fewer than 20 employees.

3.6   CONCLUSION

Whilst we can assess the risks identified by Browne LJ in *Moeliker* and acquire the evidence to support our assessment, evaluation remains imprecise. The multiplier/multiplicand approach to quantification is commonly applied and may provide the best starting point.

CHAPTER 4

EARNING CAPACITY – LOSS OF A CHANCE

4.1 INTRODUCTION

An injured claimant may have had the chance of a future career path and consequent earnings that have ended as a result of the injuries suffered. There may be no certainty that he would have obtained the job that he wished for or the earnings that would flow from it.

A broad-brush approach may be adopted where it is difficult to be precise about the claimant's likely career path but for the accident. In *McKeown v Munday*[1] HHJ Price QC stated that 'the most difficult task I have in this case is to assess what would have been her [the claimant's] working life but for the accident'. The claimant was 16 years of age when she suffered a head injury and traumatic brain injury in a road traffic accident. Her concentration had been impaired by her injuries and it was agreed that she had been deprived of the opportunity of higher education and a career as an airline pilot, which she had previously set her heart upon. In trying to resolve the difficult task of ascertaining her future career but for the accident the judge considered as a starting point her educational history. He then looked at the family history in terms of their achievements before considering the 'fierce competition' between applicants attempting to become airline pilots. Unfortunately for the claimant the judge found that her prospects were speculative. The judge then sought to identify what other loss of opportunity had been suffered as a result of the accident. He found that the claimant would have gone to university and obtained a job commensurate with her qualifications. The family history was also one of achievement. The judge assessed quantum on the basis of average rates of pay for managers, administrators and professional occupations, giving a net annual income from which he could calculate her partial loss of earnings.

At times, trying to fit the calculation of this head of damages into a mathematical computation verges on the impossible. Nonetheless, it is encouraging to see that judges attempt to produce an award even in such difficult circumstances.[2] Mr Justice Christopher Clarke, in a case

---

[1]   (Unreported) 12 March 2002, QBD.
[2]   *Appleton v Medhat Mohammed El Safty* [2007] EWHC 631, QBD.

involving a footballer whose career had been terminated as a result of clinical negligence, found that in estimating the number of possible permutations of chances the claimant had of getting a job or jobs and for how long they would last 'comes close to speculation'. However, he found that it would be unjust to decline to make an award because of the difficulty.

Where the future is more predictable, for example if the claimant has already embarked upon a particular career, the judge may quantify loss of future earnings by reference to the loss of a chance, in accordance with the principles set out in *Doyle v Wallace*[3] and *Langford v Hebran*,[4] considered further in para 4.2.

4.2   LOSS OF A CHANCE

In *Doyle v Wallace* the claimant was 19 years old when she suffered moderately severe brain damage in a road traffic accident. As a result she lost the opportunity of working as a drama teacher. The judge at first instance found that there was a 50% chance that she would have obtained the necessary qualifications and become a drama teacher, instead of undertaking less well paid clerical work.

Relying upon the House of Lords' decision in *Hotson v East Berkshire Area Health Authority*[5] the defendants argued that the claimant had to show that she would have become a drama teacher on the balance of probability.

The Court of Appeal, approving *Allied Maples v Simmons and Simmons*,[6] rejected the defendants' argument and drew a distinction between what had to be proved on the balance of probabilities and what fell within the realm of loss of a chance. In *Allied Maples v Simmons and Simmons* Stuart-Smith LJ identified three different types of situation. The first was where the defendants' act consisted of some positive act or misfeasance and the question of causation was one of historical fact; the second involved cases where the defendants' negligence consisted of an omission where causation depended not upon historical fact but upon the answer to the hypothetical question: 'what would the claimant have done if there had been no negligence?' In each case the question was one of causation according to the balance of probabilities. The third situation was where the claimant's loss depended upon the hypothetical action of a third party, whether in addition to the claimant's act or independent of it. In this situation Stuart-Smith LJ stated that the claimant need only show that he had a substantial chance of the third party acting to his benefit. This chance could be less than 50%.

---

3   [1998] PIQR Q146, CA.
4   [2001] All ER (D) 169 (Mar).
5   [1987] AC 750.
6   [1995] 1 WLR 1602.

The Court of Appeal in *Doyle* found that the claimant's situation fell into Stuart-Smith LJ's third category. Accordingly, although she could not prove on the balance of probabilities that she would have become a dance teacher, the judge was correct to include within the loss of earnings award 50% of the *additional* earnings she might have received as a teacher rather than a clerical worker.

4.3   PRINCIPLES OF ASSESSMENT

Both *Doyle* and *Allied Maples* confirm that the claimant still has to show that the chance was 'significant' or 'substantial' and not 'speculative' or 'fanciful'. The distinction is illustrated by the case of *Bonham v Hanrahan*.[7] Miss Bonham was a 'bubbly young 20 year old' at the time of the road traffic accident in which she sustained significant burn injuries. She claimed that she had thereby lost the chance of becoming a model. Prior to the accident she had been encouraged to have photographs taken by someone who purported to run a modelling agency. After the photographs were taken the claimant did not hear from the individual again and did nothing to further her career in modelling. Witness evidence was called to say that she 'could have had a future in the modelling industry at some level'. In rejecting the claim for loss of this chance the trial judge observed that many young women have a dream of a career in modelling but the dream must have 'some quantifiable reality' which in this instance it did not.

4.4   COMPLEX CASES

In *Langford v Hebran* the Court of Appeal extended the principle set out in *Doyle v Wallace* to a complex case involving multiple lost opportunities. The claimant had been a hod carrier for 10 years and for a few months had been a trainee bricklayer. He had also been the World Light Middleweight Kickboxing champion for 10 months at the time of the accident and had gone on to win his one and only professional fight. His second was cancelled because as Lord Justice Ward stated 'his opponent got cold feet at the weigh in'. The claimant was restricted by his whiplash injuries to hod carrying and kickboxing to a standard below that which he had previously been capable of. A number of scenarios were presented to the court in relation to the claimant's prospects as a professional kickboxer. These were as follows:

(1)   he would have held a national or European title;

(2)   he would have held a national or European title and then moved to the USA and won other titles;

---

[7]   (Unreported) 19 January 2001, QBD.

(3) he would have been World Champion for one year;

(4) he would have held the world title for more than two years.

The Court of Appeal looked at the four scenarios and found that the claimant had real chances of achieving each one, which they assessed as follows: scenario 1 – 80%, scenario 2 – 66%, scenario 3 – 40% and scenario 4 – 20%. In each case the claimant's loss was the chance of the *additional* earnings that he would have received if he had achieved that scenario, ie in respect of scenario 1 the calculation of past loss was as follows:

Scenario 1

If the claimant had achieved scenario 1 he would have earned £9,628.

The chance of achieving scenario 1 was 80%.

The claimant's loss was therefore:

$$£9,628 \times 80\% = £7,702$$

This method was then applied to each of the remaining scenarios as follows.

Scenario 2

If the claimant had achieved scenario 2 he would have earned £18,996.

His additional earnings over and above scenario 1 would then have been: £18,996 – £9,628 = £9,368.

The chance of achieving scenario 2 was 66%.

The claimant's loss was therefore:

$$£9,368 \times 66\% = £6,183$$

Scenario 3

If the claimant had achieved scenario 3 he would have earned £46,315.

His additional earnings over and above scenario 2 would have been: £46,315 – £18,996 = £27,319

The chance of achieving scenario 3 was 40%.

The claimant's loss was therefore:

$$£27,319 \times 40\% = £10,927$$

Scenario 4

If the claimant had achieved scenario 4 he would have earned £49,881.

His additional earnings over and above scenario 3 would have been: £49,881 – £46,315 = £3,566.

The chance of achieving scenario 4 was 20%.

The claimant's loss was therefore:

$$£3,566 \times 20\% = £713$$

The claimant's total past loss of earnings was consequently as follows:

£7,702 + £6,183 + £10,927 + £713 = £25,525. The Court of Appeal used the same methodology to calculate future loss, applying appropriate multipliers for each scenario.[8]

4.5 EVIDENCE

The principal difficulties for a claimant will be establishing a prospective career path and establishing the percentage chance of a particular event occurring. Defendants will inevitably invite the court to adopt a broad-brush approach by arguing that the whole assessment of future loss in such circumstances is too speculative. It is vital therefore, if a claimant is going persuade the judge to adopt the approach in *Langford*, that the evidence adduced in support goes far enough.

The claimant's statement is of critical importance. It should outline his proposed career path in some detail. It should list his educational and professional qualifications (supported by documentary evidence where possible) and any steps he has taken to progress his chosen career. It should also outline alternatives in the event that the chosen career is not accepted by the court.

Supporting witnesses are of almost equal importance. These witnesses should provide hard evidence of the claimant's potential and/or ambition to realise his chosen career. To that extent they can range from the professional, commenting on the claimant's prospects, to the relative confirming that 'it was always something he wanted to do'. In *Dawber v British Rail*,[9] Mr Dawber worked on the railways and had taken up

---

[8] The approach set out in *Langford* was subsequently applied by the CICA in the case of *Fergus* in July 2001.

[9] (Unreported) 12 March 2002, QBD.

playwriting. He contracted mesothelioma. At trial the director, Ken Loach, gave evidence as he was about to film the first of Mr Dawber's plays which, following the claimant's death, was shown on national television.

The claimant will have to produce evidence of his potential earnings in each scenario. This may come from a variety of sources including the New Earnings Survey, comparators or relevant professional or trade bodies. An employment expert may be of value in assessing the chance of the claimant achieving a particular position.

Detailed calculations, adopting the methodology set out above, should be served as soon as possible, and preferably with the statement of case/Particulars of Claim.

4.6   CONCLUSION

The courts are becoming more willing to award damages for future loss of earnings providing the claimant can show that there was at least a significant chance that he would achieve his ambition to pursue a chosen career. As long as the case falls within Stuart-Smith LJ's third category there is no requirement to show that the chance of a particular career being achieved was greater than 50%, but the evidence the claimant produces must be persuasive in order to avoid a finding that the claim is speculative.

CHAPTER 5

DAMAGES FOR LOSS OF CONGENIAL EMPLOYMENT

5.1 HEAD OF CLAIM

'The joy of the craftsman in his craft was beyond price'.[1]

We spend approximately 8 hours a day, 5 days a week, from the age of 16 to 60 at work. Stress from performing an occupation is now the main cause of absence from the workplace in the United Kingdom. It costs approximately £7 billion a year in lost production and is a growing problem. Conversely, for a claimant who enjoys his job, to lose employment through injuries caused in an accident creates financial loss but may also have a mental impact in respect of loss of job satisfaction. This loss is titled 'loss of congenial employment'.

This head of damage was conclusively recognised in *Morris v Johnson Matthey*.[2] In *Morris* an increase in the general damages award by £1,000 was made to reflect the loss of his craft. He had suffered hand injuries preventing him from exercising skills as a precious metal worker. He had been re-employed as an assistant store man but such work he found 'at times rather boring'. A number of subsequent cases in the 1970s and 1980s resulted in the separation of this head of damages away from general damages for pain, suffering and loss of amenity culminating in *Hale v London Underground Ltd*[3] in which Otton J stated that loss of congenial employment was a separate head of damage.

5.2 ASSESSMENT

The courts have provided no formula for assessing damages under this head. In arriving at an award, rather like general damages for pain and suffering, the courts look at the age of the claimant, the job that he has lost and the background evidence in relation to his enjoyment of the job. In the 1980s and early 1990s it was perceived that there was a maximum award of £5,000. Older claimants, in particular, would receive much less.

---

[1] Edmund Davies LJ in *Morris v Johnson Matthey & Co Ltd* (1967) 112 Sol Jo 32.
[2] Edmund Davies LJ in *Morris v Johnson Matthey & Co Ltd* (1967) 112 Sol Jo 32.
[3] [1993] PIQR Q30.

5.3   EVIDENCE

The claimant has to show that he has lost employment that was congenial. Some claimants will fail to do this because they will not be able to show that their employment was enjoyable. It is therefore important that the claimant's proof of evidence is comprehensive in considering the factors that give rise to this head of damage.

This is demonstrated by the claimant in *Lane v The Personal Representatives of Deborah Lake (decd)*[4] in which the claimant construction site project manager lost his employment but was able to show the High Court Judge that he had always been a hard worker who enjoyed his work in the building industry. His Lordship stated:

> 'He told me with feeling that he loves his work, always wanted to be a carpenter and that when he was a lad he used to love going onto sites with his father. I suspect it is one of the things he misses most.'

A sum of £5,000 was awarded. The claimant was able to show that despite commencing his working life as an apprentice joiner and carpenter, he subsequently had achieved a City and Guilds Craft Certificate in Carpentry and Joinery with a credit for his written work and distinctions in assignments and on course-work assessments; and then subsequently obtained the Advanced Crafts Certificate in Carpentry once more with credits in site procedure, site practice and course-work assessment.

The need for the claimant to demonstrate the congeniality of the employment was further demonstrated in *Hanks v The Ministry of Defence*.[5] The claimant had been a naval pilot who suffered a neck injury resulting in his discharge from the Navy and ended his anticipated career of flying jets, for which he had begun training. He was able to show the court that at school he had joined the RAF section. On joining the Navy a report on his progress concluded 'during his time in the Royal Navy, Hanks has ably demonstrated he has excellent all-round qualities and an abundance of potential. He is an officer that the Service can ill-afford to lose'. Royce J accepted that he was very much looking forward to 16 years flying with the Royal Navy and thereafter working as a pilot in civil aviation. An award of £9,000 was made.

5.3.1   The proof of evidence

(1)   The nature of the job;

(2)   the qualifications of the claimant to perform that job;

---

[4]   (Unreported) 18 July 2007, QBD, John Leyton Williams QC, sitting as a Judge of the High Court.
[5]   [2007] EWHC 966, QB.

(3) the intellectual or physical requirements of the job that make it challenging;

(4) the level of skill that the claimant has had to acquire to perform the job;

(5) the training that he has undertaken both in-house and externally to do the job better;

(6) the career development/job prospects;

(7) the job security;

(8) the length of time that the claimant has performed the job;

(9) the environment in which the claimant performs the job;

(10) the social factors associated with the work, eg camaraderie, team working, etc;

(11) whether the job has a vocation, eg public servants;

(12) whether the job has a perceived value to the general public.

The claimant's personnel file may well provide valuable information in terms of his performance at work and his prospects. Equally it may harm his claim for damages by suggesting he is de-motivated and does not enjoy the work.

5.3.2   Witness evidence of colleagues

The claimant may well say that he enjoys a job. Supporting evidence from colleagues confirming that he does and/or that they equally do when performing the same tasks will be helpful.

5.3.3   Witness statement of the claimant's partner

Spouses are usually all too well aware of whether the injured person enjoys their work or not and can provide a succinct analysis of how much the job meant to their partner.

5.3.4   Certificates/qualifications

Documentary proof of educational/training qualifications will be within the claimant's possession and should be disclosed.

5.4 QUANTIFICATION OF CLAIM

Past awards provide a useful starting point. Ensure that the appropriate inflation factor is applied to work out the current level of damages. Previous cases will not provide the full picture but will give the fundamental information as to the age of the claimant and the work that he was performing to enable a comparison to be made. Specific, subjective factors relevant to a particular claimant can then be introduced to complete the valuation of the head of damages.

In *Willbye v Gibbons*[6] it was suggested by counsel for the defendant that awards for loss of congenial employment rarely exceeded £10,000. Kennedy LJ responded by stating that 'in my judgment, it is important to keep this head of damages in proportion'. The claimant was awarded £5,000 but there was no indication given that awards should, in the main, fall within this financial limit.

Notably in *Hanks v Ministry of Defence*, the judge took account of this decision whilst still awarding a sum of £9,000.

Most recently the highest award under this head of damage was made by Mr Justice Christopher Clarke[7] for a professional footballer who lost the ability to play when he was approaching the peak of his playing years. The court found that 'to play professional football at the highest level is many a schoolboy's dream. To do so was the claimant's passion'. His Lordship held that 'the exceptional facts of this case justify a separate award of £25,000'.

In Lane, counsel for the defendants suggested that this head of damage was reserved for policemen, firemen and the like. The judge accepted that whilst awards are frequently made to such individuals, an award ought to be confined to 'those who truly have suffered a loss' under this head. An award should not be made merely by reference to the type of employment carried out by the claimant.

5.5 CONCLUSION

Loss of employment that is not readily replaced by an equally enjoyable position merits compensation. The courts are now willing to recognise this and awards amounting to a little over £10,000 are being achieved. Comprehensive evidence from a claimant on the loss of his employment is the key to successfully achieving an award.

---

[6] [2003] EWCA Civ 372.
[7] *Appleton v Medhat Mohammed El Safty* [2007] EWHC 631.

CHAPTER 6

PENSION LOSS

6.1 INTRODUCTION

It is well established that in personal injury cases, the claimant should receive damages for loss of earnings and expenses in a sum that will put him in the same financial position in which he would have been but for the injuries.[1] A claim for loss of pension entitlement should be considered in addition to a claim for loss of earnings. This chapter sets out when such a loss arises and how to calculate such a loss, and examines practical issues relating to this head of damage.

6.2 OCCUPATIONAL PENSION SCHEMES

During an employee's working life, monies are set aside by his employer and paid into a pension scheme. These monies accumulate until the employee retires. On retirement he has two options:

(i)   to take an annual retirement pension; and/or

(ii)   to commute (change) up to 25% of his pension fund to create a tax free lump sum together with a reduced annual retirement pension.

If an individual loses his employment as a result of injury or disease then the payments into his pension fund will cease on the date of his ill-health retirement. At that date he will receive an ill-health pension as occupational pension schemes usually provide for a reduced pension in the event of early retirement due to injury or ill health. He will continue to receive his ill-health pension until he reaches normal retirement age and beyond. At normal retirement age his colleagues, who continued working, will receive their retirement pension. The injured man will find that his ill-health pension is not as great (both in terms of annual pension and lump sum) as that enjoyed by his colleagues. This is his pension loss.

---

[1]   *Liesbosch, Dredger (Owners) v SS Edison (Owners)* [1933] AC 449.

The majority of employees will choose to commute part of their pension to create a lump sum because it is tax-free. In calculating pension loss it is helpful to consider loss of annual pension and loss of lump sum separately.

6.3   EVIDENCE

Certain information is necessary in order to calculate pension loss. The following list is the bare minimum required:

–   A copy of the pension scheme or at the very least the formula used to calculate pension entitlement;

–   Claimant's date of birth and age at date of trial;

–   Value of the ill-health pension at date of trial;

–   Per cent of the ill-health pension commuted and the lump sum received;

–   Age when claimant would have retired if uninjured;

–   Earnings claimant would have received at the date of trial if uninjured.

6.4   WORKED EXAMPLE

6.4.1   Simple annual pension loss

The following is a worked example of a very basic pension loss calculation. In the example given the claimant is an unmarried female:

6.4.2   Facts

Date of birth:	1.1.67
Age when started work:	20
Age at accident:	35
Age at medical retirement:	37 (2004)
Age at trial:	39 (2006)
Normal retirement age if uninjured:	60
Salary at ill-health retirement:	£15,000 per annum
Salary at date of trial:	£20,000 per annum

Annual pension: number of years service × 1/80 × salary.

Stage 1: Calculate the net annual pension loss at the date of normal retirement

The starting point is to note that the ill-health pension is deductible from the claimant's losses but only from the claim for loss of pension and not from the loss of earnings claim.[2]

(i) Pension at date of ill-health retirement when aged 37:

$$17 \text{ years service} \times 1/80 \times £15,000 = £3,188.$$

By the date of trial this has increased annually so that it is now worth £3,400 per annum

(ii) Pension at date of normal retirement (aged 60):

$$40 \text{ years service} \times 1/80 \times £20,000 = £10,000.$$

(iii) Resulting annual pension loss:

$$£10,000 - £3,400 = £6,600.$$

Stage 2: Calculate the total annual pension loss after normal retirement

The claimant is being compensated for the loss of pension she would have received at normal retirement from age 60 for the remainder of her life. The multiplier is therefore for the period from age 60 for life. This is then discounted to reflect the fact that the claimant is receiving the money early, at the date of trial (accelerated receipt).

The resulting multiplier, depending upon the claimant's age at trial, the age of normal retirement and gender, can also be read from Ogden tables 15-26 which already take into account the discount for accelerated receipt.

In the worked example the multiplier, taken from Ogden table 20, is 11.29.

The claimant's total annual pension is therefore:

$$£6,600 \times 11.29 = £67,514.$$

Stage 3: Discount for contingencies

The pension loss should usually be discounted for contingencies other than mortality. This is dealt with in more detail below.

---

[2]   *Parry v Cleaver* [1970] AC 1. *Smoker v London Fire and Civil Defence Authority* [1991] 2 AC 502, 2 All ER 449.

For the worked example a discount of 10% is assumed. The total annual pension loss is therefore:

$$£74,514 \times 90\% = £67,063.$$

6.4.3   Loss of lump sum

The claimant in the worked example was in a pension scheme which paid a lump sum of 3 x annual pension at retirement.

Stage 4: calculate lump sum loss

(i)   Lump sum at normal retirement:

$$3 \text{ years} \times £10,000 = £30,000.$$

(ii)   Discount for accelerated receipt.

As above, the claimant is receiving the lump sum early. The period from the date of trial in 2006 to the date of normal retirement in 2027 is 21 years.

Discount for fixed period of 21 years (Ogden table 27) = 0.5954.

$$£30,000 \times 0.5954 = £17,862.$$

(iii) Discount for contingencies other than mortality (10%):

$$£17,862 \times 90\% = £16,076.$$

Stage 5: Offset proportion of lump sum received at ill-health retirement

The lump sum received at ill-health retirement is essentially part of the annual pension that the claimant would have continued to receive for the rest of her life. In a simple annual pension loss claim the claimant gives credit for the ill-health pension received during the period of pension loss after normal retirement.[3] The question of how this should be applied to the lump sum was considered in *Longden v British Coal Corpn*.[4] The effect of the decision in *Longden* is that only the proportion of the lump sum (received at ill-health retirement) which is referable to the period of pension loss after normal retirement should be deducted.

In the worked example the deduction is therefore as follows:

---

[3]   See *Parry v Cleaver* and *Smoker v London Fire and Civil Defence Authority*, above.
[4]   [1998] AC 653.

(i)   At medical retirement the claimant received a lump sum of

$$3 \times £3,188 = £9,564.$$

(ii) The multiplier for the period of pension loss from normal retirement at age 60, at the date when the claimant was medically retired (age 37), is 10.60 (Ogden table 20).

(iii) The multiplier for life at the date of ill-health retirement is 27.89 (Ogden table 20).

(iv) The post-retirement proportion of the lump sum to be deducted is therefore:

$$10.60/27.89 = 38\%.$$

(v)   The amount of the lump sum received at medical retirement to be deducted from the claim is therefore:

$$£9,564 \times 38\% = £3,634.$$

(vi) The total lump sum loss is therefore:

$$£17,862 - £3,634 = £14,228.$$

6.5   DISCOUNTS

In the worked example set out above a discount of 10% to reflect contingencies other than mortality has been assumed. The justification for a discount is the possibility that the claimant may not have continued to make or receive regular pension contributions to his pension fund until his anticipated retirement. There may be many reasons for this including poor job security, redundancy, dismissal or supervening ill-health.

The approach to determining the amount of discount is inherently imprecise. In *Auty v National Coal Board*[5] the 34-year-old claimant's award was discounted by 27% for the remaining 31 years to normal retirement (or 0.871% per annum). This became something of a standard deduction until the House of Lords in *Page v Smith* approved a discount of 10% for a period of 34 years.[6]

5   [1985] 1 All ER 930.
6   [1995] 2 WLR 644. In *Phipps v Brooks Dry Cleaning Service Ltd* [1996] PIQR Q100, the trial judge applied a discount of 5% against pension loss in respect of a lost years claim for a 51 year old male who would have retired at age 60. The Court of Appeal commented that this was on the low side but did not interfere with the figure.

6.6   CLAIMANT'S CONTRIBUTIONS

Contributions to an occupational pension of the type referred to in the worked example above are usually made by both the employer and the employee. It is important to note that if a claim for an occupational pension loss is being pursued the claimant should give credit for any pension contributions that he or she would have made from earnings against the earnings loss claim.

6.7   PRIVATE SCHEMES

Not all claimants will have the benefit of an occupational final salary scheme. Some claimants will have made their own private pension arrangements. If the claimant has lost his job and can no longer make any pension contributions or has a temporary break in income due to his inability to work, there will be a shortfall in his fund at the date of normal retirement. In such cases there are two alternative approaches to calculating pension loss:

(i)   Claim the 'lost' contributions (which the claimant should then pay into his pension fund). The loss is calculated in the usual way using a multiplier and multiplicand, discounted for contingencies.

(ii)   Calculate the difference in pension at normal retirement. Again, the loss can be calculated using a multiplier and multiplicand for the period of pension loss. Alternatively, a quote can be obtained from a pension provider for the lump sum necessary at trial to make up the shortfall.

Where the claimant is able to continue contributing to his pension scheme from his loss of earnings claim and where there are no additional contributions from a third party there is no separate pension loss claim.

6.8   WIDOW'S PENSION

Many pension schemes provide for a widow's pension to be paid in the event of the claimant's death. This is often calculated as a percentage of the claimant's pension. Where the scheme provides for a widow's pension the pension loss claim should include the reduced widow's pension.

(i)   The multiplicand will be the difference between the pension that the claimant's widow would have received and the pension she will now receive when the claimant dies.

(ii)   The multiplier is the difference between the claimant's life expectancy and that of his wife, discounted for the period from the date of trial to the claimant's anticipated date of death.

Example

Male aged 40 with a life expectancy of about 41 years

Claimant's wife is aged 38 and has a life expectancy of about 47 years

Claimant's annual pension loss is £5,000 per annum

Claimant's widow is entitled to 50% in the event of his death: £2,500

Multiplier for fixed period of 6 years is 5.58

Widow's pension loss is therefore £2,500 × 5.58 = £13,950

Discount for accelerated receipt of 41 years is 0.3633

Loss is therefore £13,950 × 0.3633 = £5,068.

6.9   FATAL ACCIDENTS ACT CLAIMS

A dependency claim under the Fatal Accidents Act 1976 should include any past and/or future dependency on the deceased's occupational or private pension. However, the widow's pension, which the widow receives as a result of her husband's death, is not deductible from the damages claimed.[7]

The same consideration may apply in respect of State pension but it depends upon the entitlement of the widow to her own State pension at retirement. If the claimant widow is entitled to her own Category A State pension at normal retirement (based upon her own national insurance contributions) this will have to be deducted from the pension dependency as the claimant would have received this in any event. Conversely, if the claimant was dependent upon her husband's national insurance contributions in order to qualify for a State pension she would only have received a Category B State pension (if her husband was entitled to a Category A pension and they were both of pensionable age). In the event of her husband's death she will only ever receive the equivalent of a widow's pension. In those circumstances the widow's State pension should not be deducted from the claim.[8]

6.10   CONCLUSION

The value of pension loss claims can run into many thousands of pounds but this head of damage is frequently overlooked in personal injury

---

[7]   Section 4 of the Fatal Accidents Act 1976 (as amended) and see *Pidduck v Eastern Scottish Omnibuses Ltd* [1990] 1 WLR 993.

[8]   *Lea v Owen* unreported. Summarised in Kemp & Kemp.

claims. There is no justification for this and practitioners should therefore always investigate the claimant's pension arrangements and obtain the necessary information.

CHAPTER 7

DAMAGES FOR GRATUITOUS CARE

7.1 HEAD OF CLAIM

7.1.1 Introduction

In 1994 the Law Commission Report No 225 'Personal Injury Compensation: How much is Enough?' highlighted that four out of five injured people receiving damages claimed to need help with everyday tasks. Claims for care and assistance are sometimes mistakenly perceived to be relevant only in significant injury claims and certainly not within the fast track. In fact, many claimants will fail to be properly recompensed if a claim under this head of damage is not pursued.

If personal care is necessary, and payment for such care is made, then providing the cost is reasonable such payment will be recoverable. Gratuitous care by spouses, relatives and friends is, however, more complicated.

7.1.2 Development of head of claim

The Court of Appeal gave conflicting judgments in the space of two days in May 1973. In *Cunningham v Harrison*,[1] the claimant was injured in a road traffic accident. His wife cared for him for two years before committing suicide, a matter of three days prior to the trial, because the claimant was 'an extremely difficult' tetraplegic, Lord Denning MR stated:

> '... It is only right and just that if the wife renders services to him, instead of a nurse, he should recover compensation for the value of the services that his wife has rendered.' Such damages would be held "on trust".'

Within 48 hours a different division of the Court of Appeal in *Donnelly v Joyce*[2] considered the case of a 6 year-old boy who suffered serious leg injuries. His mother had given up her part time work to look after him. Megaw LJ stated 'his loss is the existence of the need ... for those nursing

---

[1] [1973] 1 QB 942.
[2] [1974] 1 QB 454.

services, the value of which for purposes of damages ... is the proper and reasonable costs of supplying those needs'. He continued to conclude 'the loss is the plaintiff's loss'.

The confusion was clarified by *Hunt v Severs*[3] when Lord Bridge stated '... the reasoning in *Donnelly* diverts attention from the award's central objective of compensating the carer'. The House of Lords was concerned to ensure that the voluntary carer received recompense for his or her services. The carer husband to the injured wife was also the tortfeasor. She was prevented from obtaining damages on his behalf because he had been responsible for the cause of her injuries.

Therefore, a claim for care services provided by a relative gratuitously is justifiable and the carer is entitled to receive the monies claimed unless he is also the tortfeasor.

7.1.3   Definition of care

It is important to clarify the difference between care and services provided by a volunteer with the claimant's loss of capacity to undertake housework or other household activities (see further at Chapter 10).

Recent assistance in defining 'care' was given by May LJ in *Evans v Pontypridd Roofing Ltd*.[4] The claimant had fallen from a roof whilst he was at work and suffered a serious limitation of movement in his cervical spine. His life had been devastated by the injury and he would need help with all daily activities. His wife was his main carer. The Court of Appeal did not interfere with the trial judge's view that the claimant wanted and needed 'a chat at night' which was described as 'important pillow talk'. His wife was an emotional crutch for him. In addition, she undertook strip washing, partial washing, undresssing and re-dressing. She washed his hair, tended to his use of a commode and helped him out of and back into his chair. Also, because of the potential suicide risk, she ensured that he fell asleep before she did in order to ensure that he did not harm himself. In addition, she performed the sort of tasks that are more routine, namely the preparation and cooking of meals, shopping, laundry and jobs concerned with the maintenance of the house.

The court dismissed the approach of Stuart Smith LJ in *Fitzgerald v Ford*[5] when he stated 'in many cases the actual nursing or physical assistance may only take a few hours distributed throughout the day or night. For the rest of the time it was spent in preparation and cooking of meals, shopping, laundry, jobs concerned with the maintenance of the house, all of which have to be done for the carer and any other members of the family in any case'.

---

3   [1994] 2 AC 350.
4   [2001] EWCA Civ 1657, [2002] PIQR Q5, CA.
5   [1996] PIQR Q72, CA.

In *Evans* the court found that the judge had not made an over-assessment of the services provided by Mrs Evans and 'it is neither necessary nor to be expected that a full time carer should spend every hour of the day or night engaged in providing physical services'.

In other words, care can be wide-ranging. Mrs Evans was 'fiercely dedicated to her family'. She provided '24-hour care'.

The decision in *Mills v British Rail Engineering Ltd*,[6] is often cited by defendants in an attempt to suggest that damages under this head should only be awarded in serious cases. The judgments in that case are interpreted to create a three-stage test for an award of damages, namely:

(1)   that the claimant 'would otherwise require nursing care' (per Dillon LJ);

(2)   that the care provided should go 'distinctly beyond that which is part of the ordinary regime of family life' (per Staughton LJ); and

(3)   that taken in the round 'it must only be in a very serious case that an award is justified' (per Staughton LJ).

This test was carefully examined by His Honour Judge McDuff QC in *Giambrone v JMC Holidays Ltd*.[7] In that case, a number of children had suffered from gastro-enteritis or similar illnesses resulting from food they had eaten at a hotel on holiday. Their parents had to provide constant care for them over periods from two to three weeks to a couple of months. The defendants argued that such care did not satisfy the *Mills* criteria. In the *Mills* case the wife cared for her husband prior to his death from an asbestos-induced lung cancer. The cases are indeed starkly different. However, despite this, awards were made in respect of the care provided to the children.

The judge analysed the three stages of the test as follows:

(1)   The *Oxford English Dictionary* defines 'to nurse' as including 'to attend to a sick person'. The parents of the children did exactly that. There is no requirement for any technical expertise in respect of such attendance.

(2)   It is not part of the regime of ordinary life for parents to spend their time looking after sick children for 'in ordinary life' children are not sick, they go to school. Accordingly, in looking at the *Mills* case, if Mr Mills had been unwell some months prior to his contraction of the asbestos illness, Mrs Mills would still have cared for him. Would

---

6   [1992] 1 PIQR Q130.
7   *Giambrone v JMC Holidays Ltd* [2003] All ER(D) 202 (Jun).

caring for her husband therefore become part of the 'ordinary regime for family life' for the Mills family?

(3)   The words 'it must only be in a very serious case that an award is justified' do no more than to emphasise that the illness/injury must be sufficiently serious to give rise to a need for care and attendance significantly over and above that which would be given anyway in the ordinary course of family life. There is no inference, therefore, that the nature of the injury must be particularly serious.

This approach is logical and consistent. In *Giambrone*, but for the defendant's negligence the parents would not have had to spend time attending on their sick children. It is only right, therefore, that such care and attendance is compensated.

In the children's cases, jury awards of between £150 and £275 were made.

In the Court of Appeal[8] the defendants put their appeal on two bases:

(i)   there should be no award for care except in a very serious case;

(ii)   in order to qualify for an award, the relative must prove care that went 'distinctly beyond that which was part of the ordinary regime of family life'.[9]

Giving the lead judgment on behalf of a unanimous court, Brooke LJ upheld the judgment and the awards of the Deputy High Court Judge. He rejected the first strand of the defendants appeal on the basis that such a finding would result in arbitrary justice with decisions on whether a case was sufficiently 'serious' varying from case to case and from judge to judge.

Equally, in relation to the second argument, his Lordship found that:

> 'Anyone who has had the responsibility of the care of a child with gastro-enteritis of the severity experienced by these children will know that they require care which goes distinctly beyond that which is of the ordinary regime of family life.'

The decision in Mills is therefore put firmly into its proper context. Notably, his Lordship made a closing comment expressing concern at the disproportionate cost of proving these small elements of damages in gastro-enteritis claims and suggested that perhaps an award of £50 per week for a child suffering from the condition would be appropriate.

---

8   [2004] EWCA 158.
9   Dillon J in *Mills v British Rail Engineering Ltd* [1992] PIQR Q130.

7.2 QUANTIFICATION OF CLAIM

In smaller cases the courts look to a 'jury award' of what is a reasonable sum in respect of providing the weekly level of care. In bigger value cases a multiplicand/multiplier approach is adopted. Evidence is obtained of the hourly rates for nursing care to produce a calculation of an annual figure to which the multiplier is applied. It is important to ensure that the rates are understood as these can differ widely between the National Joint Council, British Nursing Association and Whitely rates. Your care/ occupational therapy expert should cater for these within their report.

In *Housecroft v Burnett*,[10] O'Connor LJ stated: 'the courts should look at it (the capital sum) as a whole and consider whether, on the facts of the case, it is sufficient to enable the plaintiff, amongst other things, to make reasonable recompense to the relative'.

In looking at how to assess 'the proper and reasonable cost', the court in the same case looked at two extremes, namely:

(1) the full commercial cost of employing someone to do what the relative does; and

(2) assessing the care at nil as if it had all been performed under the National Health Service system.

Neither of which is accurate and the court found that 'each case must be considered on its own facts'.

One therefore looks to the level and extent of care provided by the volunteer. This can prove unfair to relatives and the courts have provided confusing guidance on this point. The following should be noted in terms of volunteer carers:

(1) The courts make no allowance for the anti-social hours worked by a gratuitous carer.

(2) The rates applied to relatives may be reduced because they lack the experience of the professional carer. This should be avoided. In many cases the gratuitous carer gains a level of experience which is equal to the professional carer. In *Hogg v Doyle*[11] Turner J stated that the wife had probably been doing the work of two full time nurses and on that basis he assessed the damages payable in respect of her unpaid services at 1.5 times the net earnings she would have earned in employment as a nurse. This decision was questioned by Stuart Smith LJ in the *Fitzgerald* case (see para 7.1.3).

---

[10] [1986] 1 All ER 332.
[11] (Unreported) 6 March 1991, CA.

(3)   If the gratuitous carer gives up employment, one must contrast the extent of the care claim with a claim for loss of earnings. The former tends to be the upper limit of damages that will be recoverable irrespective of the level of loss of earnings (see *Fitzgerald*).

(4)   Ensure that the rates of care applied in the case are appropriate. There are different rates applied to levels of skill of carers and it is important that the basic rate of a professional carer is not used in a case such as Mrs Evans where she was providing a highly specialised level of skill despite being a gratuitous carer.

7.2.1   Discounting gratuitous care

Professional carers pay tax and national insurance. They have expenses of travel and clothing. It is therefore unreasonable to allow the claimant to claim the gross cost of care and assistance provided by the gratuitous carer. The commercial rate on which the calculation has been calculated must therefore be discounted to provide a proper level.

The courts tend to apply a broad-brush approach to the discount figure. Over the years discounts have varied from 14%[12] to 33%.[13] The 'norm'[14] is perceived to be 25%. In fact many of the decisions do not properly reflect the leading case of *Housecroft* in which an arbitrary reduction of £3,000 per annum effectively created an award of 82% of the commercial value of professional care. The Court of Appeal did not interfere with Kilner-Brown J's decision in that case. Despite this, *Housecroft* is frequently cited as authority for a discount of 25% to 33%.

Since the decision there have been a number of cases which have reduced the level of the discount below 25%. In *Fairhurst v St Helen's and Knowsley Health Authority*[15] because of the level of special skills provided by the carers His Honour Judge Clarke QC found that the services should be valued 'somewhat closer to the full commercial rate than might otherwise have been appropriate'. In *Page v Sheerness Steel plc* the level of care was rounded down representing 94% of the commercial value of gratuitous care. In *Lamey v Wirral Health Authority*,[16] the judge looked to the quality of the care and not just its quantity. If the quality is high then the discount will be reduced.

The courts have been unwilling to lay down strict guidelines for practitioners, leaving the judge with the discretion to achieve a fair result. In the Evans case, May LJ stated 'in my judgment there is no scientific basis for a strictly mathematical answer to this question. Nor is the

---

[12]   *McCamley v Cammel Laird Shipbuilders* [1990] 1 WLR 963, [1990] 1 All ER 854.
[13]   *Nash v Southmead* [1993] PIQR Q156.
[14]   *A v National Blood Authority* [2001] 3 All ER 289.
[15]   [1995] PIQR Q1.
[16]   (Unreported) 1997, *Kemp & Kemp* (A4-120).

exercise upon which the court is engaged amenable to such an answer'. His Lordship upheld the discount of 25% made by the judge at first instance on the basis that 'there were no grounds in the present case for making a discount which was greater or less than the *normal*'. Despite this, his Lordship later contradicts the approach by stating 'it would not, in my view, be appropriate to bind first instance judges to a conventional formalised calculation ... but I do not think that this can be done by means of a conventional percentage, since the appropriate extent of the scaling down and the reasons for it may vary from case to case'.

In other words, the discount percentage is not fixed. The claimant must show that the level of care is of a quality that merits a discount of no more than the basic rate of tax plus a little extra for expenses, ie 20%–25%. The argument should, if the level of care is of such high quality, be that the discount should be smaller.

7.2.2 Future care

In cases in which a claim for future care forms a part, this single head of damages will often compete with loss of earnings as the largest individual item within a claimant's schedule of loss. Unsurprisingly, the High Court has had to consider a number of issues in respect of the computation of the head of damage in deciding what is a reasonable care package. As a starting point Lord Lloyd[17] stated 'claimants are entitled to a reasonable standard of care to meet their requirements, but that is all'.

7.2.2.1 Care rates

The hourly rate depends on two factors, namely the area in which the care is to take place and the nature of the carer. The test is what is reasonably required and it is not for the claimant to have to search to find the lowest rate within a region. In *Iqbal*[18] the defendant's expert advised that the rates that the claimant ought to recover were £9.50 and £10.50 for day and waking night care. The claimant's expert allowed £10/hour during the week and £12 at weekends which, in fact, were the rates being paid by the parents of the injured child. Sir Roger Bell found that 'I do not believe that there is any obligation on parents in the position of Mr and Mrs Iqbal to creep up pound by pound in the hope of saving the defendant a pound or so an hour. They are entitled to shorten the process by offering a good rate. In my judgment, the evidence of practical experience points overwhelmingly to £10 and £12 being reasonable rates which it is necessary to pay in order to confidently achieve the required continuing of competent, willing carers'.

---

[17] *Wells v Wells* [1999] 1 AC 345.
[18] *Iqbal v Whipps Cross University Hospital NHS Trust* [2006] EWHC 3111.

It is pleasing to see that the court will not be interested in the odd few pence or a pound per hour. It is important in such serious injury cases that the carers are appropriate for the needs of the victim and the family unit.

7.2.2.2 Aggregation

The 2007/8th edition of Facts and Figures includes the National Joint Council pay rates for local authorities, spinal point 8. This replaces BNA Marble Arch rates. The rates that appear in the tables are composite rates, thereby avoiding the need to calculate different rates for care provided during weekdays, at night, at weekends and on bank holidays. Use of the Annual Survey of Hours and Earnings Figures 2006 (ASHE 6115) incorporates the composite rate. Whilst there is an inference from a number of authorities that the courts are moving towards application of the composite rate, there is no direct authority in support.

In recent years the courts have adopted a 58-week notional year for the calculation of future care. The additional weeks cover sick leave, the higher rates on bank holidays, paid holiday and down time for training days. Judicial support for the figure can be seen in *Iqbal* and by Lloyd Jones J in *Sarwar 2*.[19]

7.2.2.3 Directly employed carer or agency residential carer

In *Corbett v South Yorkshire Strategic Health Authority*,[20] His Honour Judge Bullimore sitting in Sheffield County Court had to consider the alternative care packages which differed in price between £70,690 and £105,625. The former was an agency residential care package, the latter a directly employed package. His Honour rejected the former on two bases, namely:

(1) as the claimant required a considerable amount of care, a single carer would find the role extremely demanding and it would be unattractive to a carer who was of the type required,

(2) the resident carer regime breached the Working Time Regulations.

Most recently Flaux J[21] had to consider the nature of the care package for a claimant who suffered paraplegia following a road traffic accident. He found that the most appropriate care package involved a flexible '4-man team approach' with two carers present for 4 hours a day rejecting the agency carer package in preference to the directly employed package. His Lordship was influenced by a number of factors including the unreasonable reliance on the claimant's wife, the doubtful availability and

---

[19] [2007] EWHC 274.
[20] (Unreported), 4 May 2007, QBD, LS Law Med 430.
[21] *Burton v Kingsbury* [2007] EWHC 2091 (QB).

unacceptable turnover in agency overlap carers, the fact that the resident carer package would not attract the right sort of carer and the lack of safety during the transfer periods.

With further support for the directly employed package given in *Iqbal*, the future of the agency care package appears to be in some doubt.

7.2.2.4 Care packages and indexation

The bulk of future care costs consist of the earnings of the people who provide the care. Historically the earnings of commercial carers have increased faster than prices. Therefore, the implementation of a periodical payments order based on the retail prices index will likely fail to keep pace with the expenditure necessary to provide the appropriate level of care.

Indexation is a critical issue in respect of periodical payments as it is designed to provide inflation-proofing to ensure that the annual payment meets its needs. There are a number of methods of indexation but in respect of future care it appears that one method is finding favour above the others.[22]

In recent times the courts have considered the following methods of applying indexation:

(1) Indexation to the RPI

The RPI captures average price inflation across households. It relates to the purchase of good and services and consumption and does not relate to the purchase of labour in the household production of care services. McKay J[23] stated that 'indexing future care costs to RPI will result in a significant and possibly substantial shortfall'.

(2) Average Earnings Index

This index is dominated by earnings in other occupations and sectors outside of care which have no relation to a carer's earnings. In fact the average level of aggregate hourly earnings at £13/hour in 2006 is above the level of hourly earnings typically paid to carers. Whilst McKay J, given the choice of RPI or AEI indicated that he would be *'tempted'* to go with AEI despite the fact that there is a degree of bias, it is evident that both he and HHJ Bullimore in Corbett were of the view that the AEI is not a reliable indicator of the growth of a carer's earnings.

---

22   *Thameside and Glossop Acute Services NHS Trust v Thompstone* [2007] EWCA Civ 5.
23   *RH v United Bristol Health Care NHS Trust* [2007] EWHC 1441.

(3) Aggregate Annual Survey of Hours and Earnings (ASHE)

Once more the problem with these figures is that they include data from all occupations.

(4) Aggregate Annual Survey of Hours and Earnings (ASHE) SOC 6115 Care Assistance and Home Carers.

Mrs Justice Swift in *Thompstone,*[24] McKay J and HJJ Bullimore all used this measure to replace the RPI. McKay J stated 'I regard 6115 as the most accurate match to the target expenditure; it is of undoubted authority, coming from the ONS (Office of National Statistics); it is statistically reliable ... and is markedly superior to RPI.'

This earnings series provides the most precise match in terms of occupation and level of earnings. It is divided into 11 centiles which cover a range of earnings to reflect different qualifications, skills, responsibilities, type of care and terms and conditions of employment. The ASHE annual figures are now quoted regularly by nursing experts. In conclusion, Lloyd Jones J in AB found that there were a number of 'real advantages in the use of ASHE 6115 for indexation for periodical payments in respect of costs of care in the present case'. Their use was entirely justified by the achievement of greater precision which is in the interests of both the claimant and second defendant.

The Court of Appeal recently decided in favour of the use of the ASHE 6115 index[25]. The appellants argued that ASHE 6115 was not a suitable measure to use as an index for a variety of reasons which included the following:

(1)   the index did not contain exclusively care costs and therefore did not accurately target the particular carers in issue in a case;

(2)   a weighted average wage rate did not relate to the actual position of a single carer;

(3)   the index could be distorted by the entry of large numbers of higher paid workers; and

(4)   growth rates in levels of income varied considerably from year to year so the index could not be relied on to measure change over time.

Additionally, the appellants sought to argue that the Damages Act 1996 permitted modification of the RPI index in an order for periodical payments in ''exceptional circumstances'. Secondly, that the modification permitted by Section 2(8) of the Act did not permit replacement of the

---

[24]   [2006] EWHC 2904.
[25]   *Thameside and Glossop Acute Services NHS Trust v Thompstone* [2007] EWCA Civ 5.

RPI index with an alternative such as the ASHE 6115 index. Thirdly, that a party seeking to substitute an alternative index had to identify and prove the merits of the alternative.

The Court of Appeal unanimously dismissed the appellants' arguments. It upheld the decisions of the courts of first instance and also made it clear that the NHSLA and other defendants in catastrophic injury cases ought now to accept that there had been an "exhaustive review" of their objections and, unless a future defendant was able to adduce evidence in argument that was significantly different from that heard in this case, it would not be appropriate to re-open the issue in any future proceedings.

In dealing with the three issues highlighted above, the court relied on the earlier decision of *Flora v Wakom (Heathrow) Ltd*[26] finding that exceptional circumstances were not necessary, modification did include the substitution of an alternative index, and that it was "always bad" to make a claimant make a specific choice for it was a matter for the court to carry out a comparative exercise in relation to indices to decide which was appropriate.

The appellants have sought permission from the Court of Appeal to appeal to the House of Lords and the respondents have objected. The Court of Appeal has yet to decide whether it will grant or refuse permission.

7.2.2.5 *Residential care and the local authority*

The Court of Appeal[27] found that in a case in which the claimant required residential care the local authority has a responsibility to provide such care free of charge and, therefore, recovery of damages in respect of such care effectively provides a windfall.

In *Crofton v NHS Litigation Authority*[28] the Court of Appeal had to consider whether the same approach would apply where the claimant required domiciliary care. They upheld the High Court decision which followed the line adopted in *Sowden*. The court stated:

> 'we say only that we can see no good policy reason why the care costs in a case such as this should fall upon the public purse. We can see no good policy reason why damages which are about to be awarded specifically for the provision of care to the claimant, needed only as a result of the tort, should be reduced, thereby shifting the burden from the tortfeasor to the public purse. We recognise that the mechanism by which these ends could be achieved with justice might be complex and difficult. But, as we say, these are policy issues and are a matter for parliament' [para 90].

---

[26] [2006] EWCA 1103.

[27] *Sowden v Lodge; Crookedale v Dury* [2004] EWCA Civ 1370.

[28] [2007] EWCA Civ 71.

Despite this, the Court of Appeal also went on to recognize that in principle payments by third parties which a claimant would not have received but for his injuries have to be taken into account unless they come within one of the established exceptions.[29] The mechanism by which this can be achieved has caused further problems. In Crofton the multiplier was reduced. In *Burton v Kingsbury*[30] Flaux J ordered that the annual cost of care be reduced by the amount that the local authority paid.

It is important to remember with all aspects of care that the court is looking to ensure that a claimant's reasonable requirements for lifelong care are met. Should there by any anxiety that the local authority care would not meet these reasonable requirements, then the court should award compensation to be paid by the defendant so that purchase of care on the open market can be pursued.

7.2.3   Summary

In the case of a gratuitous carer who has suffered no loss of earnings:

(1)   The care must be of a level of care and assistance beyond purely the routine. Whether it needs be to the extent suggested in *Mills* is doubtful.

(2)   The judge will make some discount from the commercial value of the care which has been provided.

(3)   There is no conventional discount figure but the 'norm' is perceived to be 25% (currently).

(4)   The greater the quality of the care provided and the devotion, skill and extent of the care given, the better the argument that the discount should be reduced.

In the case of a gratuitous carer who has incurred loss of earnings:

(1)   Ascertain the loss of earnings incurred.

(2)   Was it reasonable for the carer to give up work to look after the claimant?

(3)   If so, contrast the extent of the loss of earnings with the claim for care and the ceiling is the commercial value of the care provided (see *Lamey*) although this is not an absolute bar to a larger award if it was reasonable for the carer to give up work.

---

[29]   See *Sowden v Lodge* (above) at para 91.
[30]   [2007] EWHC 2091.

(4) Interest will attach to past care.

7.3   EVIDENCE

7.3.1   The claimant's statement

This should outline the restrictions and limitations on everyday life. It should describe life before the accident and contrast it carefully with his/her current existence and the loss of independence.

7.3.2   The carer's statement

The spouse/parent/family member or relative should prepare a detailed statement outlining the same contrast between life prior to and post accident. The carer should detail a day/week/month in the life of the carer and the assistance that has to be provided to the injured claimant. The statement should demonstrate to the court the intensity of the devotion of the carer to the claimant, whilst not forgetting to outline any effects, physical and mental that the care regime has on the carer. (Note: in *Housecroft* the carer committed suicide three days before the trial.)

7.3.3   Statements from other relative/neighbours

Care may not solely be provided by a single carer. Other relatives and friends/neighbours may assist and they should be proofed accordingly. Likewise, other relatives can describe the care provided by the principle carer and the effect of the devotion given to the claimant, any effects on the carer and any detriment that the current regime inflicts on the carer.

7.3.4   Expert evidence

A report from a care specialist or occupational therapist is important in the more serious cases. A specialist will attend upon the claimant and produce a report dealing with care needs of the claimant, how they are catered for presently and ought to be catered for into the future. The report will contain the appropriate rates for professional care as well as dealing with aids and equipment to assist in the care regime as damages for care and assistance and, in particular, the future claim can be the biggest single item of damage. *Peet v Mid Kent Health Authority*[31] obliges the parties to instruct a joint care expert. In practice, particularly in larger cases, the parties often seek to rely upon their own expert.

---

[31]   [2001] EWCA Civ 1703, [2002] 3 All ER 688, [2002] 1 WLR 210.

7.3.5   Video evidence

Consider obtaining a video of a day in the life of the seriously injured claimant to provide the judge with a true picture of the limitations on the claimant's existence and the assistance he/she needs.

7.3.6   Medical experts

Ensure that the medical expert reviews the report of the occupational therapist/care expert and agrees its content. It is important that the claimant's experts are ad idem in relation to the claimant's limitations and the need for care and assistance both currently and into the future.

7.4   CONCLUSION

Damages under this head can, in many cases, be significant. A reduction in the discount rate from 25%–20% can have a massive impact on the level of damages that the claimant receives. Equally, the level of damages must provide adequate compensation to cover the situation whereby the voluntary carer is no longer available for whatever reason. For instance, a carer husband may one day leave his wife. The evidence needs to be carefully put together to ensure that the judge has a true picture of the level of care and assistance provided gratuitously by the volunteer carer.

In less serious cases the level of care and assistance can be easily proofed and a simple calculation produced to which the court's broad-brush approach can be applied to produce a lump sum. This may be as little as a few hundred pounds, but providing the level of care has been beyond the give and take of daily life it will be recompensable.

CHAPTER 8

DAMAGES FOR LOSS OF HOUSEKEEPING AND RELATED SERVICES (DIY/DECORATING/GARDENING ETC)

8.1 HEAD OF CLAIM

The claimant's loss is the inability to perform certain tasks as a result of his injury or disability. The inability to perform housework etc was historically seen as irrelevant. Fortunately the Royal Commission on Civil Liability and Compensation for Personal Injury ('Pearson Report', Cmnd 7054-1) did not agree, taking the view that a person who loses the capacity to render services to others suffers a real loss. A housewife may not have lost money by not being able to perform housekeeping duties, but she has lost 'monies worth'.

It is now settled that the claimant can recover damages for the cost of replacing these services as a separate head of damage (see *Daly v General Steamship Navigation Co Ltd*)[1] The rationale is that a housewife 'is just as much disabled from doing her unpaid job as an employed person is disabled from doing his paid one ... she is, in principle, entitled to be compensated for her loss in a similar way' (Brandon J). Tasks which commonly fall into this category are decorating, DIY, gardening, car maintenance, household maintenance, window cleaning and housekeeping, but the list is not exhaustive.

The task should benefit the household. In *Swain v London Ambulance Service NHS Trust*[2] an injured man previously valeted his wife's car which was her own property used for her sole benefit. No damages were awarded by the court as it did not benefit the household. If the task in question had freed up the wife to perform some other task for the benefit of the household, arguably the claim would be treated differently.

8.2 PRINCIPLES OF ASSESSMENT

The claimant has to establish the following:

(1) Prior to his accident/injury he performed the task(s) in question.

---

[1] [1981] 1 WLR 120, (1980) 125 SJ 100, [1980] 3 All ER 696, [1980] 2 Lloyd's Rep 415.
[2] (Unreported) 12 March 1999.

(2)   As a result of his injury/disability he can no longer perform that task(s) or can no longer perform it to the extent he was previously able to.

(3)   The task(s) in question will now have to be carried out by some other person.

Past loss can be calculated in one of two ways:

(1)   Where the claimant has employed professionals to carry out the task in question (for example decorating his house), he may recover the cost of their services but only the cost of labour (not materials, as he would have had to pay for these anyway) and only to the extent that the outlay is for work he would have done himself but for his injury.

(2)   If the claimant has relied upon friends or family to carry out the task in question (decorating or cutting the lawn etc) then he can recover the value of the work carried out. This is usually based upon commercial rates which are then discounted for tax, national insurance, travelling expenses etc in the same way as a claim for gratuitous care.

In either case the loss claimed is subject to the test of reasonableness. The claimant cannot recover the cost of employing a Formula 1 engineer to service his car if he could reasonably have had the work done locally at much less cost. Similarly, the value of assistance provided by friends or family is unlikely to exceed the reasonable commercial cost of having the work done.

No claim can be made in respect of *past loss* where no work has been done, either professionally or by friends or family.

The claimant can recover the cost of commercial or gratuitous services *post trial* irrespective of whether he intends to employ anyone to undertake these tasks.

> 'It is really quite immaterial, in my judgment, whether having received those damages, the Plaintiff chooses to alleviate her own housekeeping burden, which is an excessively heavy one having regard to her considerable disability to undertake household tasks, by employing the labour which has been taken as the basis of the estimate on which damages have been awarded, or whether she chooses to continue to struggle with the housekeeping on her own ...' (per Bridge LJ in *Daly*).

8.3 EVIDENCE/QUANTIFICATION

Past loss must be supported by the following evidence:

(1) Lay witness evidence from the claimant and/or others of the tasks that he undertook before his injury. This should be sufficiently detailed to enable the judge to ascertain the extent of the work done and how often it was carried out. (It is no use the claimant's statement simply recording that he has been unable to decorate since the accident. The statement should give some indication of the size of house and how often the claimant decorated.) The claimant should also refer to any particular skills he may have (for example as a professional electrician/plumber etc) which enabled him to undertake far more of the household maintenance than usual.

(2) Medical evidence to support the contention that he has been unable through injury or disability to perform those tasks. This may be implicit from the nature of the injuries but if it is not obvious the claimant's solicitors may need to seek confirmation of the extent of the claimant's disability in relation to DIY etc from the medical expert.

(3) Evidence of the costs of having the work done. Either proof of expenditure for work done by professionals or quotes from professionals (decorators, architects or surveyors) for the cost of the work carried out by friends or family. In the case of friends and family it is advisable to obtain a statement from the person in question setting out what he has done and when.

In respect of future loss the claim is based upon the commercial cost of having the work done regardless of whether the claimant intends to employ professionals. The evidence required to support the claim is essentially that set out above but it is important also to set out any plans the claimant may have had for the future: for example to 'do up the house' when he retired or to 'spend more time in the garden'. Defendants often contend that a claimant would only have been able to manage a limited amount of DIY/decoration in addition to his employment and family commitments. Conversely, in retirement the claimant will have far more time on his hands to do these things.

8.4 QUANTIFICATION

It should usually be possible to determine future loss on the basis of a multiplier/multiplicand.

The multiplicand will represent the annual cost of employing professionals as set out above. It may therefore be necessary to obtain a number of quotes to cover all aspects of the services lost, ie decorator, gardener, garage mechanic etc.

Claimants have frequently relied upon supposedly 'conventional figures' as multiplicands for loss of ability to undertake services such as DIY/decorating and gardening. There has been some support for such figures in the courts. In *Page v Sheerness Steel*[3] the trial judge valued future services at £1,000 per annum in respect of a claimant who had previously undertaken all the decorating inside and out, fitted a kitchen and bathroom, undertaken all the plumbing and paved the back garden. Nevertheless, the claimant still has to prove his loss and should not therefore depend upon 'conventional figures' without some evidence to back up the extent of the services claimed.

The multiplier is determined in the same way as for other future losses, taking the age of the claimant at the date of trial and using the Ogden tables to determine the appropriate multiplier for the period of loss. Invariably, it will be argued that the claimant would not have been physically capable of undertaking DIY/decorating/ gardening etc for the rest of his life. Some discount will therefore usually be applied to reflect the limit imposed by advancing age and inevitable infirmity.[4] However, there is no hard and fast rule as to the appropriate upper age limit. This question is dependent to a large extent on the medical evidence. If, but for his injury, the claimant was fit and well, displaying a vigorous enthusiasm for DIY, a judge is far more likely to accept that he would have continued to undertake such tasks himself for years to come than if he already suffered from a number of disabling complaints.

Where the various factors make it impossible to use a multiplier/ multiplicand approach the court may award a lump sum for future loss.[5]

8.5 FATAL ACCIDENTS

Dependency claims for loss of services are calculated in exactly the same way as for living claimants, save that the multiplier is taken from the date of death (less the period of past loss) and not from the date of trial. Since services such as DIY and decorating form part of the indivisible contribution the deceased made to the household there is no deduction in respect of his expenditure for his own personal benefit as there would be for a dependency on earnings or pension.

---

[3] [1996] PIQR Q26 at Q42, per Dyson J.
[4] See Court of Appeal decision in *Page v Sheerness Steel* [1997] PIQR Q1 at Q56.
[5] *Worrall (D) v Powergen plc* [1999] PIQR Q103.

8.6 LOST YEARS

For a living claimant with a reduced life expectancy there is no claim in respect of inability to perform DIY/decorating/gardening etc in the 'lost years'.[6]

---

[6] *Phipps v Brooks Dry Cleaning Service Ltd* [1996] PIQR Q100, CA.

CHAPTER 9

HOUSING

9.1 HEADS OF CLAIM

An accident may have implications on the claimant's housing requirements. There are three potential heads of claim:

(1) *New accommodation* – in more serious cases the claimant's existing accommodation may become unsuitable and there may be a need to move into new accommodation, for example a paraplegic may require a bungalow.

(2) *Adaptation of existing accommodation* – sometimes it is possible to convert existing housing, for example by providing a downstairs toilet or a stair-lift.

(3) *Increased home running costs* – claimants with significant physical disabilities frequently spend an increased amount of time in the home, are immobile and feel the cold more. Additional heating may be recoverable on a multiplier/multiplicand basis.

9.2 NEW ACCOMMODATION

9.2.1 When should an application for new accommodation be made?

There are often compelling reasons for investing in new accommodation before trial:

–   After an accident the claimant may be housed in accommodation which is unsuitable and dangerous – for example, the claimant may be unable to negotiate stairs safely as a result of his injuries.

–   It may not be possible to set up a care regime until after the move into the new accommodation.

–   It is often in the period immediately after the accident that there is the greatest scope for recovery. It is usually in everyone's best interests, including the defendant's, to fund a move at an early stage. It is important for the claimant to have as much say as possible in his own destiny at the earliest moment. If things are left, it may be years later, well after the trial has taken place, before the necessary steps are taken to move the claimant into appropriate accommodation.

In most cases, a claimant will not be in a position to fund a move. In such cases a substantial interim payment may well be appropriate (see 'Interim Payments').

9.2.2 Quantification of claim

The claimant has to be compensated for incurring the increased cost of the new accommodation. Balanced against this, the capital asset is likely to be secure and inflation proof, albeit that it will not be realised for a very long time and probably not until after the claimant's death. A pragmatic formula is used by the courts, which is sometimes referred to by the name of the leading case *Roberts v Johnstone*.[1]

The court makes certain assumptions. It is assumed that the claimant will pay for the additional accommodation out of his own capital, and that the capital will be risk free and protected against inflation as house prices tend to rise. Neither the capital costs of buying the new accommodation nor the mortgage repayments on the new property are recoverable.

The claimant has lost the income which the capital would have earned over the period of the award, after the deduction of tax. But the lost income is not calculated by reference to a commercial rate of interest. Normally interest includes two elements: a reward for taking a risk with capital and a reward for foregoing the use of the capital for the time being. The courts have decided that as only the second of these two elements is applicable, the lost interest can only be claimed at a reduced rate. Damages are assessed by taking a percentage of the net additional capital cost of the accommodation and multiplying it by an appropriate multiplier, usually life. The resulting figure is based on the amount that would have been generated had the claimant invested the additional sum in Index Linked Government Securities, sometimes referred to as ILGS, which are low risk investments. The approach was confirmed by the House of Lords in *Thomas v Brighton Health Authority*.[2]

There has been, and continues to be, considerable debate about the appropriate discount rate. For the time being at least this was settled by the Lord Chancellor in June 2001 when he used his powers under s 1 of the Damages Act 1996 and set the rate at 2.5%.

---

[1]   [1989] QB 878.
[2]   [1999] 1 AC 345, per Lord Lloyd.

The additional costs of moving including estate agent's fees and legal expenses and subsequent additional expenses such as property maintenance, council tax and gardening are recoverable as separate items of special damage.

As there is no provision for the capital cost of suitable accommodation many claimants tend to utilise other heads of damages to fund the cost. With the introduction of periodical payments it remains to be seen to what extent Judges are more reluctant to make substantial interim awards if this is likely to significantly impact on the ability of the trial judge to make an order for periodical payments.

An illustration of the calculation is set out below.

9.2.3 Evidence

This is a head of loss which on its own can generate a significant sum. It is critical that the claim has a sound foundation in the medical evidence. The test is whether the new accommodation is reasonably necessary. Sometimes it is difficult to draw the line between what is reasonably necessary as opposed to desirable. In *Cassel v Riverside Health Authority*[3] Rose J allowed a claim of £32,000 for the cost of a swimming pool which was the claimant's principal source of relaxation and pleasure. The Court of Appeal disallowed this aspect of the claim as the medical evidence did not support the claim that it was 'essential therapy', per Farquharson LJ and Ralph Gibson LJ. It was properly categorised as an element of damages for loss of amenity, per Purchas LJ. Conversely, in *Willett v North Bedfordshire Health Authority*[4] the cost of a house which included a swimming pool was allowed on the basis that it was a suitable house bought at a reasonable price within an appropriate range.

In *Burton v Kingsbury,*[5] the Claimant was aged 18 at the time of the accident which rendered him tetraplegic. He was unable to use any part of his body below the shoulders, but his medical capacity survived intact. A house was purchased for £600,000 which included an indoor swimming pool. There was medical evidence that swimming helped to reduce symptoms of pain and spasticity. Flaux J held that there was no basis for concluding that the price paid for the accommodation was excessive and followed the approach in *Roberts v Johnstone.*

The claimant's main medical witness must support the need for new accommodation in clear terms otherwise the head of loss will fail. The claimant should then instruct accommodation and care experts whose evidence should, if at all possible, be co-ordinated. If the expert reports

---

[3]   [1992] PIQR Q168.
[4]   [1993] PIQR Q166.
[5]   [2007] EWHC 2091.

do not tie in, a conference with the experts is almost certainly necessary in order that areas of agreement and disagreement can be identified.

9.2.4   Local authority provision

In the most serious cases the local authority may have a duty to provide an injured person with residential accommodation. This is an area which has recently come under the spot light. Unfortunately the legislation is difficult to follow. A local authority is obliged to provide residential accommodation for adults who require it due to 'age, illness, disability or any other circumstances' and it is not available from some other source, see National Assistance Act 1948, s 21(1). If the duty arises, the assisted person is entitled to be placed in the accommodation of their choice, provided that it is suitable, available and not more expensive than the amount ordinarily paid by the local authority. It may be possible for an assisted person to be placed in a more expensive home if additional sums are paid, see National Assistance Act (Choice of Accommodation) Directions 2001, para 3; Circular LAC (2004).

In *Sowden v Lodge*[6] it was the defendant's case that a local authority residential placement was suitable. The claimant wanted a private arrangement which would cost the defendant considerably more money. The Court of Appeal stated that the test was to consider what was required to meet the claimant's reasonable needs. Detailed evidence is essential and Pill LJ emphasised:

(a)   Evidence should be obtained as to how the proposed regimes for care and accommodation would operate.

(b)   The proposals should be particularised and costed.

(c)   When issues arise efforts should be made to define and narrow them before the hearing.

(d)   If a local authority residential care with top-up is proposed the basis on which it is put forward should be explained in writing as should any attack upon its feasibility and suitability.

Claimants must co-operate with local authorities. Whilst there is no legal burden on the claimant to disprove that statutory provision will be adequate, it is prudent to call evidence to demonstrate what the claimant reasonably needs. If the claimant is not content to live in local authority residential accommodation, good reasons will have to be provided to support this. It is for a defendant who asserts that local authority residential care is suitable to set out whether such reasonable needs can be met by local authority care and whether there is any respect in which they

---

[6]   [2005] 1 WLR 2129.

accept that such care does not meet the claimant's reasonable needs. If necessary, it will then be for the claimant to assert that top-up will be required.

The more common situation is where the claimant wishes to remain at home with a private care regime, part of which is funded by the local authority. It is then necessary to consider the amount by which the damages payable by a tortfeasor should be reduced because of the local authority care provision. In principle deductions have to be made to take account of local authority contributions to care, see *Freeman v Lockett*[7] and *Crofton v NHS Litigation Authority* per Dyson LJ, paras 88–96[8] and chapter 7 on care.

One of the biggest areas of difficulty for a defendant who seeks to rely on local authority funding to reduce its liability to a claimant relates to the uncertainty surrounding any local authorities' attitude to future funding in this area.

9.3   ADAPTATIONS

The claimant is entitled to the cost of adapting his accommodation to meet his requirements following the injury. The necessary adaptations are usually dealt with in a report from an occupational therapist and/or an architect/surveyor who has visited the claimant in the property. Recommendations may include:

–   wheelchair access, ie ramps and widened doorways;

–   stairlift and/or grabrails on the stairs;

–   adaptations in the bathroom, for example walk-in shower and dryer for those claimants who are unable to use both arms easily.

In considering what is recoverable under this head of loss it is necessary to analyse the evidence. If the claimant is wheelchair bound a green house and raised flower beds may be recommended. If the main purpose is to provide an interest for the claimant this is unlikely to form part of the accommodation claim. Such a claim should be considered as a loss of amenity and/or therapy rather than a necessary expense in the cultivation of the garden.

If the adaptations result in an increase in the value of the property, which is seldom the case, credit must be given. If the adaptations result in a reduction in the value of the property, which is unusual, this is an item of special damage which is recoverable.

---

7   [2006] EWHC 102 (QB), [2006] Lloyd's Rep Med 151.
8   [2007] EWHC Civ 71.

9.4   HOME RUNNING COSTS

The claimant should claim increased expenditure in running the home. Items which should be considered are:

–   increased heating costs;

–   wheelchair damage to property and carpets which have to be redecorated /replaced more often than usual;

–   insurance: this is likely to be more if the claimant has moved to a larger home or the accident has made it necessary to have expensive equipment in the property.

Worked example

A 14-year-old schoolboy suffers a severe head injury. Current accommodation unsuitable, particularly because of stairs. Medical evidence supports move to bungalow. Live-in carer required. Accommodation expert provides figures as follows:

(1)   **Roberts and Johnson**

Cost of bungalow to be purchased	£300,000	
Value of terraced property he would have owned in any event (lifetime average)	–£200,000	
Betterment	+£20,000	
Total	£120,000	
£120,000 × 2.5% pa × 32.93 (life multiplier)		**£98,790**

(2)   **Ancillary Costs**

(i)	Legal fees including stamp duty	£1,500	
(ii)	Removal expenses	£750	
(iii)	Surveyor	£2,500	
Total			**£4,750**

(3)   **Adaptation Works**

(i)	Construct extension for carer	£5,000
(ii)	Creation of additional bedroom	£6,000
(iii)	Drainage	£1,000
(iv)	Structural alteration	£5,000
(v)	Bathroom and kitchen	£2,500

(vi)	Redecoration	£1,500	
(vii)	Paths and access	£750	
(viii)	Burglar alarm, smoke detectors and intercom	£1,250	
(ix)	Contingencies	£1,000	
	Total		**£24,000**

(4) **Additional expenditure**

(i)	VAT element on adaptation works	£4,000	
(ii)	Supervision fees	£5,000	
(iii)	Structural engineer's fees	£1,500	
(iv)	Local authority's fees	£500	
	Total		**£11,000**

(5) **Cost of Fitting Out**

Tiles in kitchen, carpets etc	£3,500	
Curtains	£750	
Total		**£4,250**

(6) **Increased running costs**

Increased running costs incurred in running the bungalow as extended and occupied by the claimant, his family and carer. Deducted from this sum are the running costs of the claimant's present family home plus a terraced house that he would have been likely to purchase had the accident never occurred.

(i)	Council tax	(£750)	
(ii)	Heating	£250	
(iii)	Telephone	£50	
(iv)	Maintenance (property); and		
(v)	Maintenance (fixed equipment)	£1,000	
(vi)	Building insurance premium	£50	
	Total	£600 pa	
	£600 pa × 32.93 (life multiplier) =		**£19,758**

Total cost

(1)	£98,790
(2)	£4,750
(3)	£24,000
(4)	£11,000

(5)	£4,250			
(6)	£19,758			
		=	£162,548	
Less betterment			£20,000	
Total				**£142,548**

9.5 SUITABLE ACCOMMODATION

It may be that accommodation that is suitable for the claimant now will not be suitable in the future, for example if the claimant starts a family. In those circumstances one or more further moves may become a necessity. The test for recovery remains what is reasonably necessary to meet the claimant's needs.

CHAPTER 10

MEDICAL EXPENDITURE AND AIDS AND EQUIPMENT

10.1 HEADS OF CLAIM

Expenditure on medical items reasonably incurred by the claimant as a result of injury is recoverable. This includes many items, for example:

- medical treatment, for example in a serious head injury case regular assessment by a neurologist and/or psychologist and/or psychiatrist in the future may be necessary;

- hospital fees where treatment has been or will be on a private basis (see para 10.1.1);

- attendances of doctors, nurses, physiotherapists, chiropodists etc;

- medicines: where large amounts of medication are being taken regularly an annual prescription should be considered;

- aids and equipment.

10.1.1 Private or NHS?

Section 2(4) of the Law Reform (Personal Injuries) Act 1948 provides:

> 'in an action for damages for personal injuries ... there shall be disregarded, in determining the reasonableness of any expenses, the possibility of avoiding those expenses or part of them by taking advantage of facilities under the National Health Service.'

A claimant may opt for private treatment and include this expense as part of his claim. The judge has to make an assessment: will the claimant probably rely on the NHS? Judges are wary about awarding future operation costs on a private basis when the same facility is available to the claimant under the NHS. The risk is obvious: the claimant may say that he will have the operation done privately and then have it done under the NHS and incur no expense. On the other hand, there are often good reasons for claimants wishing to have an operation done privately. For example, an ankle fracture may lead to osteoarthritis and an operation to fuse the joint (arthrodesis). If the claimant is working he may wish to have the operation performed privately so that it can be done at a time which is convenient to him and minimises the disruption to his work.

Since the introduction of the Rehabilitation Code in 1999 some enlightened insurers have been far more pro-active in providing private funding to expedite treatment of a claimant at an early stage when it is most needed. A copy of the 2007 version can be found in the PNBA Facts and Figures 2007/08 (I10).

10.1.2   What is reasonably necessary?

The line as to what is reasonably necessary may be difficult to draw.

- A head injured child may benefit from a computer with computer games. In the case of adults such claims will be much more difficult to support, see, for example, *Cassel v Riverside Health Authority*.[1] The child claimant will increasingly be met with the reasonable argument that they would probably have had computer games anyway.

- In *Cassel* the Court of Appeal reversed the decision of the trial judge who awarded £32,000 for the cost of a swimming pool which was the claimant's principal source of relaxation and pleasure. The decision was based on the fact that the medical evidence did not support the contention that swimming was a necessary therapy. Without compelling medical evidence a whirlpool or jacuzzi is unlikely to be recoverable. In *Burton v Kingsbury*[2] the medical evidence did support the need for a swimming pool for a tetraplegic and Flaux J awarded the full purchase price of the house including the pool (see chapter 9 housing) and the running costs of the pool which came to £4,000 p a.

- The claimant may, as a result of injuries, spend much more time in the home watching television. Increased home running costs are recoverable, but it will be difficult to prove that a claim for satellite/cable TV is reasonably necessary as a result of injuries sustained in an accident. There is likely to be considerable force in the argument that the claimant would have had satellite/cable TV anyway.

- If a medical therapy is recommended by a medical practitioner, there is unlikely to be difficulty in recovering the cost even if the treatment is unusual. In cases of post traumatic stress disorder, for example, eye movement desensitivisation therapy has now been recognised by

---

[1]   [1992] PIQR Q168.
[2]   [2007] EWHC 2091.

the National Institute for Clinical Excellence (NICE) and is for many psychiatrists the treatment of choice. This treatment is not easily available on the NHS.

- The cost of alternative therapies may be more difficult. Judges are increasingly inclined to allow the costs of acupuncture, chiropractors and osteopaths where the claimant can demonstrate that it has been of benefit, occasionally even in cases where it has not been recommended by a medical practitioner. It will, however, be more difficult to obtain damages for the cost of more innovative types of treatment such as aromatherapy

- In an amputation case the cost of light weight, high quality prosthetics can run into hundreds of thousands of pounds and it is vitally important to obtain good quality expert evidence from a reputable source. Even some orthopaedic consultants are out of touch with modern developments in this field.

10.2 QUANTIFICATION OF CLAIM

The capital cost of the item required should be claimed. An assessment should be made as to when the equipment will need replacing so that the replacement cost of the equipment can be claimed. The general principle is best illustrated by example.

Example A

Claimant aged 50 at trial had her leg amputated as a result of a road traffic accident. Attempts to fit an artificial leg failed. She is able to move only short distances on crutches, otherwise she needs a wheelchair. She has a 30 year life expectancy. An occupational therapist may recommend the following items:

Calculation

PNBA *Facts & Figures 2007/08*, schedule A3 for periodic multipliers at 2.5% discount. Multiplier for life for 50-year-old female at 2.5% discount (see Ogden tables 2) = 23.37

Item	Replacement Cost	Capital
Lightweight easily erected wheelchair		£1,400
Replacement every 5 years 3.98 × £1,400	£5,572	
Heavy duty wheelchair		£3,500

Item	Replacement Cost	Capital
Replacement every 5 years 3.98 × £3,500	£13,930	
Insurance for wheelchair 23.37 (life multiplier) × £50	£1,168	£50
Crutches @ £25 per pair		£25
Replacement every 2 years 10.34 × £50	£517	
Bath allowing easy access		£2,500
Delivery and installation Replacement every 20 years 0.61 × £2,900	£1,769	£400
Bathroom stool		£80
Replacement every 3 years 6.81 × £80	£545	
Electrically operated recliner		£1,100
Replacement every 10 years 1.87 × £1,100	£2,057	
Bed incorporating mattress inclinator and variable posture mattress		£2,500
Replacement every 10 years 1.87 × £2,500	£4,675	
Microwave		£350
Replacement every 10 years (see text below) 1.87 × £350	£654	
Kitchen stool		£55
Replacement every 5 years 3.98 × £55	£219	
Service Call		£12
Replacement every 3 years 6.81 × £12	£82	
Mobile Phone (see text below) 22.48 × £120 pa	£2,698	
Chair		£2,250
Replacement every 5 years 3.98 × £2,250	£8,995	

Item	Replacement Cost	Capital
Door opener intercom with twin channels		
Installation		£125
Replacement every 10 years 1.87 × £125	£234	
Lifeline – purchase		£225
24-hour monitoring and reactive service 23.37 × £225	£5,258	
Total	£48,373	£14,572
Replacement costs =	£48,373	
Capital costs =	£14,572	
TOTAL	£62,945	

Example B

This method is still used by many practitioners using a Capital and Annual Cost.

Item	Replacement	Capital Cost
Lightweight easily erected wheelchair		£1,400
Replacement every 5 years	£280	
Heavy duty wheelchair		£3,500
Replacement every 5 years	£700	
Insurance for wheelchair	£50	£50
Crutches @ £25 per pair		£25
Replacement every 2 years	£12.50	
Bath allowing easy access		£2,500
Delivery and installation		£400
Replacement every 20 years	£145	
Bathroom stool		£80
Replacement every 3 years	£26.66	
Electrically operated recliner		£1,100
Replacement every 10 years	£110	
Bed incorporating mattress inclinator and variable posture mattress		£2,500

Item	Replacement	Capital Cost
Replacement every 10 years	£250	
Microwave		£350
Replacement every 10 years	£35	
Kitchen stool		£55
Replacement every 5 years	£11	
Service Call		£12
Replacement every 3 years	£4	
Mobile Phone	£120	£120
Chair		£2,250
Replacement every 5 years	£450	
Door opener intercom with twin channels		
Installation		£125
Replacement every 10 years	£12.50	
Lifeline – purchase		£225
24-hour monitoring and reactive service	£90	
TOTAL	£2,296.66	£14,692.00

Multiplier for life for 50-year-old female at 2.5% discount (see Ogden tables 2) = 23.37

£2,296.66 × 23.37 = £53,672.94

Capital costs =   £14,692.00

Total   £68,364.94

Of the two methods, Example A is more accurate and to be preferred, as example B can lead to over-recovery. This can be illustrated using the example of the bath. In the above example the claimant has a life expectancy of 30 years. The bath will therefore only require replacement once. The capital cost now is £2,500 + £400. The periodic multiplier for replacement in 20 years time is 0.61: £2,900 × 0.61 = £1,769. Total claim: £2,900 + £1,769 = £4,669.

If the multiplicand is annualised the claim will include 10 years' contribution towards a third bath which will not be required. The capital cost now is £2,500 + £400 as above. The annual multiplicand is $1/20$ × £2,900 = £145. The multiplier for life is 23.22. The replacement costs are therefore 23.22 × £145 = £3,366.90. Total claim: £2,900 + £3,366.90 = £6,266.90.

In the above example there is likely to be a dispute about the cost of the microwave and the mobile phone which may well be items which the claimant would have had irrespective of the accident.

10.3 EVIDENCE

In all cases, it must be demonstrated by the medical evidence that the treatment or therapy or equipment is necessary. Obtaining satisfactory evidence requires close co-ordination between the parties involved, which is often easier than it sounds. It is prudent to wait until the future condition and prognosis of the claimant is known before considering what further non-medical reports are needed. In borderline cases, it is at this stage that it is necessary to consider whether the claimant's accommodation is suitable, or can be adapted to make it suitable.

10.3.1 Low-value cases

In a smaller case, a separate report from a care expert and/or occupational therapist may not be proportionate. The claimant may seek the assistance of organisations which help disabled people such as the Disabled Living Foundation (DLF)[3] in order to assess what more could be done. If expenditure on aids and equipment is thought to be necessary, questions should then be put to the medical expert to obtain support for the items: the burden is on the claimant to prove the case. In smaller cases Defendants have been known to object to a report on care/occupational therapy at case management, only for the claimant to be confronted at a hearing with the argument that there is no evidence to prove the claim for aids and equipment and/or level of care.

10.3.2 Medium-value cases

In an intermediate case, a care expert can sometimes usefully cover a modest aids and equipment claim as well as the proposed care regime.

10.3.3 High-value cases

In a larger case, a report from an occupational therapist, who can visit the claimant in the home, should be considered in addition to a care report. The occupational therapist should assess the medical evidence, witness the claimant in the home environment and consider the suitability of the accommodation. Reports from occupational therapists may recommend a large number of items, as in the above example. The principal medical expert should be asked to comment on the report in order to establish that the recommendations are reasonably necessary. Even in large clinical negligence cases, in the absence of special circumstances, the non-medical

---

[3]   Disabled Living Foundation (DLF) telephone (0845) 130 9177 [www.dlf.org.uk].

expert evidence should now normally be restricted to a single jointly instructed witness, see *Peet v Mid Kent Healthcare NHS Trust*.[4]

---

[4]   [2002] 1 WLR 210, in particular the judgment of Lord Woolf LCJ.

CHAPTER 11

MOBILITY AND TRANSPORT

11.1 HEAD OF CLAIM

Transport is of critical importance to any disabled person as more mobility can frequently mean greater independence. Investment in this area can radically improve the claimant's quality of life and, from the defendant's point of view, reduce the care element of a claim. The following heads of claim should be considered:

(a) loss of use of car;

(b) travelling expenses;

(c) transport costs.

11.2 LOSS OF USE OF CAR

11.2.1 Damaged car

The claimant's car may have been damaged and be off the road for a period. Loss of use should be claimed on a weekly basis. The level of the award will depend on the degree of the inconvenience and hardship. In practice such awards are now rare as hire cars are usually provided.

The cost of a hire car is recoverable if an alternative car is needed whilst accident repairs are being carried out. Need can be proved in the claimant's statement because of business, social or domestic reasons. The courts are usually prepared to compensate the clamant who obtains an alternative similar vehicle by credit hire, even though it is often considerably more expensive than the normal or 'spot' rate. The claimant has an obligation to act reasonably, but it should not be forgotten that he is the wronged party and the duty is a low one. There is, for example, no obligation to ring round in order to check that the lowest price has been obtained.[1] If liability is not admitted the claimant is entitled to wait until

---

[1] The claim for a replacement vehicle may be based on special damages based upon the

his own insurers authorise the repair, provided that period is not unreasonably protracted, see *Kingfisher Care Homes v Jones*.[2]

11.2.2 Collateral benefit

The claimant may have lost his job and with it his company car. The court then has to assess the annual loss. The AA and RAC provide tables which estimate running costs. It is necessary to consider whether running and standing costs can be legitimately claimed, or whether the claim is restricted to running costs only. These tables are reprinted in *Facts and Figures* produced by the Professional Negligence Bar Association.

11.3 TRAVELLING EXPENSES

Travelling expenses to and from medical appointments, etc are recoverable. These may include a claim for mileage, parking and, if the claimant required someone to drive him, a claim for the time of that person. Reasonable costs incurred by friends and relatives visiting the claimant in hospital will be recovered if the judge finds that the visits aided the recovery of the patient, or that additional services were being provided to the patient, eg assistance with eating, or helping the patient go for walks. Expenses incurred as a result of 'normal' visits which arose out of affection for the patient when the time was largely spent chatting would not, however, be recoverable, see *Havenhand v Jeffrey*.[3]

11.4 TRANSPORT COSTS

In the case of a seriously injured claimant, a claim for past and future transport costs may be appropriate. After an accident a claimant may find himself without the ability to travel independently. A claim for a suitable car should be considered as this can make a massive difference to the claimant's life.

11.5 QUANTIFICATION OF CLAIM

Provided the foundation is laid in the medical evidence the following may be recoverable.

11.5.1 Adaptations to claimant's car

Adaptations to allow a wheelchair to be carried or power steering may be recoverable.

---

cost of the hire, or general damages based on the spot hire charge for a comparable vehicle, see *Bee v Jenson* [2007] EWCA Civ 923 per Longmore LJ at para 20.

[2] (Unreported) 12 March 1998, CA, per Millet LJ.

[3] (Unreported) 24 February 1997, CA.

11.5.2　Acquiring new vehicle

Additional expenditure incurred in buying a reliable car and changing it more regularly than before the accident. A new car has additional benefits such as lower running costs and a manufacturer's warranty.

In *Woodrup v Nicol*[4] the claimant sustained serious injuries resulting in paralysis from the level of the sternum downwards. He retained movement in the upper limbs, but he also suffered from spasticity and was subject to involuntary and severe spasms. The need for a car was accepted by both parties. The Court of Appeal held that the award should be a capital figure which if properly invested would finance the purchase of a new motor car that would be replaced every four years. When the car is replaced the notional trade in value of the new car (as opposed to the car the claimant would have had anyway) should be deducted.

In *Goldfinch v Scannell*[5] the Court of Appeal held that it was appropriate to award damages reflecting the difference in capital depreciation between a new and second hand car and apply the multiplier to future loss based on a proportion of the annual capital depreciation of a suitable vehicle from AA statistics.

It was held in *Sarwar v Motor Insurers' Bureau*[6] and *Burton v Kingsbury*[7] that where the claimant had been rendered tetraplegic the cost of a Chrylser Voyager at nearly £40,000 was recoverable.

11.5.3　Expenses caused by travelling greater distances

In *Woodrup*, Wright J allowed a claim for an additional 10,000 miles p a as the claimant travelled long distances to see his friends who were living in different parts of the country. This was halved by the Court of Appeal on the basis that the claimant would travel less as he grew older and he became more involved in the farm he was now operating.

In cases where the claimant cannot drive his main contact with the outside world may be in trips out with a carer. There is a good argument that this additional mileage is reasonably necessary and recoverable. A good recent example of the calculation can be found in *Sarwar v Ali & MIB*[8]. In this case additional insurance of £4,437 p a was also allowed in order to cover at least one carer of under 25, less the £750 p a that the claimant would have spent on car insurance anyway.

---

[4]　[1993] PIQR Q104.
[5]　[1993] PIQR Q143.
[6]　[2007] EWHC 274 & 1255 (Lloyd Jones J).
[7]　[2007] EWHC 2091.
[8]　[2007] EWHC 1255.

Example

Claimant is 49 year old male and needs a reliable hatchback in order to travel to see friends and have sufficient additional room to store prosthetics. Replacement every 3 years, final replacement when he is 70 years old,

Statistics taken from Facts & Figures PNBA 2007/8

(1) Cost of new VW Golf 1.6 S FSI 5 door =	£14,500 (F & F I9)	
Proportion of price lost at each replacement =		
0.59 + 0.01 = 0.60 (F & F, I9)		
0.60 x £14,500 =	£8,700	
Multiplier for 21 years (3 yearly @ 2.5%) = 5.26 (F & F, A3)		
5.26 x £8,700 =		£45,762
(2) Credit has to be given for price of VW Polo Claimant currently owns using the same calculation		
Cost of VW Polo 1.2 E 64 3 door =	£8,200	
Proportion of price saved at each replacement = 0.64		
0.64 x £8,200 =	£5,248	
Multiplier for 21 years (see above) = 5.26		
5.26 x £5,248 =		£27,604
5 door VW Golf less saving on VW Polo		£18,158
(3) Estimated additional 5,000 miles pa by reason of disability		
19.88 pence per mile (F & F I6) × 5,000 = £994.00 pa × 22.27 (life multiplier for 49 year old male at 2.5%)		£22,136
Total cost of future transport		**£40,294**

11.5.4   Running costs

A distinction must be drawn between claims for running costs alone and claims including running costs and standing charges. If the claimant would have had a car anyway only running costs, including the additional depreciation which results from the increased mileage, are recoverable.

11.5.5 Motability

The claimant should investigate 'Motability', a government sponsored organisation which can give advice on all aspects of transport for the disabled. It is only available to those in receipt of certain state benefits, eg by using the higher rate mobility component of the disability living allowance the claimant may be able to enter a leasing or hire purchase agreement on a new car. For further information see www.motabilityonline.co.uk.

CHAPTER 12

MENTAL INCAPACITY AND THE COURT OF PROTECTION

12.1 INTRODUCTION

The law and practice relating to 'mentally incapable' claimants was overhauled by the Mental Capacity Act 2005. The Act took effect in October 2007. There are corresponding changes to the CPR (r 21),[1] new Court of Protection Rules[2] and a Code of Practice.

This chapter is concerned with the application and effect of the new regime. It is concerned only with mental incapacity and does not address the position of minors.

12.2 MENTAL CAPACITY ACT 2005

12.2.1 Principles

The stated principles of the Act are as follows:[3]

(1) A person must be assumed to have capacity unless it is established that he lacks capacity. (Whether a person has capacity is determined on the balance of probabilities and the burden of proving incapacity rests with the party asserting incapacity.)

(2) A person is not to be treated as unable to make a decision unless all practicable steps to help him to do so have been taken without success. (The court will be concerned to know whether steps have been taken to provide the claimant with advice from his family, medical and/or legal advisers.)

(3) A person is not to be treated as unable to make a decision merely because he makes an unwise decision. (Anyone can make an irrational or rash decision, but this is not the test of capacity under the Act.)

---

[1]   Civil Procedure (Amendment) Rules 2007.
[2]   Court of Protection Rules 2007.
[3]   Section 1.

(4)   An act done, or decision made, under this Act or for the benefit of a person who lacks capacity must be done, or made, in his best interests.

(5)   Before the act is done, or the decision is made, regard must be had to whether the purpose for which it is needed can be as effectively achieved in a way that is less restrictive of the person's rights and freedom of action.

In essence, the objective of the Act is to be less restrictive of an individual's right to make decisions for himself where possible. The Act establishes a new Court of Protection, as a superior court of record with increased powers and the new Office of Public Guardian, which has supervisory and regulatory functions.

12.3   THE TEST FOR CAPACITY

The first question is whether the claimant lacks capacity. For both parties this is crucial as no settlement or compromise of the claim is valid without court approval if the claimant lacks the requisite capacity and is therefore a 'protected party'.[4]

The test for capacity under the Act is set out in sections 2(1) and 3(1):

'2(1) For the purposes of this Act, a person lacks capacity in relation to a matter if at the material time he is unable to make a decision for himself in relation to the matter because of an impairment of, or a disturbance in the functioning of, the mind or brain.'

'3(1) For the purposes of section 2, a person is unable to make a decision for himself if he is unable to (a) understand the information relevant to the decision, (b) retain that information, (c) use or weigh that information as part of the process of making the decision, or (d) communicate his decision (whether by talking, using sign language or any other means).'

Over time the common law had developed tests for capacity on a piecemeal basis as different issues came before the courts.[5] Sections 2(1) and 3(1) of the Act provide a single test for financial, healthcare and welfare decisions but this test is not inconsistent with the existing common law tests.[6] For questions falling outside the ambit of the Act the

---

4   CPR 21.10(1)(a), replacing the term 'patient'.
5   *Banks v Goodfellow* (1870) LR 5 QB 549 – capacity to make a will; *Re Beaney (decd)* [1978] 1 WLR 770 – capacity to make a gift; *Boughton v Knight* (1873) LR 3 PD 64 – capacity to enter into a contract; *Re MB (Medical Treatment)* [1997] 2 FLR 426 – consent to medical treatment; *Masterman-Lister v Brutton & Co* (No 1) [2002] EWCA Civ 1889, [2003] 1 WLR 1511- capacity to litigate; *Sheffield City Council v E* [2004] EWHC 2808 (Fam) [2005] Fam 326 – capacity to marry.
6   Mental Capacity Act 2005 Code of Practice, para 4.33; *In the Matter of MM (an adult)* [2007] EWHC 2003 (Fam), paragraph 73.

Code of Practice suggests that the test under the Act may also be applied at common law, at the discretion of the judge.[7]

In *Saulle v Nouvet*[8] the court was asked to consider whether the definition of capacity under the Act applied to the question of whether the claimant had capacity to litigate as well as the question of whether he had the capacity to manage or control money recovered in the proceedings. The judge held that although the new Act did not require the test in section 2(1) to be applied to the question of capacity to conduct the litigation, the provisions of CPR Part 21 (as amended) had that effect. Any suggestion made by the Code of Practice to the contrary was wrong.

It does not matter whether the disturbance or impairment is temporary or permanent.[9] Also, the question of what is in a claimant's best interests cannot be established merely by reference to his age or appearance, or a condition of his, or an aspect of his behaviour, which might lead others to make unjustified assumptions about what might be in his best interests.[10]

A person is not regarded as unable to understand the information relevant to a decision if he is able to understand an explanation of it given to him in a way that is appropriate to his circumstances (using simple language, visual aids or any other means).[11] This consideration ties in with the principle of ensuring that all practicable steps have been taken to assist the claimant to understand the information necessary for the decision he is making.

The fact that a person is able to retain the relevant information for a short period only does not prevent him from being regarded as able to make that decision.[12] Relevant information includes information about the reasonably foreseeable consequences of deciding one way or another or failing to make the decision.[13]

As with the common law, the test of capacity under the Act is therefore both time ('at the material time') and issue ('the matter') specific.[14] Timing was considered in *Saulle v Nouvet*. The claimant disclosed video evidence which demonstrated that there were periods when, in the court's judgment, he had the necessary capacity. Expert and lay witness evidence suggested that there were other times when he probably lacked sufficient capacity. However, there was no evidence that the claimant had taken important decisions when he lacked capacity and he had sufficient control over his actions to take important decisions when he was properly able to

---

[7]   Mental Capacity Act 2005 Code of Practice, para 4.33
[8]   [2007] EWHC 2902 (QB).
[9]   Section 2(2).
[10] Section 2(3).
[11] Section 3(2).
[12] Section 3(3).
[13] Section 3(4).
[14] Mental Capacity Act 2005 Code of Practice, para 4.4.

do so. Accordingly, the judge found that the claimant did not lack capacity within the meaning of section 2(1) of the 2005 Act.

In *Bailey v Warren*[15] the court was concerned with the claimant's capacity to deal with a particular issue. The brain-injured claimant was held not to have been a patient and was therefore found to have had capacity in relation to the compromise of liability, in respect of which he had been given simple advice, but to have been a patient and therefore without capacity in relation to quantum, which was complex and involved a continuing responsibility for managing the resulting substantial damages.

12.4   BEST INTERESTS

Section 4 of the new Act sets out the matters relevant to the question of what is in the 'best interests' of the protected party and the obligations on the person making the determination at the material time. The list includes consideration of all the relevant circumstances:

- whether the protected party might at some time in the future have capacity in relation to the matter in question and if he will, when that might be

- he must in so far as is reasonably practicable permit and encourage the protected party's participation in the act or decision in question or improve his ability to participate in that act or decision

- he must consider the protected party's past and present wishes or feelings, any beliefs or values that would be likely to influence his decision if he had capacity and other factors he would consider if he was able to do so.

The person making the determination is also obliged to take into account, if practicable and appropriate to consult them, the views of anyone named as a person to be consulted about the matter in question or matters of that kind, anyone engaged in providing care for the protected party or any person interested in his welfare, any donee of a lasting power of attorney and any deputy (see below) appointed by the court.

12.5   PROTECTION FROM CIVIL LIABILITY

Section 5 of the Act provides a measure of protection against liability to those charged with responsibility for caring or treating an individual who lacks capacity. This protection is qualified by a number of requirements:

---

[15]   [2005] PIQR P15.

- reasonable steps have to be taken to establish whether that individual lacks capacity in relation to the matter in question;

- the person acting must reasonably believe the individual lacks capacity in relation to that matter;

- it must be reasonable to believe that it is in that individual's best interests for that act to be done.

Section 5 does not abrogate liability for negligence, criminal liability or for acts that would still have been unlawful even if the individual concerned had consented.

12.6 COURT OF PROTECTION

The new Court of Protection (CoP) has jurisdiction for welfare and health care as well as property and financial matters. The CoP is now a superior court of record with the same status as the High Court.[16] It is based in London but will sit in Bristol, Birmingham, Cardiff, Manchester/Preston and Newcastle upon Tyne.

Under Section 16, the CoP has the power to determine whether an individual has the capacity to make a particular decision and to make decisions about an individual's personal welfare[17] and/or his property and affairs[18] if the necessary conditions in sections 1 (the principles) and 4 (best interests) are satisfied.

The CoP also has the power to appoint deputies to take such decisions.[19] The role of deputy therefore replaces and expands the old role of 'receiver'. In appointing a deputy to act the court is required to have regard to the principles that it is preferable for any decision to be made by the court rather than the deputy and that the deputy's powers should be as limited in scope and duration as is reasonably practicable in the circumstances.[20] The CoP can make orders, give directions and appoint a deputy of its own motion.[21] It can revoke the appointment of a deputy or vary the powers conferred on the deputy in appropriate circumstances.[22] The CoP also has the power to call for reports from the Public Guardian, Court of Protection Visitor, local authority or NHS body.[23]

---

[16] Sections 45–47.
[17] Section 17.
[18] Section 18.
[19] Sections 16(2)(b), 19.
[20] Section 16(4).
[21] Section 16(6).
[22] Section 16(8).
[23] Section 49.

'Welfare' is defined in section 15 and includes such matters as place of residence, contact with specified person(s) and the giving or refusing of consent to medical treatment. However, it does not include personal family matters such as marriage or civil partnership, sexual relationships or divorce.[24] Note that the powers of the deputy in relation to welfare are restricted (see section 20).

'Property and affairs' is defined in section 16 and includes decisions about the control, management, acquisition and disposal of property, the carrying on of business or trade, dissolution of partnerships, performance of contracts, discharge of debts or other obligations, settlement of property or the execution of a will, the exercise of any power vested in the individual and the conduct of litigation brought by or against the individual whose capacity is in question. Again, the powers of the deputy in relation to property and affairs are limited by the Act (see section 20).

12.7 PUBLIC GUARDIAN

The new Office of the Public Guardian will keep a register of all orders appointing deputies and will be responsible for their supervision.[25] The Public Guardian has the power to call for a Court of Protection Visitor[26] to visit a deputy and/or to call for a report on the deputy and/or the claimant in question.

12.8 LITIGATION BY OR ON BEHALF OF PROTECTED PARTIES

Regard should be had to the detailed provisions in CPR 21 and the accompanying Practice Direction.

CPR 21.1 defines a 'protected party' as someone who lacks capacity within the meaning of the Mental Capacity Act 2005. A protected party must have a 'litigation friend' to conduct proceedings on his behalf.[27] The litigation friend may be a deputy who has been appointed under the 2005 Act with power to conduct proceedings on the individual's behalf[28] or some other suitable person as long as that person can satisfy the requirements of CPR 21.4(3), ie he can fairly and competently conduct the proceedings on behalf of the protected party, has no adverse interests to the protected party and undertakes to pay the protected party's costs if necessary.[29]

---

[24] Sections 27–29.
[25] Section 50(1)(b) and (c).
[26] See: Section 61 generally.
[27] CPR 21.2(1).
[28] CPR 21.4(2).
[29] CPR 21.4(3).

Any step taken in proceedings before the protected party has a litigation friend has no effect without a court order.[30] Similarly, no settlement, compromise, payment or acceptance of a payment into court is valid without the court's approval.[31] The same requirement exists for the apportionment of an award made under the Fatal Accidents Act 1976[32] and in respect of voluntary interim payments.[33]

If the court has not already appointed a litigation friend the procedure set out in CPR 21.5 should be followed. If the litigation friend is a deputy with the power to conduct proceedings on behalf of the protected party he must, at the time the claim is made, file a copy of the order from the CoP which conferred that power.[34] A litigation friend who has not been appointed by court order or who is not a deputy must, at the time the claim is made, file a 'certificate of suitability', stating that he satisfies the requirements of CPR 21.4(3)(see paragraph 12.23 above). He must also consent to act, state that he knows or believes that the claimant is a protected party and set out the grounds for that knowledge/belief, attaching any medical evidence upon which he relies.[35] This document should be served on the person authorised to conduct proceedings on the protected party's behalf, or in the absence of such a person, on the individual with whom the protected party resides or who is responsible for his care.[36] The litigation friend must file a certificate of service.[37]

The court has the power to appoint a litigation friend. The procedure set out in CPR 21.6 and 21.8 should be followed. The application should be supported by evidence and the proposed litigation friend must satisfy the requirements of CPR 21.4(3). The court also has the power to exclude a person from acting or continuing to act as a litigation friend, terminate the appointment of a litigation friend or substitute a litigation friend.[38]

An application for approval of any settlement or compromise, whether made before or after proceedings have been commenced, requires an opinion on the merits of the settlement or compromise from counsel or solicitor in all but the clearest cases. The court will also require the instructions on which the advice was based (unless these are apparent from the advice) and any financial advice. The court will want to know whether periodic payments have been considered in respect of any claim for future loss, and, if the settlement includes provision for periodic

---

[30] CPR 21.3(4).
[31] CPR 21.10(1).
[32] PD 1.6.
[33] PD 1.7.
[34] PD 2.3(1).
[35] PD 2.3(2).
[36] See also generally CPR 6.6.
[37] PD 2.2 (2).
[38] CPR 21.7.

payments, the court must be provided with the terms of the settlement or compromise and a draft consent order.[39]

A point may arise where the protected party acquires or regains capacity to conduct the litigation. However, the appointment of the litigation friend continues unless and until the court orders otherwise. The protected party, litigation friend or another party to the proceedings may apply for an order ending the appointment of the litigation friend. Once the order is made the protected party must serve notice on all other interested parties, giving his address for service and stating whether he intends to continue with the proceedings.[40]

Where damages are recovered by or on behalf of the protected party, or a payment into court is accepted, the court will give directions for the management of the money recovered.[41] These may provide for the payment of the whole or part of the damages into court to be invested, but before giving directions the court must first consider whether the protected party is also a 'protected beneficiary' (ie a protected party who lacks the capacity to manage and control any of the money recovered on his behalf in the proceedings).

12.9   INDEPENDENT MENTAL CAPACITY ADVOCATE

For those without support or representation the Act provides for the appointment of an Independent Mental Capacity Advocate to support and represent the protected party in respect of applications relating to medical treatment, accommodation in an NHS institution or local authority accommodation.[42]

12.10   FEES

Each application to the Court of Protection (Court of Protection Fees Order 2007, Part 9) will incur a fee of £400.00.[43] If a hearing is required an additional £500.00 becomes payable. The fees are not payable in respect of an application by the Public Guardian or if the applicant is in receipt of a qualifying benefit,[44] unless, in respect of the benefit exception, the applicant has received damages in excess of £16,000.00 which has been placed in a PI Trust so as to be disregarded for the purpose of determining eligibility for benefits.

---

[39]   PD 6.3–6.9.
[40]   CPR 21.9.
[41]   CPR 21.11, PD 8.
[42]   Sections 35–39.
[43]   Court of Protection Fees Order 2007.
[44]   Qualifying benefits are listed in reg 8(3).

A fixed fee of £125.00 is payable where the court appoints a deputy in accordance with the provisions of section 16 of the Act. Supervision fees incurred by the Public Guardian are also payable depending upon his assessment of the level of supervision required. Type I (highest) will attract an annual fee of £800.00. Type II (medium) will attract an annual fee of £175.00. Type III (minimal) incurs no fee.[45]

The deputy is also entitled to be recompensed for his reasonable expenses and, if the court so directs when appointing him, to remuneration for the performance of his functions.[46]

If the litigation friend has incurred expenses he may apply to recover those expenses from any damages recovered, as long as the expense was reasonably incurred and reasonable in amount.[47]

12.11 CONCLUSIONS

The various provisions relating to those lacking sufficient capacity either to litigate or to manage and control a substantial award of damages are complex and present a potential minefield for the unwary. Nevertheless, practitioners must be on the look out for any sign that the claimant may not have the requisite capacity. Cases of severe brain injury or psychiatric injury will be obvious. However, many cases involve minor damage with subtle but potentially devastating consequences. When in doubt, it is always advisable to obtain appropriate expert medical evidence from a neurologist, neuro-psychologist or consultant psychiatrist.

---

[45] The Public Guardian (Fees, etc) Regulations 2007.
[46] Section 19.
[47] CPR 21.12.

CHAPTER 13

DAMAGES IN RESPECT OF DEATH

13.1   GENERAL

There are two separate and distinct claims:

(a)   The claim on behalf of the deceased's estate (Law Reform (Miscellaneous Provisions) Act 1934).

(b)   The claim brought by the deceased's dependants in respect of their own loss (Fatal Accidents Act 1976 (as amended)).

13.2   CLAIMS ON BEHALF OF THE ESTATE

13.2.1   Law Reform (Miscellaneous Provisions) Act 1934

A deceased's claim survives for the benefit of the estate regardless of whether the *death* was caused by the defendants' breach of duty/negligence. Heads of damage usually include the following:

(1)   pain and suffering;

(2)   past loss of earnings;

(3)   past care/services;

(4)   miscellaneous losses including medical expenses, travel and probate.

Claims may also include damages in respect of funeral expenses.

A claimant may have suffered an injury that reduces his life expectancy, resulting in a loss of potential earnings or pension he would otherwise have received in the lost years. A living claimant may recover damages for those losses but this head of damage does not survive for the benefit of the estate.

13.2.2 Pain and suffering

This is calculated in accordance with conventional principles and is therefore dependent upon the claimant's personal awareness of pain and suffering.[1]

A particular problem arises in respect of damages for pain and suffering where the death was instantaneous or occurred very shortly after the accident in question. The court may still make an award but it is likely to be modest.[2]

The claimant must adduce some evidence to support the claim: *Hicks v Chief Constable of the South Yorkshire Police*[3], where a claim by victims of the Hillsborough disaster was rejected on the basis that the evidence indicated that the pain and suffering (from asphyxia) for which damages might have been awarded was so short lived that it should be considered as part of the death itself and not result in an award.

13.2.3 Loss of earnings up to the date of death

This is calculated as past loss on established principles as for a living claimant.

13.2.4 Care and services up to the date of death

The basis for a claim for care/services provided by others is that the damages are held in trust for the carer. The same principle applies to the claim on behalf of the estate.

As for lost earnings, the claim runs up to the date of death.

13.2.5 Miscellaneous

Any discrete items of loss or expenditure incurred by the deceased prior to death should be included within the claim.

13.2.6 Funeral expenses

Funeral expenses usually form part of the Fatal Accidents Act claim if the dependants have incurred the expense. However, in *Bateman v Hydro*

---

[1]   *Lim Poh Choo v Camden and Islington Area Health Authority* [1980] AC 174 at 183.

[2]   See *Rose v Ford* [1937] AC 826. (Claimant survived for four days after the accident although spent the greater part of that time in a coma. Damages fixed at £20; *Roughead v Railway Executive* [1949] WN 280. Deceased died the day after the accident but was able to speak to his solicitor in that time. Damages fixed at £250 (2002 – worth about £5,300).)

[3]   [1992] PIQR P 63.

Agri (UK) Ltd,[4] the judge held that the claimant, who was suffering from mesothelioma and was expected to die within three months, could recover the prospective costs of his funeral.

13.3 CLAIMS ON BEHALF OF DEPENDANTS

Heads of damage usually include the following:

(1) damages in respect of bereavement;

(2) damages for loss of dependency;

(3) funeral expenses.

13.3.1 Who may bring the claim?

The action must be brought by and in the name of the executor or administrator of the deceased. If there is no executor or administrator *or* no action is brought within six months of the date of death by and in the name of the executor or administrator the action may be brought by and in the name of any of the dependants. Only one action can be brought under the Act.

No action may be brought if the victim has already settled his claim, or obtained judgment, prior to death.[5]

13.3.2 Damages in respect of bereavement

This is a statutory award (FAA 1976, s 1A). For deaths occurring on or after 1 April 2002 the award is £10,000 and from 1 January 2008, £11,800. Before April 2002, £7,500 and before 1990, £3,500.

Damages for bereavement may only be claimed by the spouse of the deceased unless the deceased was an unmarried minor at the date of death in which case the award may be claimed by both parents, divided equally, if he was legitimate or by his mother alone if illegitimate. The Act is applied strictly in respect of the age of the deceased at the date of death.[6]

There is no other basis for apportioning the award of damages for bereavement.[7]

---

[4] (Unreported) 15 September 1995.
[5] *Thompson v Arnold* [2007] EWHC 1875 (QB).
[6] *See Doleman v Deakin* (1990) *The Times*, 30 January.
[7] *Griffiths v British Coal Corporation* (unreported) 6 February 1998, per Turner J.

13.3.3 Dependency

The dependency claim invariably includes a claim for loss of earnings/pension/other income but may also include claims in respect of loss of care and services of a spouse or parent.

13.3.4 Dependants

Fixed by statute:

(a)   wife or husband or former wife or husband;

(b)   any person living with the deceased as husband or wife for a period of at least two years prior to death and still living with the deceased in that capacity immediately before the date of death;

(c)   any parent or other ascendant;

(d)   any person treated by the deceased as a parent;

(e)   any child of the deceased;

(f)   any person who, in the case of any marriage to which the deceased was at any time a party, was treated by the deceased as a child of the family in relation to that marriage;

(g)   any brother, sister, uncle or aunt of the deceased or their children.

Note that illegitimacy is not a bar to recovery as the Act specifies that an illegitimate child shall be treated as legitimate of the mother and reputed father.

13.3.5 Multiplier

The established approach is to calculate the multiplier at the date of *death* and then treat the period from death to trial as past loss, leaving the balance of the multiplier for future loss from the date of trial.[8]

This approach can lead to injustice, particularly where there is a significant delay between death and trial.[9]

The Ogden Working Party and the Law Commission have suggested that losses prior to trial should be treated as past loss, and the multiplier for

---

[8]   *Cookson v Knowles* [1979] AC 556, [1978] 2 All ER 604, [1978] 2 WLR 978, [1978] 2 Lloyd's Rep 315. Confirmed in *Graham v Dodds* [1983] 2 All ER 953, [1983] 1 WLR 808.

[9]   *Corbett v Barking, Havering & Brentwood Health Authority* [1991] 2 QB 408.

future losses post-trial should be calculated from the date of *trial*. However, thus far attempts to displace the clear authority of *Cookson* have been unsuccessful.[10]

The proper approach therefore appears to be:

(a) calculate the multiplier at the date of death;

(b) discount this for contingencies other than mortality. The general approach is set out in the introductory notes to the Ogden Tables, 6th Edn – See Chapter 2, Loss of Earnings para 2.4.2);

(c) calculate past dependency to the date of trial;

(d) calculate future dependency using the balance of the multiplier.

13.3.6 Different working lives

Most couples have different retirement dates or life expectancies. Where, but for the accident, the deceased's life expectancy was greater than the dependant's, the multiplier will have to be reduced to take account of the dependant's life expectancy as this will more accurately reflect the true period of dependency.

This is achieved by calculating the multiplier for each period and using the lower of the two multipliers.

This approach applies equally to different periods of dependency, for example in the case of a child or spouse/partner whose dependency will cease before the Deceased's predicted retirement age/life expectancy.

Example

The deceased dies at age 60, his wife is aged 68. The deceased's lifetime multiplier at the date of death is 16. His wife's lifetime multiplier is 13.8. The appropriate multiplier for dependency for life is 13.8.

13.3.7 Multiplicand

A conventional approach has developed for calculating the multiplicand which is applicable to most cases.

---

[10] See *Wilkens v Press Construction* (unreported), 30 November 2000; *White v ESAP Group (UK) Ltd* [2002] PIQR Q76 and *MS v ATH* [2003] QB 965.

13.3.8   Couple with no dependent children, surviving spouse not working

Past: The loss represents that part of the deceased's earnings which would have been for the benefit of the dependant, either as part of a shared expense (electricity, rent or mortgage, etc) or an individual benefit (clothes, food). The conventional figure is two-thirds or 66.66% of the deceased's income.[11]

Future: The balance of the multiplier × multiplicand at the date of trial.

Example

Income £15,000 pa for each of 2 years after the death and prior to trial. Multiplier of 5.5.

Past loss: 2 × £15,000 × 66.66% = £20,000.

Future loss: 3.5 × £15,000 × 66.66% = £34,996.50.

13.3.9   Couple with dependent children, surviving spouse working

Where the family has dependent children the multiplicand is usually treated as three-quarters or 75% of the lost income until the dependency of the children ceases[12] (this can be beyond the age of majority, particularly in cases where the children go on to university or college). Accordingly, more than one calculation may be required.

Where the spouse was also working, it is assumed that both incomes were pooled and the family was dependent upon the joint income.

The loss is therefore the joint income × the dependency (66.66% or 75%) less the continuing income of the surviving spouse.

Example

Deceased's income would have been £15,000 in each of 2 years after the death and prior to trial. Spouses' income £10,000 in each year. Two children aged 10 and 12 at the date of trial. Multiplier for loss until younger child ceases full time education (aged 21) 9.6. Balance of multiplier 3.

Joint annual income: £25,000.

Annual figure while children still dependent: £25,000 × 75% = £18,750.

---

[11]   *Harris v Empress Motors Ltd; Cole v Crown Poultney Packers Ltd* [1983] 3 All ER 561, [1984] 1 WLR 212.

[12]   *Coward v Comex* (unreported) 1988, Kemp & Kemp M2-232.

Annual dependency while children still dependent: £18,750 – £10,000 = £8,750.

Annual figure after children no longer dependent: £25,000 × 66.66% = £16,665.

Annual dependency after children no longer dependent: £16,665.00 – £10,000.00 = £6,665.

Past loss: 2 × £8,750 = £17,500.

Future loss (first period): 7.6 × £8,750 = £66,500.

Future loss (second period): 3 × £6,665 = £19,995.

13.3.10   Factors affecting multiplicand

The conventional approach set out above is appropriate for most cases. However, it is based upon an assumption about the way in which family income is used. Ultimately the more precise approach is to calculate as accurately as possible the actual dependency taking into account the income and the outgoings of the deceased. It is the complexity and impracticality of doing this that justifies the conventional approach.

There are cases where the conventional approach is still not appropriate, for example where the joint income is so small that virtually all of it is used for the benefit of the family as a whole, with little or no part kept back for the deceased's own benefit. In such a case the 66.66% or 75% should be increased appropriately. Where the deceased's income was substantial and only a modest part was used for the benefit of the spouse/family, again the calculation should be modified. For a high income family in certain circum-stances a higher percentage may still be justified.[13]

13.3.11   Collateral benefits

The loss may not necessarily be limited to the deceased's income. The deceased may also have had the use of a company car, payment of domestic telephone bills etc. Such losses are recoverable and should be included as part of the dependency claim.

13.3.12   Claimant's loss

In addition to the loss of the deceased's income, the claimant may also establish that his or her own source of income was affected by reason of

---

[13]   *Farmer v Rolls Royce Industrial Power (India) Ltd* (unreported) 2003: the dependency in this case was 85%.

the death. The circumstances where this arises are rare in practice and must arise out of the relationship between the claimant and the deceased.

In *Oldfield v Mahoney*,[14] the loss of a wife diminished the claimant's prospects of promotion as a housemaster, a position normally reserved for married men. Neild J concluded that the claimant's married status gave him a particular qualification for that job and the loss of his wife had removed that qualification leading to a measurable loss of future income.

13.3.13   Pension loss

Dependency upon pension also arises after the date of retirement. Pension loss is dealt with elsewhere but the following points should be noted.

Section 4 of the FAA 1976 prevents benefits which have accrued or may accrue as a result of the death from being taken into account. In practical terms this means that a widows' pension is not to be deducted in calculating dependency on pension. However, the pension the widow would have received irrespective of the death will still be taken into account in the normal way.

The multiplier for pension loss may be calculated in a number of ways. Usually it is the lifetime multiplier, less the multiplier for earnings loss. The difference represents the multiplier for dependency on pension without the need for further discount for accelerated receipt.

There is no reason in principal why the State pension should not form part of the loss.[15] Note: the calculation depends upon whether the dependent spouse was entitled to a State pension in her own right or whether her pension was to be paid as part of the deceased's entitlement based upon his national insurance contributions and following his death she receives a widow's benefit.

13.3.14   Services

The claim is based upon those services provided by the deceased that now have to be performed by others, either gratuitously or for payment, ie car maintenance.

The lifetime multiplier is not appropriate for this head of loss. It is generally accepted that an individual's capacity to undertake DIY, decorating, car maintenance, gardening etc diminishes in the advancing years of life. Conventionally this is reflected by reducing the multiplier either by discounting the lifetime multiplier or determining a multiplier

---

[14]   (Unreported) 1968, Kemp & Kemp M3-123.
[15]   *Lea v Owen* (unreported) 1980, summarised in Kemp & Kemp.

based upon an assumed age by which the deceased would probably have stopped being able to manage much DIY etc. It is also open to the court to make a lump sum award rather than calculate this loss on a simple multiplier/multiplicand approach.[16]

Past loss of services should generally be based upon the cost actually incurred by the claimant between death and trial. However, where the services were replaced gratuitously an assessment of their value will have to be made. The best evidence for this is from estimates from professional providers (decorators etc). However, as with claims on behalf of living claimants a broad-brush approach has frequently been adopted by the courts. See, for example, *Page v Sheerness Steel plc*,[17] where the value of the DIY etc provided by a young claimant who undertook all the decorating inside and out, fitting out the kitchen and bathroom and all the plumbing and paving the back garden was valued at £1,000 per annum (worth bout £1,400 in 2008).

13.3.15   Loss of a mother

Loss of a mother may give rise to claims for financial dependency as set out above. Often, such claims are limited to or include a claim for the loss of the 'services of a mother'. The assessment of the value of these services is by no means straightforward and care must be exercised when considering authorities as a basis for the appropriate award of damages for the loss of a mother's services. Nevertheless, early decisions do provide a useful guide in this area of assessment as in any other.

Some awards have been based upon the notional cost of a housekeeper,[18] although the Court of Appeal in *Spittle v Bunny* observed that whilst the valuation of a mother's services in the early years might properly be based upon the notional cost of hiring a nanny, this became less appropriate as the child grew older and entered school age.

In *Spittle* the trial judge awarded £47,000 to a 3 year old girl when her unmarried mother died at the age of 28. The father took no responsibility for the child. The claim was for loss of dependency to age 22. The award was reduced on appeal for the reasons set out above to £25,000.

Lewis v Osborne:[19] Sedley J also departed from a multiplier/ multiplicand approach. He awarded a 1 year old girl £40,000 for the loss of her mother.

Bacon v White:[20] the court awarded a 2 year old child £30,000 for the loss of his mother, who also worked as a nurse.

---

[16]   See, eg, *Worrall (D) v Powergen plc* [1999] PIQR Q103 at 107.
[17]   [1996] PIQR Q26.
[18]   See *Hay v Hughes* [1975] QB 790 and *Spittle v Bunny* [1988] 1 WLR 847.
[19]   (Unreported) 1995, Kemp & Kemp M4-071/1 and M4-136.
[20]   (Unreported) 1998, Kemp & Kemp M4-072/1 and M4-137.

Hayden v Hayden:[21] the Court of Appeal upheld an award of £20,000 to a girl aged 4 for the death of her mother. The claimant was one of five children but no claim was advanced on behalf of the others.

Re TG and J:[22] CICB awarded three children aged 5, 3 and 2 at the date of death, damages ranging from £21,250 to £29,750 in respect of the loss of their mother. The awards were based upon the commercial cost of a nanny but about 25% was in respect of financial dependency. The mother was not working at the date of death but had a good work record and was likely to have returned to work in the future.

The cases summarised above suggest that awards are generally limited. An obvious exception is *Martin v Grey*,[23] in which the trial judge used an annual multiplicand of £22,500 per annum to a child aged 12 at the date of death.

Where the surviving spouse has given up work to care for the children, it may be appropriate to award the value of the loss of earnings, although damages are usually limited to the likely cost of employing professional help unless circumstances permit. In *Mehmet v Perry*[24] the court allowed as the value of services the earnings of the surviving father who gave up well-paid work to care for his children, a number of whom suffered from a rare medical condition necessitating constant care.

In a number of cases the courts have made a separate, modest, award for the loss of services of a wife or mother over and above the cost of a replacement nanny or housekeeper.[25] In *Topp v London Country Bus (SW) Ltd*[26] the trial judge assessed the value of the loss of services of a wife, over and above the financial dependency, as £2,000. The award to the husband in *Johnson v British Midland Airways Ltd*,[27] was £2,500.

13.3.16　Apportionment

As set out above, there is only one claim permitted under the FAA 1976. Accordingly, damages have to be apportioned between the various dependants. Settlements on behalf of minors must also be approved by the court.[28]

The apportionment of damages as between the surviving spouse and the children will depend upon the relationship between them.

---

[21]　[1992] PIQR Q111.
[22]　(Unreported) 1990, Kemp & Kemp M4-070.
[23]　(1999) 99 (3) QR 8.
[24]　[1977] 2 All ER 529, DC.
[25]　See *Regan v Williamson* [1976] 2 All ER 241.
[26]　[1992] PIQR P206, [1993] 3 All ER 448.
[27]　[1996] PIQR Q8.
[28]　CPR, r 21.10(1).

There is some authority for the proposition that the award to the minors should be 'such sum as he might have expected to receive ... if his father had not died, which sum would have been *over and above* the cost of his keep, which ... is included in the dependency of his mother' *per* Borham J in *Thompson v Price*[29] [emphasis added]. This suggests that the bulk of the award for the maintenance of the children should go to the surviving parent on the basis that she has the responsibility for continuing to maintain the children.

Thompson is no longer entirely authoritative as a deduction was made from the child's award in that case for the fact of the surviving mother's remarriage. Remarriage is no longer relevant due to the effect of s 4 of the Fatal Accidents Act 1976 (as amended). It is also noteworthy that the precise figures for apportionment in that case were agreed.

The question of apportionment was considered by Latham J in *R v CICB*.[30] Historically and following *Thompson* the approach of the courts to apportionment between dependants had been pragmatic, seeking to give as much available cash as possible to the surviving spouse in order to provide ready access to the fund necessary for the upkeep of the dependent children. However, Latham J considered that:

> '... the principle appears to me to be clear. The principle is that each person who can properly be described as a dependant is entitled to the value of his or her dependency. The value of that dependency will obviously depend upon, so far as the children are concerned, their age and the financial circumstances in which the family may be at any given time.'

A reasonable and simple starting point for the assessment of the dependency of each child may be extrapolated arithmetically from the dependency calculation. Essentially, that part of the dependency referable specifically to the children is represented as the difference between 75% and 67%: 8%. In practice the courts should consider the individual dependency of each child in assessing the amount to be apportioned, and will therefore modify the strict arithmetic approach to the evidence.

13.3.16.1   Reduced Life Expectancy

A claimant may have a reduced life expectancy as a result of his injuries or disease. He will therefore be prevented from earning or using his income in the 'lost years' of reduced life expectancy.

It is now well established that the surviving claimant can in such circumstances recover damages for his loss in the lost years.[31] In a conventional calculation the multiplicand is usually taken to be 50% of

---

[29]   [1973] 2 All ER 846.
[30]   (1994) *The Times*, 8 February.
[31]   *Pickett v British Rail Engineering* [1980] AC 136.

the Claimant's anticipated net income during the period of reduced life expectancy. The multiplier is that appropriate to the period of reduced life expectancy, discounted for accelerated receipt.

This claim does not survive for the benefit of his estate.[32]

---

[32] *Gammell v Willson* [1982] AC 27, in which such a claim was allowed in the House of Lords, was reversed by an amendment to the FAA 1976.

CHAPTER 14

INTEREST

14.1 STATUTORY PROVISIONS

The power to award interest on damages for personal injuries derives from s 35A of the Supreme Court Act 1981 with s 69 of the County Courts Act 1984:

> '(1) Subject to rules of court, in proceedings (whenever instituted) before the High Court for the recovery of a debt or damages there *shall* be included in any sum for which judgment is given *unless the court is satisfied that there are special reasons to the contrary* simple interest, at such rate as the court thinks fit or as the rules of court may provide, on all or any part of the debt or damages in respect of which judgment is given, or payment is made before judgment, for all or any part of the period between the date when the cause of action arose and ... the date of the payment ... the date the judgment.'

14.2 PRINCIPLES

An award of damages is intended to:

> 'as nearly as possible put the party who has suffered in the same position as he would have been in if he had not sustained the wrong'.[1]

Interest itself does not form part of the award of compensation but is designed to meet the fact that the claimant has been kept out of money which was rightfully his:

> 'Interest should not be awarded as compensation for the damage done. It should only be awarded to a plaintiff for being kept out of money which ought to have been paid to him'.[2]

It is that fundamental principle which underpins the award of interest on damages.

---

[1]   *Livingstone v Rawyards Coal Co* (1880) 5 LR App Cas 25; *Lim Poh Choo v Camden and Islington Health Authority* [1979] 2 All ER 910.
[2]   Per Lord Denning MR in *Jefford v Gee* [1970] 1 All ER 1202.

14.2.1   General damages

Interest on damages for pain, suffering and loss of amenity runs from the date of *service* of the proceedings.

Interest on damages for pain, suffering and loss of amenity is currently 2%.[3]

14.2.2   Special damages

In claims for damages in respect of personal injury the rate is fixed by the prevailing special account rate. The various rates in force from time to time are set out in the table in *Facts & Figures*. Since 1 February 2002 the rate has been 6% per annum.

14.2.3   Full or half rate

The issue most likely to arise in practice is whether to apply the rate in full on any particular head of damage.

The logical approach would be to calculate interest on each item of loss separately. In practice this would frequently be unworkable, particularly in respect of items of loss continuing from day to day or over a long period.

An expedient approach to calculating interest on items of continuous loss from the date of accident to the date of trial was given by the court of appeal in *Jefford v Gee*.[4]

> 'In all ordinary cases ... it would be fair to award interest on the total sum of special damages from the date of the accident until the date of trial at half the [special account] rate ...'.

The alternative, as stated above, would be to calculate interest on each week's loss. However, in order to avoid this level of detail Lord Denning suggested:

> 'More rough and ready, the total loss could be taken from the accident to trial: and interest allowed only on half of it, or for half the time, or at half the rate.'

Applying interest at half rate from accident to trial is still not appropriate for one-off payments (ie damaged clothing) or where losses are incurred

---

[3]   *Lawrence v Chief Constable for Staffordshire* [2000] TLR 562, CA.
[4]   [1970] 2 QB 130. See also *Dexter v Courtaulds Ltd* [1984] 1 All ER 70, [1984] 1 WLR 372.

over a limited period of time and the period of loss ends some time before trial (ie cost of taxis for a few months or where the claimant has returned to work).[5]

The following methods may then be used as circumstances dictate:

(a)   interest at full rate from the date of loss to trial;

(b)   interest at full rate from the mid-point of the period of loss to trial; or

(c)   interest at half rate during the period of loss and then at full rate from the end of that period to trial.

Ultimately, practitioners should remember that the court has discretion in relation to the amount and period of interest and may depart from the principles set out above, although it is unlikely to do so in practice.

14.2.4   Interim payments

The claimant should only recover interest on his actual loss. If prior to trial some of that loss has been made good by way of interim payments, these should be taken into account in the calculation of interest.

Similarly, where a particular item of loss has been met by the defendants directly, there is no good reason why this item should attract interest in the claim.[6]

The conventional approach is for an interim payment to be treated first as compensation in respect of special damage. Interest runs at half rate on continuing losses until the date of the interim payment and thereafter at half rate on the balance of the continuing losses.

If the interim exceeds the amount of special damage due on the date it is paid, the balance of the interim is treated as compensation in respect of general damages for pain and suffering.[7]

Where, however, the claimant receives interim payments after judgment has been entered but before the claim has been quantified, it has been held at first instance that interest accrued by the claimant on the interim payments received is not to be deducted from the interest due to the claimant on his losses.[8]

---

[5]   Per May LJ in *Prokop v DHSS* [1985] CLY 1037, CA.
[6]   See, eg, *IM Properties Ltd v Cape and Dalgleish (A Firm)* [1999] QB 297.
[7]   *Bristow v Judd* [1993] PIQR Q117 at 130.
[8]   *Parry v NW Surrey Health Authority* [2000] TLR 2.

14.2.5   Benefits

Deductible benefits paid during the period of loss are not to be taken into account in calculating interest, any more than they are taken into account in the calculation of damages themselves.[9] Accordingly, it is the total loss, before deduction of benefits, that attracts interest.

However, the award of interest on damages for loss of earnings falls within the definition of 'compensation for earnings lost' and is therefore also subject to reduction on account of deductible benefits.[10]

14.2.6   Factors affecting the court's discretion

(1)   Delay: *Read v Harries*:[11] a case in which the judge found inexcusable delay by the claimant in failing to provide proper information to the instructing solicitor. In dealing with interest the trial judge concluded that there was no reason why the action should not have been tried three years earlier in October 1991. In the event he awarded interest only up to that date.
       However, *Adcock v Cooperative Insurance Society Ltd*,[12] suggests that this power to reduce the award of interest should only be used in exceptional circumstances, ie where the defendant has been pressing for trial.

(2)   Conduct: ie where a party has deliberately withheld relevant information.

(3)   Part 36: the court has power to award interest at a higher rate where a defendant fails to beat a claimant's Part 36 offer.[13]

14.2.7   Payments by volunteers

Where an employer has continued to pay sums equivalent to the claimant's wages, should these be offset against the loss of earnings claim in calculating interest? In *Davies v Inman*,[14] the court refused to deal with interest in this way rather stating that the employer should be treated as a volunteer who has made good the loss. The employer had been kept out of

---

[9]   *Wisely v John Fulton (Plumbers) Ltd*; *Wadey v Surrey County Council* [2000] 1 WLR 820, HL.
[10]   *Griffiths v British Coal Corpn* [2001] EWCA Civ 336, [2001] 1 WLR 1493.
[11]   [1995] PIQR Q34. See also *AB v British Coal Corpn* [2006] EWCA Civ 1357, in which the CA confirmed the power of the managing judge of a group litigation scheme to impose interest payments on defendants in order to encourage the efficient processing of claims.
[12]   [2000] Lloyd's Rep IR 657, (2000) *The Times*, 26 April.
[13]   CPR, r 36.14(3)(a).
[14]   [1999] PIQR Q26.

pocket and had a legal right to recover the sums advanced from the claimant. Essentially, therefore, the award of interest was held on trust for the defendants.

14.3 PROCEDURE

The claim for interest must be pleaded in full as a claim for interest on all damages at half rate may lead to under-compensation.

More significantly, the defendants may make a Part 36 offer based upon the half rate claimed. Although the claimant may successfully obtain an amendment allowing a claim for interest at full rate, he may nevertheless still face costs sanctions because of the undervaluation of the claim.

CHAPTER 15

BENEFITS

15.1 STATUTORY FRAMEWORK

15.1.1 Social Security (Recovery of Benefits) Act 1997

The Social Security (Recovery of Benefits) Act 1997 came into force on 6 October 1997 by SI 1997/2085. Its provisions apply to 'compensation payments' made on or after that date. Accordingly, the Act applies to all existing claims and all claims that were unresolved on that date.

The exception to this general rule is in relation to compensation payments made in pursuance of an earlier agreement or court order.

The Act applies to all claims for damages in respect of personal injury or disease, and includes MIB claims. Certain payments are 'exempted' from the provisions of the Act (see Schedule 1, Part 1). There is provision for these to include small payments but the necessary regulations have not yet been introduced. Also exempted are insurance payments, redundancy payments and certain trusts.

15.2 PRINCIPLES

The object of the relevant legislation is to prevent a claimant recovering for the same loss twice. In the simplest case, a claimant may be off work and lose wages and thereby become entitled to earnings related benefits. If he also recovers damages in respect of the lost earnings he will be better off financially than he would otherwise have been if he had not been injured.

A defendant liable for the loss should nevertheless be responsible for making good that loss but only once.

The scheme designed to prevent this double recovery is contained in the Social Security (Recovery of Benefits) Act 1997. This provides for certain 'relevant' benefits to be deducted from specified heads of damage, and for the benefits to be repaid by the defendant to the Secretary of State.

15.3   HOW DOES THE ACT OPERATE?

Benefits are deductible *only* from damages in respect of loss of earnings, cost of care (including gratuitous care) and loss of mobility. Only the 'relevant benefits' specific to that head of damage are deductible and only from that head of damage, ie the benefits listed in Schedule 2 in respect of loss of earnings are only deductible from damages for loss of earnings.

The value of deductible benefits are withheld by the defendant from the damages payable as these form part of the benefits recouped by the State.

The heads of compensation and the relevant benefits are set out in the table in Schedule 2:

Calculation of Compensation Payment

(1) *Head of compensation*	(2) *Benefit*
1. Compensation for earnings lost during the relevant period	Disability working allowance Disablement pension payable under s 103 of the 1992 Act Incapacity benefit Income support Invalidity pension and allowance Jobseeker's allowance Reduced earnings allowance Severe disablement allowance Sickness benefit Statutory sick pay Unemployment supplement Unemployment benefit
2. Compensation for cost of care incurred during the relevant period	Attendance allowance Care component of disability living allowance Disablement pension increase payable under s 104 or s 105 of the 1992 Act
3. Compensation for loss of mobility during relevant period	Mobility allowance Mobility component of disability living allowance

Notes

1.

(a)   References to incapacity benefit, invalidity pension and allowance, severe disablement allowance, sickness benefit and unemployment benefit also include any income support paid with each of those benefits on the same instrument of payment or paid concurrently with each of those benefits by means of an instrument for benefit payment.

    (b)   For the purpose of this Note, income support includes personal expenses addition, special transitional additions and transitional addition as defined in the Income Support (Transitional) Regulations 1987.

2.   Any reference to statutory sick pay –

    (a)   includes only 80 per cent of payments made between 6 April 1991 and 5 April 1994, and

    (b)   does not include payments made on or after 6 April 1994.

3.   In this Schedule 'the 1992 Act' means the Social Security Contributions and Benefits Act 1992

Example

A claimant has received £2,000 by way of Incapacity Benefit and no care related benefits. His claim for damages includes a claim for £1,500 in respect of loss of earnings and £1,000 in respect of the cost of care. Only £1,500 of the benefits may be withheld from the damages by the defendant in respect of the loss of earnings claim and nothing in respect of the care claim.

15.3.1   Period

Only benefits paid within 'the relevant period' are deductible. Section 3 of the Act sets an upper limit of five years from the date of the accident or injury, or, in the case of disease, five years from the date when a claimant first claims a listed benefit in consequence of the disease. Otherwise 'the relevant period' ends on the date of judgment/assessment of damages or settlement.

15.3.2   Requirements

The party paying, 'the compensator', is required to apply to the Secretary of State for a 'Certificate of Recoverable Benefits' prior to making any compensation payment. Assuming the application is made correctly, a certificate should be issued within four weeks of the application being received.

15.3.3   Certificate of recoverable benefits

The certificate should specify for each recoverable benefit the amount that has been paid and/or is likely to be paid up to a specified date and, if the benefit is continuing, the rate, period and intervals at which each benefit is likely to be paid.

15.3.4   Defendants' liability

A 'compensation payment' is defined as a payment to or in respect of any other person in consequence of any accident, injury or disease suffered by the other (section 1(1)(a)). There is currently no lower limit on the amount of compensation paid before the provisions of the Act apply.

Where a defendant makes a compensation payment he is liable to repay the Secretary of State an amount equal to the total amount of recoverable benefits. So if any compensation payment is made the defendant becomes liable to repay the whole of the recoverable benefits.

Note that only those benefits listed in Schedule 2 have to be repaid.

Note also that even if the claimant's claim does not include a claim in respect of loss of earnings, care or mobility, the defendant still has to repay the *total* of those benefits received by the claimant.

Similarly, if a claimant's award is reduced on account of contributory negligence, the defendant is still liable to repay the total amount of the recoverable benefits.

15.3.5   Tactics

Damages in respect of pain, suffering and loss of amenity are effectively ring-fenced from deduction of benefits. It follows from the above that a claimant may want to maximise damages for pain and suffering when negotiating a settlement. Conversely the defendant will want to minimise the general damages part of the settlement in order to reduce his overall liability.

15.3.6   Practical effect for a claimant

The defendant becomes liable to pay damages to a claimant for accidental injury. The damages include claims in respect of loss of earnings, care and mobility. The claimant has received benefits in respect of one or more of the listed heads of damage. The defendant then pays the claimant the damages due but withholds such amount of the relevant benefits up to a maximum of the value of the claim under each head. The effect of this is that the claimant may recover nothing under a particular head of damage if his benefits relating to that head of damage exceeded his damages under that head.

15.3.7 Are benefits relevant to the calculation of damages?

No. Section 17 states that in assessing damages in respect of any accident, injury or disease, the amount of any benefits paid, or likely to be paid, is to be disregarded.

15.3.8 Is the amount of benefit received relevant to the calculation of interest?

No. In calculating interest on damages the amount of benefits received or likely to be received in respect of that particular head of damage is to be disregarded (see *Wisely v John Fulton (Plumbers) Ltd; Wadey v Surrey County Council).*[1]

15.3.9 Are relevant benefits deductible from interest on damages?

Yes. If the amount of benefits exceeds the damages paid, any interest due in respect of that head of damage will also be reduced by the relevant benefit (see *Griffiths v British Coal Corpn).*[2]

15.3.10 Can a claimant claim the value of a lost benefit?

Yes. If a claimant is already in receipt of benefits for an unrelated disability and those benefits are replaced by benefits paid in respect of the relevant accident, injury or disease (which are then deductible from the damages claimed) the claimant may claim the value of the benefits lost (see *Hassall and Pether v Secretary of State for Social Security;*[3] *Neal v Bingle).*[4] For example, a claimant is in receipt of £140 per week incapacity benefit due to some pre-accident disability. Following the accident the claimant receives different benefits and loses his incapacity benefit. The Schedule of Loss in such a case should include a claim in respect of the lost incapacity benefit.

15.3.11 Damages excluded from the operation of the Act

The following damages are excluded from provisions of the Act:

(1) Pain and suffering.

---

1 [2001] 1 WLR 820; *Wadey v Surrey County Council* [2000] 144 SJ LB 197.
2 [2001] 1 WLR 1493, 60 BMLR 188.
3 [1995] 1 WLR 812, [1995] 3 All ER 909, [1995] PIQR P292.
4 [1998] QB 466, [1998] 2 All ER 58, [1998] 2 WLR 57, 40 BMLR 52.

(2) *Smith v Manchester*. This is an award for future loss of earnings.

(3) Loss of Congenial Employment. This forms part of general damages which are effectively ring fenced.

(4) Pension loss – where this relates to future loss.[5]

(5) DIY/Services. This is distinct from the claim for care.

15.4 REVIEWS

The Secretary of State may review any certificate of recoverable benefits if he is satisfied that the certificate was issued in ignorance of or was based upon a mistake as to a material fact or that a mistake has occurred in the preparation of the certificate (s 10).

Upon review, the Secretary of State may either confirm the certificate or issue a varied certificate. However, the amount of recoverable benefits may not be increased unless this is required because of incorrect information.

15.5 APPEALS

Either party may appeal a certificate of recoverable benefits on the grounds that the amount, rate or period is incorrect or on the ground that listed benefits paid otherwise than in respect of the accident, injury or disease, have been brought into account. This last ground is likely to be used by defendants where, in particular, it is asserted that the benefit should never have been paid at all.

The appeal cannot be made until the claim has been disposed of (this includes cases involving an order for provisional damages) and the defendant has discharged his liability to the Secretary of State.

The Secretary of State is obliged to refer such cases to the Medical Appeals Tribunal (MAT) where the appeal raises issues as to the amount, rate or period of benefit and/or whether listed benefits have been paid otherwise than in respect of the accident, injury or disease.

Any party may appeal the decision of the MAT on a point of law to a Social Security Commissioner.

---

[5] See *Nizami v London Clubs Management Ltd* [2004] EWHC 2577 (QB), in which McKinnon J characterized the claim for pension loss as 'compensation for lost earnings' within the meaning of the Act, as the pension loss claim was based upon the contributions that the claimant would have made from his earnings.

15.6 PRACTICE ON JUDGMENT

The judgment should specify the amount awarded under each of the relevant heads of damage (s 15(2)).

If the case is settled by consent there is no such requirement (s 15(1)).

15.7 PART 36 OFFERS AND BENEFITS

The rules governing Part 36 offers and benefits are set out in CPR, r 36.15 and the accompanying practice direction.

When the defendant makes a Part 36 Offer he must state whether the offer is made without regard to any liability for recoverable benefits[6] or that it is intended to include any deductible benefits.[7]

If the offer is intended to include deductible benefits the follows steps are required:

(a)   the defendant must apply for a CRU certificate;[8]

(b)   the offer must state the gross amount, the name and amount of any deductible benefit by which the gross amount is reduced and the net amount after deduction of the relevant benefits;[9]

If the defendant has not yet received the CRU certificate at the date the offer is made he must provide the name and amount of any deductible benefit and the net amount after deduction of the relevant benefits not more than 7 days after receipt of the certificate.[10]

Note: where the offer is intended to include deductible benefits for the purpose of determining whether the claimant has beaten the Part 36 payment, it is the *gross* amount that is considered by the court.[11]

The claimant should make a decision about the defendant's Part 36 offer as soon as possible – where following a Part 36 offer an application is made for the money in court to be paid out the court may treat the money in court as being reduced by any further recoverable benefits paid to the claimant since the date of the payment into court.[12]

---

[6]   CPR, r 36.15(3)(a).
[7]   CPR, r 36.15(3)(b).
[8]   CPR, r 36.15(5).
[9]   CPR, r 36.15(6).
[10]   CPR, r 36.15(7).
[11]   CPR, r 36.15(8).
[12]   CPR, r 36.15(9).

The compensator should ensure that the amount of benefit received is set off *only* against the appropriate head of damage in respect of which benefit has been paid. Benefits should not be brought into account generally. Any adjustment of the certified amount is a matter for the compensator to pursue.[13]

The notice should be clear. In *Hilton International Hotels Ltd v Smith*[14] the defendant made a payment into court in the sum of £6,000. The notice stated that the £6,000 was in addition to £40,124 of recoupable benefits so that the gross amount was £46,124. The claimant accepted the payment. The certificate was then appealed and reduced to nil. The claimant sought recovery of the £40,124 repaid by the Secretary of State to the defendants. It was held on appeal that the claimant was entitled to this sum as the notice was unequivocal in its terms and there was no evidence that the claimant was aware that the defendants had made a mistake.

If there is any ambiguity the claimant may within seven days request clarification of the notice from the defendant, or if the clarification requested is not forthcoming within seven days of the request being received apply for an order.[15]

---

[13] *Williams v Devon County Council* [2003] EWCA Civ 365.
[14] [2001] PIQR P14.
[15] CPR, r 36.8.

CHAPTER 16

PROVISIONAL DAMAGES

The power to award provisional damages is an exception to the general rule that damages are assessed once and for all. Its object is to ameliorate the potential for injustice in under- or over-compensating the claimant.

16.1 STATUTORY PROVISIONS/RULES

Provisional Damages are governed by s 32A of the Supreme Court Act 1981 with s 51 of the County Courts Act 1984 and CPR, Part 41.

16.2 PRINCIPLES

16.2.1 When will provisional damages be awarded?

Section 32A of the Supreme Court Act 1981 (s 51 of the County Courts Act 1984) provides:

> 'This section applies to an action for damages for personal injuries in which there is proved or admitted to be *a chance* that at some *definite or indefinite time in the future* the injured person will, as a result of the act or omission which gave rise to the cause of action, develop some *serious disease or suffer some serious deterioration* in his physical or mental condition.'

The prerequisites to the making of an award are therefore:

(1)   a claim for provisional damages in the particulars of claim/ statement of case;

(2)   injury resulting from the breach of duty which gave rise to the necessity for an immediate award;[1]

(3)   a chance of some further disease or deterioration.

---

[1]   Historically, provisional damages orders have frequently been made in claims arising from the development of asymptomatic pleural plaques caused by asbestos exposure. Claimants invariably have an increased risk of developing a number of potentially disabling or fatal respiratory conditions. As a result of the majority decision of the HL in *Johnston v NEI International Combustion Ltd* [2007] UKHL 39 such a claim can no longer be pursued on the basis that asymptomatic pleural plaques do not amount to actionable injury.

In making the award the court first assesses damages on the assumption that the risk conditions will not occur, and then specifies the risk conditions which entitle the claimant to make a further application for damages.

16.2.2 'Chance'

'Chance' is not defined in s 32A, but has been considered in a number of cases. In *Willson v Ministry of Defence*,[2] Scott Baker J defined chance as something 'measurable rather than fanciful'. Roch LJ in *Curi v Colina*,[3] said that chance meant a possibility but no more than a possibility.

If the disease/deterioration is probably going to arise the section should not apply because a judge could and should deal with the future potential complication or sequelae.

It is important to note that the claimant does not need to do more than establish the existence of a chance of the risk condition. He does not need to prove causation or attribution, such matters being specifically left over until a further application is made.[4]

16.2.3 'Definite or indefinite time in the future'

The court must specify a period within which an application for further damages may be made.[5] Frequently, it is not possible to ascertain with sufficient precision the period over which the disease or deterioration may develop. In such cases the court has the power to direct that the relevant period is 'for the duration of the life of the claimant'.[6]

The court may make an order in respect of more than one disease or deterioration, and specify a separate time period for each.[7] The period in question may be extended on application by the claimant if a current medical report is filed.[8] No application for further damages may be made

---

[2]   [1991] 1 All ER 638 at 642b.
[3]   (1998) *The Times*, 14 October, CA. See also *O'Kennedy v Harris* (unreported) 1990, in which the trial judge made a provisional damages order in respect of the risk of epilepsy developing where the risk ranged from 1.5% to 0.015%.
[4]   CPR, PD41, para 2.5 and *Hurditch v Sheffield Health Authority* [1989] QB 562, at p 878f–g. *Pendleton v Cooperative Wholesale Society Ltd* (unreported) 2001. See also *Mann v Merton and Sutton Health Authority* (unreported) 15 November 1999, [1989] CLY 1229. *Hurditch* was distinguished in *Green v Vickers Defence Systems* (2002) Times, 1 July: a consent order for provisional damages included a statement of facts which provided for recovery of damages in full, thereby precluding the defendant from raising the issue of causation when the claimant made a further application for damages.
[5]   CPR, r 41.2(2)(b).
[6]   CPR, PD41, para 2.3.
[7]   CPR, r 41.2(2)(c).
[8]   CPR, r 41.2(3) and PD41, para 3.5.

after the expiry of the period specified.[9] It is important to note that the claimant may make only one application in respect of each specified disease or type of deterioration.

16.2.4 'Serious disease/deterioration'

The disease(s) or deterioration(s) in respect of which an application may be made must be identified.[10] They should also be clear cut.

In *Willson* (above) Scott Baker J refused to award provisional damages in respect of the possibility of osteoarthritis developing, concluding that the section envisaged a clear and severable risk rather than ordinary or continuing deterioration. In *Patterson v Ministry of Defence*[11] Simon Brown J made an order in respect of the 2–3% chance of the claimant developing mesothelioma, but not in respect of the 5% chance that his pleural thickening would progress and cause increased breathlessness. The judge was unconvinced that any progression of the claimant's pleural thickening would produce a serious deterioration within the meaning of s 32A.

In practice, in cases concerning progressive disabling conditions such as asbestosis or pleural thickening, where there is a risk of future deterioration, parties often agree that the right to seek further damages will not arise until a particular level of disability has been reached. The court may also order the inclusion of a progressive condition if a clearly defined threshold can be specified.

The word 'serious' applies not only to the disease/deterioration but also to the impact of that condition upon the particular claimant. Examples of this may be life expectancy, earning capacity or a claimant's ability to undertake domestic tasks.

16.2.5 Discretion

The claimant has the right to a final award if he chooses but the making of a provisional damages award is in the court's discretion. The magnitude of the risk of the disease/deterioration and the nature of the disease/deterioration will be taken into account in deciding whether to exercise that discretion (*H (a child) v Thompson Holidays*[12].

The court will not always make an order if it could result in potential injustice to either party. In an exceptional case the development of the risk condition may lead to a significant reduction in the overall value of the claim, for example as a result of the early death of the claimant. In

---

[9]   CPR, r 41.3(1).
[10]   CPR, r 41.2(2)(a).
[11]   (Unreported) 29 July 1986, [1987] CLY 1194.
[12]   [2007] EWHC 850.

Molinari v Ministry of Defence[13] W Crowther QC, sitting as a deputy High Court judge, suggested that in such an extreme case the court may refuse to make a provisional damages award.

The circumstances in which the Court will exercise its discretion will inevitably vary depending on the facts. In *Garth v Lloyd Grant and MIB*[14] HHJ Hickinbottom, sitting as a Judge of the High Court, refused to make a provisional damages award in respect of a claimant whose injuries necessitated hip replacement surgery but that surgery carried risks of either palsy or infection. The decision appears to have been made on the basis that the risk conditions would have failed to improve the claimant's present state, rather than qualify as a serious deterioration. However, in *H (A Child) v Thomson Holidays*[15] Cox J made a provisional damages order in respect of a child whose injuries meant that she was likely to require kidney transplant in the future but that surgery carried a risk of failure. The judge found that if the surgery failed that would amount to a serious deterioration in her condition.

16.2.6　Fatal accidents

Where a claimant is awarded provisional damages and subsequently dies as a result of the act or omission which gave rise to the original cause of action an award of provisional damages does not operate as a bar to an action under the Fatal Accidents Act 1976.[16]

16.2.7　Dependency

Where part of the original award of provisional damages and/or further damages awarded prior to death was intended to compensate the claimant for pecuniary loss in a period which falls after the date of his death, this will be taken into account in assessing dependency under the Fatal Accidents Act 1976.[17]

An award of further damages made after death cannot include an amount for loss of income.[18]

16.3　PROCEDURE

The Particulars of Claim must include a claim for provisional damages, including a statement to that effect and the grounds for claiming them.[19]

---

[13]　[1994] PIQR Q33.
[14]　(Unreported) 25 May 2007, High Court.
[15]　*H (A Child) v Thomson Holidays* [2007] EWHC 850 (QB).
[16]　Damages Act 1996, s 3(2).
[17]　Ibid, s 3(3).
[18]　Ibid, s 3(4).
[19]　CPR, r 16.4(1)(d).

When provisional damages are awarded certain documents should be preserved as the 'case file'. These should be set out in a schedule attached to the judgment and include copies of the judgment, statements of case/particulars of claim, transcript of any oral judgment, the medical reports relied upon and a transcript of any parts of the claimant's own evidence which the judge considers necessary.

Where provisional damages are agreed by consent, an application for a consent order should be made in accordance with CPR, Part 23. If the claimant is a child or a patient the court's approval is required. Instead of the transcript the case file should include an agreed statement of facts and agreed medical reports.

In either case the court will keep the case file for the duration of the specified period but the parties should also keep a copy of the case file.[20]

The claimant must give notice to the defendant and, if possible, the defendant's insurers of his intention to apply for further damages.

Where a defendant fails to file an acknowledgement of service and fails to file a defence the claimant may not enter judgment in default unless he abandons his claim for provisional damages. Instead the claimant should apply for directions.[21]

16.4   PART 36 OFFERS AND PROVISIONAL DAMAGES

A defendant may make a Part 36 offer in respect of a claim which includes a claim for provisional damages.[22]

The Part 36 Offer notice must specify whether the defendant proposes that the settlement should include an award of provisional damages. If the defendant agrees to a provisional damages award the notice must state:

(1)   that the sum paid into court is in satisfaction of the claim on the assumption that the injured person will not develop the disease/deterioration specified in the notice; and

(2)   that the offer is subject to the condition that the claimant must make any claim for further damages within a limited period and specify what that period is.

If the claimant accepts the Part 36 payment he must, within seven days of doing so, apply to the court for an order for an award of provisional

---

[20]   CPR, PD41, para 3.6.
[21]   CPR, PD41, para 5.1.
[22]   CPR, r 36.6.

damages under CPR, r 41.2. The money in court will not be paid out until the court has disposed of this application.[23]

---

[23] See *Green v Vickers Defence Systems* (2002) *The Times*, 1 July, [2002] All ER (D) 48 (Jun).

CHAPTER 17

PERIODICAL PAYMENTS

17.1   INTRODUCTION

Traditionally, damages in personal injury cases have been awarded on a once and for all, lump sum, basis. This has its attractions for claimants and defendants. Once the award has been made there is a clean break, both parties know where they stand and can organise their affairs accordingly.

On the other hand, it has long been recognised that as this approach involves predicting the future it is unsatisfactory and in every case is likely to result in over or under compensation, see *Lim Poh Choo v Campden & Islington Area Health Authority*.[1] There are other disadvantages. Many claimants have no experience of investing large sums of money to produce the necessary return which is assumed in the calculations. Even if prudently managed, the money awarded may run out, for example if care costs continue to exceed the rise in the Retail Prices Index (RPI). Conversely, there may be gross unfairness to the defendant if the claimant dies shortly after the award is made.

17.2   RATIONALE OF PERIODICAL PAYMENTS

The logic is compelling. In the past, the parties have been compelled to use uncertain estimates of life expectancy when assessing future loss. Under the periodical payments system the courts assess the annual future needs of the claimant which rise with inflation. These payments are then made for the rest of the claimant's life and never run out.

17.3   STRUCTURED SETTLEMENTS

Attempts have been made to find an alternative, more refined, approach which takes account of at least some future developments. Judicial endorsement of these attempts started in Britain in 1989 when the first structured settlement received judicial approval. Structured settlements were, however, of limited application. They were only made in cases where

---

[1]   [1980] AC 174 per Lord Scarman.

the award was large (in practice this usually meant an award of over £1 million) and both parties agreed. The power of the court to approve structured settlements was removed on 1 April 2005 when periodical payments were introduced, see Civil Procedure (Amendment No 3) Rules 2004.[2] Structured settlements are now of historical interest only.

17.4   The legislation

Section 2 of the Damages Act 1996 as amended by s 100 of the Courts Act 2003 now provides that a court awarding damages for future pecuniary loss in respect of personal injury:

-    must always consider whether or not to make an order for periodical payments

-    may make such an order without the consent of the parties

Damages under other heads of loss, such as past loss, or pain suffering and loss of amenity, may be included in a periodical payments order if the parties agree, see s 2(2).

The power to make a periodical payments order must be exercised having regard to all the circumstances of the case and in particular the form of the award which best meets the claimant's needs, see CPR 41.7. 'Needs' are to be interpreted broadly and include those things which the claimant needs in order to enable him (or those looking after him) to organise his life in a practical way. This will include finding suitable accommodation. The Court of Appeal stated in *Thompstone v Tameside and Glossop Acute Services NHS Trust*[3] that the test was an objective one. The judge must have regard to the wishes and preferences of the parties, but:

> 'The judge's mind should be focused not on what the claimant prefers but on what best meets the claimant's needs; the two are not necessarily the same' [para 107].

17.5   Security

There would obviously be considerable injustice to the claimant if the payments were not made throughout the duration of the order. The court may not make an order for periodical payments unless satisfied that the payments are 'reasonably secure', see s 2(3). The Act gives some assistance by stating that the continuity of payment under the order is reasonably secure if:

-    it is protected by a Ministerial guarantee under s 6 of the Act

---

[2]   Civil Procedure (Amendment No 3) Rules 2004, SI 2004/3129.
[3]   [2008] EWCA Civ 5.

- it is protected by a scheme under s 213 of the Financial Services and Markets Act 2000

- the source of the payments is a government or a health service body.

It is possible for a defendant that falls outside these definitions to purchase an appropriate life annuity for the benefit of the claimant. This would be protected by the Financial Services Compensation Scheme, see s 4 of the Act. Alternatively it would be for the defendant to prove to the court that another method of funding was reasonably secure.

17.6 INDEXATION

When periodical payments were introduced parliament anticipated that the claimant's annual award would normally rise in accordance with the RPI, see s 2(8), although sub section (9) provided for the disapplication of sub section (8) in undefined circumstances. The adoption of the RPI as the appropriate index has proved to be controversial. In cases where the claimant has been seriously injured the future care claim is often the largest head of damage. The RPI is a measure of changes in prices. Providing for carers is largely dependant on wage costs which in the last 40 years have risen at a faster rate than prices. Claimants have now successfully challenged the use of the RPI as the appropriate index.

The issue was fully argued in *Thompstone v Tameside and Glossop Acute Services NHS Trust*[4] by Swift J who heard extensive expert evidence. She held that the RPI was a measure of changes in prices which if applied to periodical payments, a large proportion of which were wages, would not adequately compensate the claimant. Instead of the RPI the index which was most likely to adequately compensate the claimant was found to be by using the Aggregate Annual Survey of Hours and Earnings (ASHE 6115). It was appropriate, fair and reasonable for the court to modify the effect of s 2(8) by providing for the amount of periodical payments to vary by reference to the 75th percentile of ASHE 6115. ASHE 6115 was also adopted as the appropriate index at first instance in *RH v United Bristol Health Care NHS Trust*[5] and *Corbett v South Yorkshire Strategic Health Authority*[6] and *Sarwar v Motor Insurers' Bureau.*[7]

The Court of Appeal has now endorsed the use of ASHE 6115.[8] Waller LJ giving the judgment of the court stated that:

---

[4]   *Thompstone v Tameside and Glossop Acute Services NHS Trust* [2006] EWHC 2904, QB.

[5]   *RH v United Bristol Health Care NHS Trust* [2007] EWHC 1441.

[6]   (Unreported) 4 May 2007, QBD, LS Law Med 430.

[7]   [2007] EWHC 274.

[8]   See *Thameside and Glossop Acute Services NHS Trust v Thompstone* [2008] EWCA Civ 5.

'100. We hope that as a result of these proceedings the National Health Service, and other Defendants in proceedings that involve catastrophic injury, will now accept that the appropriateness of indexation on the basis of ASHE 6115 has been established after an exhaustive review of possible objections to its use, both in itself and as applied to the recovery of costs of care and case management.'

The Court of Appeal also stated that in the absence of new evidence or significantly different argument it would not be appropriate to re-open the indexation issue.

In the initial stages of working with ASHE 6115 it is likely that expert evidence will be required. The Court of Appeal expect, however, that within a short period of time the relevant material will 'appear in practitioners' works and rapidly become familiar to the specialists who practice in this area', see para 98. The hope is that it will then be possible to dispense with expert evidence on indexation.

The Defendant is petitioning the House of Lords for permission to appeal. Subject to this point the way forward is now to use the ASHE 6115 for indexation, which is likely to make periodical payments orders more attractive to claimants.

17.7 PERIODICAL PAYMENTS OR LUMP SUM DAMAGES

17.7.1   Advantages of an award for periodical payments

(a)   greater financial security for the claimant who is able to predict the payments receivable. The money will not run out. This is particularly important where life expectancy is likely to be long;

(b)   the risk of over or under compensation is reduced;

(c)   there is a degree of flexibility as the court may make provision at the time of the hearing for step changes in the level of the annual payment. This will be frequently be necessary, for example:
-     when it is likely that the claimant's condition will deteriorate;
-     when relatives (frequently parents) take it upon themselves to care for a disabled claimant for as long as they are able, after which the cost of professional carers will be necessary;

(d)   tax advantages as payments in the hands of the claimant are without deduction:
-     tax: future periodical payments are tax free in the hands of the claimant, see s 329 of the Income and Corporation Taxes

Act 1988 as amended by s 100(2) of the Courts Act 2003. This
is the equivalent provision as that which previously existed
under structured settlements;

- benefits: future periodical payments will be disregarded in
calculating the claimant's welfare benefits, see Social Security
Amendment (Personal Injury Payments) Regulations 2002
(SI 2002/2442) and the National Assistance (Assessment of
Resources) (Amendment) (No 2) Regulations 2002 (SI 2002/
2531);

(e)   reduction in the risk that the money will be used inappropriately.
Relatively few claimants have experience in investing large sums of
money. A lump sum may be dissipated, or invested unwisely. At the
other extreme the claimant fearing a lump sum may run out may be
excessively frugal;

(f)   managing a large sum of money effectively is likely to involve its own
expense. Under the periodical payment regime this risk is born by
the provider;

(g)   unless the Defendant's appeal to the House of Lords in *Thompstone*
is upheld ASHE 6115 will be the normal measure of indexation and
periodical payments will become more attractive to claimants;

(h)   if the claimant dies soon after the periodical payment order it used
to be said that the claimant's dependants, who have looked after him,
would receive far less than under a lump sum order. Rule 41.8(2)
envisages a periodical payment that continues after the claimant's
death for the benefit of relatives. This also takes away the problem
which may arise when a claimant who has been awarded a significant
lump sum dies early and there is an inheritance which has to be
divided between relatives and friends.

17.7.2   Advantages of a lump sum award

(a)   Flexibility: unforeseen developments can be catered for. Funds may
be required to meet a one off significant expenditure, such as the
purchase a property, which the award was not designed to cover.

(b)   A clean break from the defendant. This may help the claimant move
on after an accident.

(c)   It is possible that the claimant may be able to achieve returns that are
higher than those on offer under the periodical payments scheme.
Now that the Court of Appeal have endorsed the use of ASHE 6115,
this is unlikely.

(d)   Some claimants prefer having control over their own funds which they can invest themselves.

(e)   In smaller personal injury cases where the award is less than £100,000 there are few advantages in securing an order for periodical payments. In such cases the costs of administration have to be considered.

(f)   Even if an order for periodical payments is made the claimant will require a significant lump sum as a contingency fund.[9]

17.8   Variable orders

There is a restricted power to make an award of periodical payments which varies on the happening of certain specified events, see the Damages (Variation of Periodical Payments) Order 2005, SI 2005/ 842.[10]

If there is a chance that the claimant will:

–   as a result of the act or omission which gave rise to the cause of action develop some serious disease or suffer some serious deterioration; or

–   enjoy some significant improvement in his physical or mental condition;

the court may with the agreement of the parties, or of its own initiative, make an order that the periodical payments be varied. Before making a variable order the court must consider the defendant's financial resources, see regulation 3.

Regulation 4 of the Order makes it clear that an award of provisional damages may be made in addition to a variable award for periodical payments.

There are striking similarities between the wording used in the Order and the words used when considering provisional damages under s 32A of the Supreme Court Act, or s 51 of the County Courts Act 1984. In the case of provisional damages the courts have been reluctant to apply the wording to anything other than the clearest cases.[11] It may well be that there will be similar judicial reluctance in making orders for variable periodical payments.

The permission of the court must be sought for any future application to vary the terms of a periodical payment order.

---

[9]   See *RH V United Bristol Healthcare NHS Trust* [2007] EWHC 1441 (QB).
[10]   Damages (Variation of Periodical Payments) Order 2005, SI 2005/841.
[11]   See *Willson v Minstry of Defence* [1991] 1 All ER 638 and Chapter 16.

17.9 PROCEDURE

In any personal injury case in which there is an award for future pecuniary loss the court is obliged to consider an award of periodical payments (see s 2 of the Damages Act 1996 as amended). The court must consider and indicate to the parties as soon as is practicable whether periodical payments or a lump sum is likely to be the most appropriate form of order, see CPR 41.6. The parties may set out in their statements of case which method they prefer, see CPR 41.5. When considering whether periodical payments or a lump sum is more appropriate the court shall have regard to all the circumstances of the case and in particular the form of award which best meets the claimant's needs, see CPR 41.7.

The factors which the court must take into account are set out in 41BPD.1:

–   the scale of the annual payments taking into account any deduction for contributory negligence;

–   the form of award preferred by the claimant taking into account the reasons for the preference and the nature of any financial advice received;

–   the form of award preferred by the defendant including the reasons given.

The range of issues which must be addressed in the order itself are set out in CPR 41.8. These include:

-   the annual amount awarded, how each payment is to be made during the year and at what intervals;

-   how the annual sum is broken down into income based losses and recurring or capital costs;

-   the period for which the periodical payments are to be made;

-   the appropriate index.

If periodical payments are being considered by a claimant a report from an independent financial adviser is essential, although in practice this is not usually obtained until the litigation is reasonably well progressed. Even in a relatively straightforward case it is hard to know how useful a financial adviser's report will be until liability issues, including contributory negligence, have been determined.

In a substantial case the claimant will usually instruct an independent financial adviser to report on the order which best meets the claimant's needs. In *Thompstone* the Court of Appeal made it clear that faced with such evidence it would only be rarely that a defendant would call its own expert evidence to show that the form of order preferred by the claimant will not best meet his needs, see paragraphs 110–112. The courts do not want to become bogged down with evidence on satellite issues.

17.10   CONCLUSIONS

The system of periodical payments has been in place for a relatively short time. In that short time there have been major practical problems, most significantly with the court's attempts to ensure that an award of periodical payments is linked to an appropriate index. In *Thompstone* the Court of Appeal attempted to lay the indexation issue to rest. Some tentative early observations can be made:

– When introduced the Department of Constitutional Affairs expressed the wish that periodical payment orders would become the 'norm'. This has not yet happened.

– Although the court has power to impose a periodical payments award on the parties so far, perhaps not surprisingly, judges have been reluctant to impose such orders against the wishes of the parties.

– In cases where there is a reduction in the award for contributory negligence and it is known that the award of damages will not be adequate to fully compensate the claimant, many claimants understandably wish to preserve the greatest possible flexibility and request a lump sum award.

– Unless the Court of Appeal judgment in *Thompstone* is successfully appealed, now that an index which is more favourable to claimants has been established, periodical payments are likely to become more popular with claimants.

– The use of variable periodical payments is likely to be restricted.

CHAPTER 18

INTERIM PAYMENTS

18.1 AUTHORITY

The rules on interim payments are an exception to the general principle that a defendant has a right not to be held liable to pay until liability has been established by a final judgment. Once proceedings have been commenced it is possible to apply for one or more interim payments prior to the trial. This procedure is frequently overlooked and can be of great practical benefit. Claimants should always be advised that the power exists, as they otherwise may not be aware of it. The relevant rules are to be found in CPR, rr 25.6–25.9. As always, pre-CPR cases should be regarded with caution, but as the new rules closely follow the old rules with only subtle differences, the cases on RSC 29, rr 10 and 11 are still relevant.

18.2 PRINCIPLES

18.2.1 When should an application be considered?

It is not possible to obtain an order for an interim payment in a small claims case, see CPR, r 27.2(1)(a). The court has power to make an order in fast track cases, but such an application will rarely be appropriate given the likely value of the case and the relatively short time that will elapse before the final hearing. An application for an interim payment can be of particular benefit in multi-track cases. For example, in the following circumstances:

–   Where the claimant is struggling financially as a result of his injuries. He may, for example, be falling behind on his mortgage repayments as a result of being unable to work.

–   Where the trial will not be heard for a considerable time, perhaps because the final prognosis is uncertain.

–   In injuries of the utmost severity, where it is necessary to establish the claimant in new accommodation with a care regime as soon as possible.

18.2.2 Cases of the utmost severity

In cases of the utmost severity it is important to consider an application for a large interim payment at the earliest opportunity. This can be of enormous practical benefit to struggling carers, who are often family members doing their best in difficult circumstances. There are also tactical benefits in having the claimant's accommodation and care regime set up before trial. If the scheme is working, a judge may be reluctant to interfere. It is difficult for a defendant to oppose this approach.[1] In any event the defendant may prefer to see how the system works in practice and accurately assess its costs rather than speculate on projected care packages which frequently differ markedly.

In head injury cases, and cases involving serious physical injuries, it may be necessary for the claimant to move into single-storey accommodation. Applying for an interim payment to cover a move into different accommodation and the adaptation of that accommodation may mean an application for an interim payment of several hundred thousand pounds. If there is a risk that an interim payment may be too high the defendant's position can be secured by the claimant undertaking to apply for the purchase of a property and executing an equitable charge in favour of the defendant.[2] The court will avoid making orders for interim payments which will limit the trial judge's ability to make an order for periodical payments at the final hearing, see *Richmond v East and North Hertfordshire NHS Trust*.[3]

18.2.3 Threshold conditions

An application for an interim payment in a personal injury action may only be made if certain threshold conditions are met.

(1) The defendant:
    (a) has admitted liability; or
    (b) has had judgment entered against him for damages to be assessed or for a sum of money (other than costs) to be assessed; or
    (c) if the action proceeded to trial the claimant would obtain judgment for substantial damages against a defendant, see r 25.7(1).

It may be that the claimant will succeed against one defendant, but there is doubt as to which one. Where two insured defendants blame each other it is possible to obtain an interim payment against either defendant, even though the court has yet to determine which of them is liable, see r 25.7(3). This is a change introduced by the CPR.

---

[1] See *Campbell v Mylchrest* [1999] PIQR Q17.
[2] See *Harris v Ellen* [1995] CLY 1649, CA.
[3] [2007] EWHC 1999 (QB) and see CPR 41.4.

Where the factual issues are complicated or where difficult points of law arise, an application for an interim payment is not appropriate.[4]

(2) All the defendants must be either:
  (a) insured in respect of the claim; or
  (b) the defendant's liability will be met by an insurer acting under s 151 of the Road Traffic Act 1988, or an insurer acting under the Motor Insurers Bureau (MIB) Agreement or the MIB itself; or
  (c) the defendant is a public body, see r 25.7(1)(e)(ii).

Under the CPR, it is no longer possible to obtain an interim payment against a defendant who does not fit into these categories, for example a wealthy uninsured individual who is a defendant.

18.2.4 Discretion

The court has a discretion whether to make an order for an interim payment at all, and if so, the amount. The discretion is very wide. The only guidance that is given in the CPR is that the court must not order an interim payment of 'more than a reasonable proportion of the likely amount of the final judgment', see r 25.7(4). Claimants gain some assistance under the CPR where the defendant now has an obligation to serve a counter-schedule admitting undisputed losses, see PD16, para 13.2.

In *Stringman v McArdle*[5] the Court of Appeal held that:

– it was of no concern to the judge what is done with the money once it is in the hands of the claimant;

– the claimant did not have to demonstrate any particular need over and above a general need to be paid the damages as soon as reasonably possible;

– where there is delay until the final disposal, it will generally be appropriate and just to make an order.

There is no specific requirement in CPR Part 25 for the claimant to state the purpose for which the money is required. However, the Practice Direction[6] requires an application for an interim payment to be supported by evidence dealing with the items or matters in respect of which the interim payment is sought. The Practice Direction purports to have

---

4 See *Schott Kem v Bentley* [1991] 1 QB 61, per Neill LJ. Although this was a commercial case, it is submitted that the principle holds good in a personal injury action where the facts are unclear.
5 [1994] 1 WLR 1653.
6 CPR, 25BPD para 2.1(2).

introduced a change in the substantive law, something which the CPR were not designed to do. A judge is, however, more likely to be persuaded to exercise the discretion favourably to the claimant if it is proved that the interim payment is for a sensible purpose which may benefit the claimant.[7]

It is necessary to specifically address the conditions of CPR 25.7(4). In a recent case liability was agreed at 70% and as the infant claimant's medical condition had not stabilised there was going to be a delay of at least two years before trial. There was a serious dispute between the experts on diagnosis, causation and prognosis and consequently the value of the claim: the claimant's value was in excess of £1.4 million, the defendant's £260,000. Langley J felt it was safe to conclude that, after apportionment, £180,000 was the 'likely amount of the final judgment'. In considering what amounted to a 'reasonable proportion', the time that had already elapsed since the accident and would elapse prior to trial were significant factors. In this case the judge held that a reasonable proportion was 75% of £180,000, see *Spillman v Bradfield Riding Centre.*[8]

The court will avoid making orders for interim payments which will limit the trial judge's ability to make an order for periodical payments at the final hearing, see *Richmond v East and North Hertfordshire NHS Trust.*[9]

Conditions should not be imposed on an interim payment. In *Wright v Sullivan*[10] the claimant suffered a brain injury when she was knocked down by the defendant's car. Liability was compromised on a 70/30 basis in the claimant's favour. Wakerley J ordered an interim payment of £50,000 to meet the costs of a case manager. He rejected the defendant's suggestion that the interim payment order should be made conditional upon the case manager being jointly instructed. However, he also held that although the case manager was a witness as to fact, she should regard herself as owing the same duties to the court as an expert witness under CPR 35. The Court of Appeal was not prepared to make the interim payment conditional. The case manager owed her duties to the claimant alone, and her legal advisers should be able to attend a conference with her. The Court of Appeal disagreed that CPR 35, which provides extensive rules for expert witnesses, applied to a witness of fact and deleted this part of the judge's order.

In *Richmond v East and North Hertfordshire NHS Trust*[11] the claimant was born in July 2004 with severe brain damage, for which the defendant admitted liability. She required 24-hour care and her life expectancy was 2–7 years. The claimant's schedule of loss was £1,664,000 and an interim

---

7   See *Campbell v Mylchrest* [1999] PIQR Q17 and CPR, 25BPD, para 2.1.
8   [2007] EWHC 89.
9   [2007] EWHC 1999 (QB) and CPR 41.4.10
10   *Wright v Sullivan* [2005] EWCA Civ 656, CA.
11   [2007] EWHC 1999.

payment of £1,250,000 (approximately 75% of the full value) was sought. The Defendant's valuation of the claim was £810,000 and an interim payment of £450,000 was offered. The court made an award of £750,000 being 75% of the likely damages that would be awarded at the final hearing. It was also emphasised that the award of the interim payment should not prejudice the ability of the trial judge to make an order for periodical payments.

The defendant may oppose an application for an interim payment on a number of grounds:

(1) the threshold conditions have not been met;

(2) there is serious doubt that the claimant will recover enough to warrant an interim payment. CPR, r 25(7)(1)(c) states that the judge must be satisfied that the claimant 'would obtain judgment for a substantial amount of money'.

(3) quantum: the judge must consider a set-off or counterclaim and contributory negligence.

18.3   VOLUNTARY INTERIM PAYMENTS

Funds may be necessary to cover immediate expenses (ie nursing care or rehabilitation) before the time when the court can order an interim payment (see below). Claimants' advisers should seek voluntary payments from the defendant where need dictates. The advantage to the defendant is that he may reduce the ultimate award of interest. The defendant may also seek some input into the care regime or rehabilitation as a condition for making a voluntary payment.

18.4   PROCEDURE

The procedure is set out at CPR, r 25.6. An application for an interim payment cannot be made before the end of the period for filing an acknowledgement of service (14 days after service of the claim form or particulars of claim, whichever is the later, see CPR, r 10.3). The application must be served on the defendant at least 14 days before the hearing of the application and be supported by evidence. If the defendant wishes to rely on written evidence at the hearing he must file and serve the evidence upon which he wants to rely at least seven days before the hearing. If the claimant wishes to rely upon evidence in reply it must be served on the defendant at least three days before the hearing.

Part 23 of the CPR deals with general rules about applications. A copy of the application notice must be served on each respondent (r 23.4(1)). The respondent is the person against whom the order is sought (r 23.1(a)). The application must be served as soon as practicable after it is filed (r 23.7(1)(a)). Every application should be made as soon as it becomes necessary or desirable to make it (PD23, para 2.7). It is good practice to make the request for an interim payment in writing and allow 14 days for compliance prior to making an application to the court.

The evidence to accompany the application should be either in the form of a witness statement with a Statement of Truth or an affidavit. The evidence should deal with the following (see 25BPD, para 2.1):

(1)   the sum of money sought;

(2)   the items or matters in respect of which the interim payment is sought;

(3)   the sum of money for which final judgment is likely to be given;

(4)   the reasons for believing that the threshold conditions are satisfied;

(5)   any other relevant matters;

(6)   details of special damages and past and future loss;

(7)   in a claim under the Fatal Accidents Act 1976 details of the person(s) on whose behalf the claim is made and the nature of the claim;

(8)   any documents in support of the application, including medical reports, should be exhibited.

An application for summary judgment and for an interim payment may be made at the same time. An application for summary judgment may be made if the defendant has no real prospect of successfully defending and there is no other compelling reason why the case should be tried (see CPR, r 24.2). It is unlikely that an interim payment will be awarded where unconditional leave to defend has been given.[12]

18.5   PRACTICAL POINTS

18.5.1   Benefits

If the defendant is liable to repay benefits, the defendant should apply to the Secretary of State for a Certificate of Recoverable Benefits (the CRU Certificate). A copy of the CRU Certificate should be filed at the hearing of the application for an interim payment. The judge's order should set

---

[12]   See *British and Commonwealth Holdings Plc v Quadrex Holdings Inc* [1989] QB 842, per Browne-Wilkinson VC.

out the amount by which the payment to the claimant has been reduced in accordance with the CRU Certificate. Payment to the claimant will be made of the net amount, although the order should also state the gross amount and the benefits repayable, see 25BPD, para 4.

18.5.2 Court of Protection

Where an interim payment application is made on behalf of a minor or a patient the money should be paid into court and application made to the court for payment out when the money is required. In larger cases, when the Court of Protection is involved, an application should be made to that court.

18.5.3 Repayment, variation and adjustment

Occasionally an interim payment is awarded which is too high. CPR, r 25.8 provides detailed rules for repayment, variation, discharge or other adjustment of an interim payment. If a repayment is made the court can order the claimant to pay interest from the date the money was paid.

18.5.4 Payment by instalments

The court may make an order for an interim payment by instalments (CPR r 25.6(7)). The court order should set out the total amount of the payment, the amount of each instalment, the number of instalments and to whom the payment should be made.

18.5.5 Restriction on disclosure

The fact that an interim payment has been made shall not be disclosed until after all issues on liability and quantum have been resolved, unless the defendant agrees (see CPR, r 25.9).

CHAPTER 19

INVESTMENT OF DAMAGES

19.1 INTRODUCTION

An award of damages may constitute the largest single financial payment that most claimants will receive in their lifetime. There is a tendency for friends and colleagues to think of the damages as a 'windfall' or a 'bonus'. The courts take a different view. In the words of Lord Blackburn in *Livingstone v Rawyards Coal Co*:[1]

> 'I do not think there is a difference of opinion, it has been a general rule that, where any injuries be compensated by damages, in settling the sum of money to be given for reparation of damages you should as nearly as possible get that sum of money which will put the party who has been injured, or who has suffered, in the same position as he would have been in if he had not sustained the wrong for which he is now getting his compensation or reparation.'

There is no windfall element to UK damages.

In multi-track cases, and particularly in cases involving loss of employment through injury, the award is often designed to compensate the claimant for life. Evidence produced in *Wells v Wells* demonstrated that damages awards based on a multiplier of future losses ran out before the claimant's financial needs ended. The consequent reduction of the rate from 4.5% to 2.5% increased multipliers significantly but it continues to be a source of anxiety as to whether the money will run out before the end of the claimant's life. Careful investment of damages remains an imperative.

19.2 INVESTMENT ADVICE

19.2.1 Accident victim

A solicitor must advise his client to take independent financial advice from an independent financial adviser or stockbroker. He need do nothing more.

---

[1] (1880) 5 LR App Cas 25 at 39.

19.2.2   'Patient'

For a definition of 'patient' see Chapter 12 on the Court of Protection.

The Public Guardianship Office (PGO), which is the administrative arm of the Court of Protection, has clear principles on investments. It appoints firms of brokers to a panel. The PGO is becoming more relaxed about the appointment of non-panel brokers. The PGO has agreed to put out to tender the provision of panel broker work. This is to the advantage of Independent Financial Advisers and the claimant can now have an ongoing relationship with an advice team from the commencement of his claim to its conclusion and for the remainder of his life. That said, the PGO favours a portfolio split between cash on special account, equities and collective investments – a medium- to high-risk portfolio.

19.3   CLAIMING DAMAGES FOR INVESTMENT ADVICE AND FUTURE PRIVATE CLIENT LEGAL COSTS

All too often elements of damages that do not naturally fall within the personal injury arena are omitted from a claim to the cost of the claimant. In high value cases it is important to consider whether to build in to the claim the following costs:

(1)   Cost of providing advice on the legal mechanism by which funds must be managed, ie private trust versus Court of Protection.

(2)   Cost of tax advice and the production of annual tax returns.

(3)   Cost of estate planning and the preparation of a statutory will if the claimant is a patient.

(4)   Future conveyancing costs.

(5)   Costs of investment advice.

(6)   Cost of matrimonial advice in the event that it can be shown that the end of the claimant's relationship with his or her spouse has been caused by the effects of the accident.[2]

(7)   Cost of a Court of Protection application, solicitors-general management, administration and disbursements.

---

[2]   However in *Pritchard v JH Cobden Ltd* [1987] 2 WLR 627 the Court of Appeal refused to award damages under this head.

19.3.1   Evidence

To assist a judge in understanding the nature of the costs of investment of damages, a statement from a specialist is recommended. This provides a succinct explanation of the likely costs in what, to lawyers and judges, is a complex area of mathematics and financial planning.

19.3.2   Financial management and children

In cases involving children under 18, the damages must be managed to ensure that funds are available to apply for the child's ongoing care and welfare.

The most common form of investment mechanism is a trust fund. Parents of the child can act as the trustees and become responsible for applying the trust fund for the benefit of the child. Legal advice should be taken not only in ensuring the correct trust is set up, but also in respect of the ongoing responsibilities of a trustee in respect of investment, accounting and taxation.

If a child is under a mental disability, a Court of Protection Order may be appropriate. This will certainly be the case if the child, on attaining the age of 18, will not be mentally capable of managing his own financial affairs.

The child may be entitled to certain welfare benefits as may the parent or carer. Advice can be obtained from the Benefits Agency or a specialist in welfare benefits. Many means-tested benefits may be available even where there is a claim for damages. This is particularly so where funds are placed in trust or fall within the jurisdiction of the Court of Protection.

The child cannot make a will until the age of 18. If damages have been received then at 18 there will be an estate to distribute. A will ensures that any funds held by the child are properly disposed and not left to the legal rules of intestacy. This can include gifts to friends, family and charities who may not otherwise benefit. Additionally, it may avoid potential inheritance tax liabilities. Again, if the child does not have the adequate mental capacity to execute a will then an application to the Court of Protection can be made for a will to be executed on their behalf.

19.4   SPECIAL NEEDS TRUSTS

The payment of damages above £6,000 can have an adverse effect upon a claimant's means-tested benefits. Prior to 1 October 2006, arrangements could be made for a special needs trust to be in place at the time of the settlement of the claim to ensure that the damages were paid into a trust to be held by the trustees for the benefit of a claimant. The claimant would, therefore, not receive the money directly, he would not have to advise the DWP and he would be entitled to continue to receive benefits as the income received from the trust was disregarded for the purposes of the claimant's capital entitlement.

The position changed on 1 October 2006.[3] The new terminology is a 'personal injury trust'. The Regulations permit a one year period in which the claimant is entitled to receive the money and spend the award. Such a period is called the 'disregard'. However, at the close of the year if the money is not all spent and what remains exceeds the maximum £6,000 then the means-tested benefits will be affected. Care should, therefore, be taken not to 'mix' the award damages with any other sum received to keep a clean audit trail.

It is important to note that the 52-week period commences with any payment received in relation to the injury. This can, for instance, mean an interim payment, insurance payments such as those for critical illness if they are made as a result of the injury and ex-gratia payments made before settlement by an employer.

If the claimant is in receipt of local authority care, then a trust *must* be set up as such care is means-tested. The period of disregard will not apply to receipt of payments from the Criminal Injuries Compensation Authority or the MIB.

19.5   CONCLUSION

Historically, solicitors have felt that their involvement with a client ends with the handing over of his damages cheque. This is no longer the case. Solicitors have a duty to provide advice on financial investment in all cases irrespective of a valuation.

This is an area fraught with potential difficulty for personal injury lawyers. Lawyers may feel, therefore, that their only involvement is to advise the client to seek advice from an independent financial adviser.

---

[3]   Social Security (Miscellaneous Amendments) (No 4) Regulations 2006, SI 2006/2378.

CHAPTER 20

CAUSATION

20.1 INTRODUCTION

This chapter will deal with:

(1) Basic principles of causation
- 'But for' test
- Concurrent causes
- Successive causes
- Apportionment between successive employers
- Intervening events
- Damage must be proved

(2) Contributory negligence

A detailed examination of causation is outside the scope of this book. It is, however, necessary to be aware of problem areas and this chapter highlights some of these and seeks to give some guidance.

20.2 BASIC PRINCIPLES OF CAUSATION

20.2.1 'But for' test

In order to succeed in a personal injury case based on negligence, the claimant must first establish:

(1) that there is a causal connection between the breach of duty and the damage. This is a question of fact. The claimant has the burden of showing that the breach of which complaint is made has caused the damage;

(2) that the damage is not in law too remote. In the context of personal injuries this often turns on whether a defendant should be held responsible for unforeseeable consequences. Policy plays a significant role here.

In determining factual causation, a starting point is the 'but for' test – but for the breach of duty, would the claimant have suffered damage? *Barnett v Chelsea and Kensington Hospital Management Committee*[1] provides a graphic example of this. Despite proving that the doctor was negligent in failing to diagnose arsenic poisoning when examined, the claimant did not succeed as the deceased would have died even if properly diagnosed and treated. If a claimant fails the 'but for' test this is usually fatal to a claim.

Like many broad statements of principle in this area, the 'but for' rule should not be regarded as being of universal application. It has long been recognised that strict application of the 'but for' rule may result in injustice. This has been graphically illustrated in two recent House of Lords cases in which the claimant failed the 'but for' test but nevertheless succeeded: *Fairchild v Glenhaven Funeral Services*[2] which is considered at 20.2.4.2 below, and *Chester v Ashraf*[3] where policy exceptions to the general rule have been allowed.

In *Chester*, the claimant was not properly warned about the 1–2% complication of cauda equina syndrome when undergoing a spinal operation. She underwent non-negligent surgery but developed the complication. Her evidence was that if she had been properly advised she would have postponed treatment and sought further advice. It was not proved that if she had been properly advised she would never have had the operation. Despite this the House of Lords upheld her claim by a 3–2 majority. It was enough in these circumstances to establish an increased exposure to risk. If the operation had been postponed, it would have been unlikely that the unusual complication which was confined to the particular time and circumstances would have materialised. Further, if there was no remedy it would undermine the very duty owed by the doctor.

The *Fairchild* and *Chester* cases can be regarded as narrow exceptions to the general rule where the strict 'but for' test has been replaced by other less stringent tests in circumstances where the justice of the case demands it: see *Paul Davidson Taylor v White*.[4]

20.2.2   Concurrent causes

Difficulties arise where there is more than one possible cause of the damage. These problems arise acutely in industrial disease cases where the strict rules of causation have been relaxed in order to do justice in an individual case. It is not necessary to show that the breach of duty was the sole cause of damage. The courts have dealt with problems in these areas incrementally.

---

[1]   [1969] 1 QB 428.
[2]   [2002] UKHL 22, [2003] 1 AC 32.
[3]   [2004] UKHL 41 [2005] 1 AC 134.
[4]   [2004] EWCA Civ 1511 per Arden LJ.

20.2.2.1 What if there are two causes of damage (one innocent and one guilty) and the disease is cumulative?

In *Bonnington Castings Ltd v Wardlaw*,[5] Mr Wardlaw contracted pneumoconiosis as a result of inhaling silica dust at work. The inhaled silica dust could have come from a source which did not involve any breach of duty (the innocent source) or a source which did involve a breach of duty (the guilty source). The disease was caused by gradual accumulation of dust in the lungs. Mr Wardlaw could not prove that 'but for' the guilty dust he would not have contracted the disease. Despite this the House of Lords found for Mr Wardlaw on a 100% basis as the guilty source *materially contributed* to the harmful dust inhaled.

20.2.2.2 Can a claimant be successful even where he cannot prove that the breach probably caused the damage?

In certain circumstances the claimant can succeed.[6] Mr McGhee came into contact with brick dust in brick kilns at work and as a result contracted dermatitis. Some of the exposure to brick dust was inevitable and not in breach of duty. The employer was, however, in breach of duty for failing to provide washing facilities. The claimant had to cycle home caked with grime and sweat and covered in brick dust which could have had a causative effect, although precisely how was not known. The brick dust caused the dermatitis, but the claimant could not prove that it was additional guilty exposure during the cycle home that caused the disease. As the claimant did not have to prove the impossible, it was enough to show that the breach had *materially increased the risk* of his contracting dermatitis which in the circumstances was indistinguishable from making a material contribution to the cause of his dermatitis. As it was impossible for the claimant to prove that the guilty dust was the cause of dermatitis the House of Lords were prepared to draw an inference of fact to overcome an evidential gap. This case established an important principle of law.

The courts have been reluctant to extend this approach into other areas of the law as can be illustrated by three House of Lords cases involving medical negligence.

In *Wilsher v Essex Area Health Authority*[7] a claim was made on behalf of a premature baby who became almost blind and developed retrolental fibroplasia (RLF) as a result of excess oxygen given by junior hospital doctors. In fact, there were a number of other separate and distinct possible causes unconnected with excess oxygen, and the claim failed. The claimant in this case could only have succeeded if he proved that the excess oxygen administered shortly after birth had caused the RLF.

---

[5]   [1956] AC 613.
[6]   See *McGhee v National Coal Board* [1973] 1 WLR 1 at 4–5 per Lord Reid.
[7]   [1988] AC 1074.

In *Hotson v East Berkshire Area Health Authority*[8] the doctor negligently failed to diagnose a fracture of the left femoral epiphysis for five days. The House of Lords held that as the claimant was unable to show that failure to provide treatment would probably have made any difference his claim failed. On the evidence there was a 75% chance that avascular necrosis would have developed anyway.

In *Gregg v Scott,*[9] as a result of a breach of duty, a non-Hodgkin's lymphoma was identified nine months later than it should have been. The claimant's chances of recovery were reduced as a result of the delay from 42% to 25%. By a majority, the House of Lords refused to extend the reasoning in *Fairchild.* The claimant had not proved that if he died prematurely that this was as a result of the defendant's negligence.

In *Hotson* and *Gregg* the claimants presenting condition had a separate determinate cause and it had not been demonstrated that this could probably have been overcome by timely treatment. The loss of a chance was not compensatible.

With the notable exception of the 'lack of warning' case of *Chester* (para 20.2.1 above) the claimant will not recover damages against a doctor for negligently depriving him of recovery where he can not show that the treatment, or lack of it, would probably have made a difference.

20.2.3   Successive causes

The claimant's injuries or loss may be caused by separate unrelated events. If by the time of trial the claimant has given up work, or is likely to give up work because of an unrelated medical condition, it has long been established that the on-going loss of earnings claim will be limited. The court cannot ignore independent events that are known, or which are likely to occur. The cases draw a distinction between supervening tortious and non-tortious events, which is not easy to apply.

20.2.3.1   Supervening non-tortious events

In *Jobling v Associated Dairies*[10] the claimant suffered a back injury at work for which his employers accepted liability. Three years later he suffered from an unrelated cervical myelopathy which rendered him totally unfit for work. The defendant was only liable for the initial three years until the supervening non-tortious medical problem intervened. The rationale lies in a reduction for the vicissitudes of life: the defendant should not be responsible for events which would have overtaken the claimant anyway.

---

[8]   *Hotson v East Berkshire Area Health Authority* [1987] AC 750.
[9]   [2005] UKHL 2 [2005] AC 176.
[10] *Jobling v Associated Dairies* [1982] AC 794.

This has practical application in many personal injury claims. For example, in a whiplash case in which the claimant is left with permanent spinal pain and stiffness preventing employment, the medical evidence may establish that this would have happened within a few years anyway due to unrelated constitutional problems.

20.2.3.2 *Supervening tortious events*

In *Baker v Willoughby*[11] the claimant seriously injured his leg in a road traffic accident in which liability was admitted. Before the case came to court he was shot in the damaged leg in a robbery and the leg was amputated. The defendant in the road traffic accident argued that he was responsible for the losses until the robbery, but that any losses thereafter should be laid at the door of the robbers. The House of Lords held that the defendant was liable for all the consequences of the original injury caused in the road traffic accident. To hold otherwise would mean that the robbers (even if they were worth suing) would only be liable for the additional damage caused to an already injured leg. After the shooting the claimant would then be left uncompensated for the difference between a sound leg and a damaged leg. As a matter of practicality on these unusual facts the House of Lords held that the claimant should succeed in full against the first tortfeasor.

Jobling and *Baker* are not easy to reconcile, One explanation is that where the claimant suffers from successive causes of damage where both events are tortious,causal responsibility will be attributed to the first tort. If, on the other hand, one event is tortious and one non tortious the defendant will only be liable for additional damage which can properly be attributed to his blameworthy conduct.

In *Rahman v Arearose Ltd*[12] Laws LJ saw no inconsistency between *Jobling* and *Baker* and addressed the problem in a pragmatic way. The claimant was assaulted by a violent gang as a consequence of his employer's negligence, as a result of which he suffered a serious injury to his eye. When he attended hospital, as a result of negligent surgery on the eye, he lost his vision in that eye. He also developed a severe psychiatric reaction as a result of the assault and the negligent treatment. The Court of Appeal refused to treat the negligent treatment as an intervening event which broke the chain of causation. The psychiatric reaction was a result of the attack and negligent surgery. The tortfeasor should compensate the claimant for the loss and damage for which he was responsible: it was crucial to look at the duty of care owed in order to determine the extent of the damage for which the defendant was properly liable.

The Court of Appeal has applied the 'vicissitudes of life' principle to supervening future tortious events which may well have reduced the claim

---

[11] [1970] AC 467.
[12] [2001] QB 351.

anyway. In *Heil v Rankin (No 2)*,[13] the claimant was a police dog handler who suffered a serious and frightening criminal injury in 1987 and a further minor injury in 1993. After the first incident the claimant had suffered from post-traumatic stress disorder (PTSD). After the second incident the PTSD became much worse and the claimant had to give up work. The possibilities of future tortious events which would have been likely to have curtailed the claimant's working life had to be taken into account to avoid over-compensation. The claimant's future loss of earnings claim was reduced by half to reflect the possibility that as a policeman he would probably have been confronted with criminal activity which would have exacerbated his PTSD.

20.2.4   Apportionment between consecutive employers

20.2.4.1   *Practical problems arise for practitioners, particularly in the context of industrial disease: divisible conditions*

The claimant may have had several employers each of whom have materially contributed to his injury. Is each defendant liable for the full amount of the damage or not? Where it is possible to identify the extent of the contribution that the defendant's wrong made to the damage, the defendant is liable only to that extent and no more. If a disease is related to the extent of the exposure, it will then be necessary to quantify the proportion of the damage attributable to each defendant. This can be illustrated by reference to cumulative or 'dose related' conditions such as asbestosis, work-related stress and deafness.

Asbestosis

Mr Holtby, a marine fitter who spent approximately half his working life with the defendant, was exposed over many years to asbestos leading to asbestosis. The defendant was held liable for a proportion of the full award on a time exposure basis.[14] Asbestosis is a divisible condition in which the severity of the disease is dependent in part upon the extent of exposure. This is to be distinguished from conditions such as cancer or mesothelioma where there is no direct correlation between the extent of exposure and severity of disease.

Stress-related psychiatric illness

Many stress-related illnesses have a number of different causes. The wrongdoer should pay only for that proportion of the harm suffered for which he is responsible.[15]

---

[13]   [2001] PIQR Q16.
[14]   See *Holtby v Brigham and Cowan (Hull) Ltd* [2000] PIQR Q293.
[15]   See *Hatton v Sutherland* [2002] EWCA Civ 76, [2002] 2 All ER 1 at 17.

Deafness

See *Thompson v Smiths Shiprepairers (North Shields) Ltd*.[16]

Vibration white finger

The pragmatic nature of the rules was emphasised in *Allen v British Engineering Ltd*.[17] The employer's liability was limited to the extent its negligence added to the claimant's disability. Apportionment between employers was the correct approach, but a claim should not fail solely because a claimant can not establish accurately the apportionment of injury caused between respective employers: evidence to prove apportionment must be proportionate to the amount at stake.

20.2.4.2   Indivisible conditions

Different rules exist where the medical condition is not cumulative or dose related.

Mesothelioma is a malignant tumour, usually of the pleura (the covering of the lungs). It is fatal and is nearly always the result of asbestos exposure. Mesothelioma is an indivisible conditions – because of the current limits of scientific knowledge the claimant who has been wrongfully exposed to asbestos by several employers is unable to prove which employer was responsible for the fibre(s) which mutated into a mesothelial cell. In *Fairchild v Glenhaven Funeral Services Ltd*[18] the House of Lords balanced the possible injustice to the Defendant who has not been proved by the traditional 'but for' test to have caused damage, against depriving the seriously injured claimant of a legal remedy, see Lord Bingham para 33. It was held that in limited cases successive employers found to be in breach of duty are each liable to the claimant in full as they have each materially contributed to the risk of the disease being contracted.[19] This is a further exception to the 'but for' rule (see 20.2.1 above) and an application of the reasoning in *McGhee* (see 20.2.2 above) In order to meet the justice of the case a different and less stringent test than the 'but for' test was applied.

It is likely that this exception will be kept within narrow limits, see Arden LJ in *Paul Davidson Taylor v White*.[20]

The question of apportionment was not raised before the House of Lords in *Fairchild*. In *Barker v Corus*,[21] in another mesothelioma case, the

---

[16]   [1984] QB 405.
[17]   [2001] PIQR Q101.
[18]   [2002] UKHL 22; [2003] 1 AC 32.
[19]   See *Fairchild v Glenhaven Funeral Services Ltd* [2002] 3 All ER 305.
[20]   [2004] EWCA Civ 1511; [2005] PNLR 15 at 40.
[21]   [2006] UKHL 20.

employers argued that as there had been a development in the law to cater for difficulties in proving causation in this type of case, a further rule should be developed to allow the employers to divide up responsibility for the claimant's injury between them. The House of Lords by a majority of 4:1 agreed that joint and several liability should be replaced by several liability. The damage was the creation of a risk or chance, see Lord Hoffman para 35. Although the disease itself was indivisible, the risk or chance was capable of division. The employer's liability was to be assessed by reference to the extent to which contribution had been made to the risk or chance. It was fair to limit an employer's liability to a proportion, otherwise a solvent employer may be left holding the baby because other employers had ceased to exist, become untraceable or insolvent or no relevant insurance could be found.

Because of the perceived injustice to the victims of mesothelioma the government acted quickly to reverse *Barker*. On 25 July 2006 the Compensation Act 2006 was passed. Section 3 of the Act provides that in cases of mesothelioma caused by asbestos exposure as result of the negligence or breach of duty of an employer, where it is not possible to determine with certainty which exposure lead to the disease and the employer is liable in tort, the employer shall be liable in respect of the whole of the damage. In these limited circumstances the employer is fixed with joint and several liability, see s 3 (2)(b). This does not stop one employer seeking an apportionment from another. The statute returned the law to its pre-*Barker* state. The act has, as yet, only been applied to mesothelioma claims.

Where there are multiple defendants, it is of particular importance to establish whether the damage is divisible or indivisible when a cost effective offer is made so that a defendant is not kept in the litigation unnecessarily.

20.2.5   Intervening causes

The causal connection between the wrong and the damage may be broken by an intervening cause (formerly referred to as a novus actus interveniens). An intervening cause may take one of three forms:

(1)   intervening conduct of a third party;

(2)   the conduct of the claimant;

(3)   an act of nature.

20.2.5.1   *Intervening conduct of a third party*

It is necessary to have regard to all the circumstances and in particular:

–   the impact of the intervening conduct on the chain of causation;

–   whether the intervening conduct was deliberate and unreasonable;

–   whether the intervening conduct was foreseeable;

–   whether the defendant should be held liable for the intervention (eg by creating the opportunity for a third party to intervene).

20.2.5.2   *Conduct of the claimant*

If the conduct of the claimant is wholly unreasonable and of such overwhelming impact that the defendant's wrongdoing is eclipsed, the chain of causation may be broken and the claim may fail altogether. This, however, does not often occur. If the claimant's conduct can be criticised the courts tend to look to the alternative doctrines of contributory negligence or failure to mitigate in order to limit the extent of the claim.

In *Sayers v Harlow UDC*[22] the claimant was, in breach of duty, locked in one of the council's public lavatories. She injured herself whilst returning to the floor after an unsuccessful bid to climb over the top of the door using the toilet roll holder as a foothold – the toilet roll holder moved under her foot causing her to lose her balance. The Court of Appeal found for the claimant. It was necessary to weigh the degree of inconvenience to the claimant against the risks that were being taken to do something about it. The claimant's conduct was not unreasonable, rash or stupid, although she was held to have partly contributed to her injuries and her damages were reduced by 25%.

A claimant may also diminish the recoverable loss by failing to act reasonably or by failing mitigate.

20.2.5.3   *Act of nature*

This is a doctrine of limited application and applies only in extreme circumstances.

20.2.6   **Damage must be proved**

The claimant first has to establish injury. This has recently been the subject of discussion by the courts in relation to pleural plaques. Pleural plaques constitute a physiological change in the lungs which has been

---

[22]   *Sayers v Harlow UDC* [1958] 1 WLR 623.

caused by exposure to asbestos. In 99% of cases they are asymptomatic, although in many cases the victims suffer from anxiety. Pleural plaques are markers of exposure to asbestos and a victim is at increased risk of other asbestos related diseases such as mesothelioma or pleural thickening. For over 20 years claimants in Britain with pleural plaques have received compensation through the courts. In *Johnston v NEI International Combustion Ltd*[23] the House of Lords recently held that the physiological changes were not sufficient injury to found a cause of action.

20.3   CONTRIBUTORY NEGLIGENCE

It is a well-established principle that an award of damages may be reduced because the claimant is responsible for part of the damage because of failure to take care for his own safety. The doctrine applies to actions in negligence, nuisance and breach of statutory duty. Section 1(1) of the Law Reform (Contributory Negligence) Act 1945 provides:

> 'Where any person suffers damage as a result partly of his own fault and partly of the fault of any other person or persons, a claim in respect of that damage shall not be defeated by reason of the fault of the person suffering the damage, but the damages recoverable in respect thereof shall be reduced to such an extent as the court thinks just and equitable having regard to the claimant's share in the responsibility for the damage ....'

20.3.1   Fault

Fault is defined in s 4 of the Act:

> '... fault means negligence, breach of statutory duty or other act or omission which gives rise to a liability in tort or would, apart from this Act, give rise to a defence of contributory negligence.'

Other conduct such as a breach of contract which does not involve a breach of tortious duty, or morally reprehensible conduct, is not caught by the definition. A deliberate act by the claimant may be within the definition. A prisoner who was a known suicide risk who was allowed to commit suicide in police custody was held to be 50% to blame for his death.[24]

20.3.2   The standard of care

The claimant is judged by an objectively defined reasonable standard of care. The courts frequently adopt what is called a 'common sense' approach. The application of the doctrine is best illustrated by example.

---

[23]   [2007] UKHL 39.
[24]   See *Reeves v Metropolitan Police Comr* [1998] 2 WLR 401.

20.3.3   Safety belts

In *Froom v Butcher*,[25] the claimant, who chose not to wear a seat belt, was injured in an accident caused wholly by the negligence of the defendant. The Court of Appeal took a robust approach and laid down rules of general application. If the injuries would have been prevented altogether had the claimant worn a safety belt, the damages should be reduced by 25%. If the injuries would have been a good deal less by the wearing of a safety belt, the damages should be reduced by 15%. If it would have made no difference whether or not the claimant was wearing a safety belt, there should be no deduction at all. In this case the claimant's conduct contributed to the injuries, not to the accident. In *J (A Child) v Wilkins*,[26] the Court of Appeal held that although there could be cases which fell outside the range suggested, such cases were likely to be rare. It was emphasised that the reduction of 25% for failure to wear a seat belt should not be regarded as an absolute ceiling.

20.3.4   The work context

Mere thoughtlessness or inadvertence is not enough. The court should take account of work conditions including long hours and fatigue, the slackening of attention which naturally comes from constant repetition, to noise and confusion, and preoccupation in the job at the cost perhaps of some inattention to safety.[27] A finding of contributory negligence is more likely to be made against an experienced workman than a novice.

20.3.5   Regulations

Where regulations have been introduced with the specific purpose of preventing an accident caused by the inadvertence of an employee, the courts are reluctant to make a finding of contributory negligence where the claimant's alleged fault is the very thing the employer was supposed to guard against, see *Staveley Iron & Chemical Co Ltd v Jones*.[28]

20.3.6   Dilemma created by defendant's negligent act

The more difficult the situation in which the claimant is placed by the defendant's negligent act, the less critical the courts will be of his reaction, see *Sayers v Harlow UDC* (para 20.2.5).

---

[25]   [1976] QB 286.
[26]   [2001] PIQR P12.
[27]   See *Caswell v Powell Duffryn Associated Collieries Ltd* [1940] AC 152 at 176 per Lord Wright.
[28]   [1956] AC 627, per Lord Tucker at 648.

20.3.7   Children

Courts are reluctant to find a child guilty of contributory negligence. The child's age and understanding of the dangers are relevant. The child must be assessed against an objective standard set by other similar children. In practice, children below the age of 12 are unlikely to be found guilty of contributory negligence in road traffic cases. A very young child will never be found guilty of contributory negligence.

This is a difficult area because it is impossible to set out any hard rules. It is often hard to predict whether a court will make a reduction for contributory negligence at all, and if it does make a reduction, at what level. Because of this, it is an issue which is raised by defendants in almost every case and a reduction should not be agreed upon without careful thought.

20.3.8   Miscellaneous points

In order for a deduction to be made, the claimant's conduct must be causative and blameworthy.

If the conduct of the claimant is relatively trivial, for example under 10%, it will be ignored.

If there are multiple defendants the claimant's conduct has to be assessed as against the totality of the defendants' conduct.[29]

The burden of pleading and proving contributory negligence lies on the defendant.

---

[29]   See *Fitzgerald v Lane* [1989] AC 328.

APPENDIX 1

SCHEDULE OF LOSS

IN THE HIGH COURT OF JUSTICE

QUEEN'S BENCH DIVISION

BIRMINGHAM DISTRICT REGISTRY

Between:

RONALD WEASLEY

(by his mother and litigation friend Mrs Weasley)

Claimant

and

CD

Defendant

SCHEDULE OF LOSS FOR TRIAL DATED 1ST SEPTEMBER 2008

Claimant	RONALD WEASLEY
Date of birth	1st September 1973
Date of accident	1st September 2003
Age at accident	30
Age at trial	35
Address	17 Acacia Avenue, unsuitable for Claimant's needs. Bungalow at 25 Privet Drive to be purchased
Occupation at accident	Clerk
Future occupation	Unemployable
Life expectancy	Unimpaired
Life multiplier	27.51 (Ogden Tables, 6th edition, Table 1 at 2.5 %)

Employment multiplier	20.53 (Ogden Tables, 6th edition, Table 9 at 2.5 %)
Writ issued	1st September 2005
Trial	Quantum only
Date schedule prepared	1st January 2008
Trial date	1st September 2008

A.   Pain suffering and loss of amenity

The Claimant, who was born on the 1st September 1973, was 30 years old at the time of the accident. He suffered a severe concussive head injury and an occipital fracture of the skull. On admission to hospital his Glasgow Coma Scale was reduced to 10/15 and fell to 4/15. The injury has led to brain damage. He now experiences headaches, clumsiness and lack of co-ordination. He is epileptic and prone to falls.

His concentration and memory are now poor. He has reduced intellect, poor visuo-spacial skills and a personality change with a reduction in his powers of insight and judgement. He is impulsive and vulnerable. His pre-morbid IQ is assessed at 105. He has lost up to 30 IQ points and his full scale IQ is now 75. He has frontal lobe syndrome which adversely affects cognitive, motor and social function.

He has not worked since the accident and has become depressed. He has been taking anti-depressants since this time. His personality has completely altered and he is now intolerant of others and occasionally violent.

He has developed post-traumatic epilepsy which is only partially controlled by medication.

He is unemployable.

He is and will remain a patient.

He is not safe to be left on his own and needs 24 hour care, companionship and supervision and a carer who can drive. His quality of life is grossly impaired.

The prognosis is guarded.

He relies on the reports of: (name medical experts)

General damages	£175,000
Interest at 2% from date of issue of writ	

1.9.2005–1.9.2008: 3 years × 2 % = 6%   £10,500

Total including interest   **£185,500**

B.   Pre-trial loss

(1) Loss of earnings

The Claimant worked as a clerk from 1997 until the accident on the 1st September 2003.

He had a high work ethic and was a conscientious worker. A copy of his CV is attached and marked 'RW 1'.

At the time of the accident he was earning £242.72 a week net. Had he not been injured his wages would have increased at 3% p.a. as confirmed by the letter from his former employers:

(i) 1st September 2003 –
31st August 2004:

£242.72   £12,621

minus receipts from employer   £10,000

                                           £2,621

(ii) 1st September 2004 –
31st August 2005:

£242.72 × 3% = £250.00

£250 × 52 =   £13,000

(iii) 1st September 2005 –
31st August 2006:

£250 × 3% = £257.50

£257.50 × 52 =   £13,390

(iv) 1st September 2006 –
31st August 2007:

£257.50 × 3% = £7.72

£265.22 × 52 =   £13,792

(v) 1st September 2007 –
31st August 2008:

No pay rise

£265.22 × 52 =   £13,792

Total   £56,595

The Claimant will give credit for relevant benefits disclosed on the CRU certificate.

Interest at half the special account rate:

1st September 2003 – 31st August 2008; 5 years × 3% = 15%

Interest at 15.%	£8,489
Total (including interest)	**£65,084**

(2) Care

The Claimant relies on the report of A Carer

(a) 1st December 2003 – 31st August 2004:

The Claimant remained in hospital and then at a Rehabilitation Centre for 3 months until the 30th November 2003. For the next 9 months Mr and Mrs Weasley, the Claimant's parents, assisted him in all aspects of personal care including washing and dressing. He required physical assistance and encouragement to eat food. The level of care is estimated at 10 hours a day (70 hours a week).

Hourly rate based on the aggregate rate in *Facts & Figures 2007/08* = £7.73 an hour

70 hours × £7.73 × 39 weeks =	£21,102

(b) 1st September 2004 – 31st August 2005:

During this period the Claimant's condition improved slightly. Care was provided by Mr and Mrs Weasley. The level of care is estimated at 6 hours a day (42 hours a week). Since this time he has required daily assistance with dressing, washing and eating. He has not been left on his own since the accident for more than about an hour.

42 hours × £7.94 an hour × 52 weeks =	£17,340

(c) 1st September 2005 – 31st August 2006:

42 hours × £8.18 an hour × 52 weeks =	£17,865

(d) 1st September 2006 – 31st August 2007:

42 hours × £8.43 an hour × 52 weeks =	£18,411

(e) 1st September 2007 – 31st August 2008:

Mr and Mrs Weasley continued to provide care in all aspects of daily living at 42 hours a week.

42 hours × £8.68 an hour × 52 weeks =	£18,957
Total	£93,675
Care provided voluntarily. Deduct 25 %	£70,256
Interest at 15 %	£10,538
Total (including interest)	**£80,794**

(3) Services

The services the Claimant would have performed or provided but for the accident, but in fact have been provided by others, can be realistically estimated as follows:

(a) Decorating and DIY:

The Claimant was an accomplished decorator, DIY enthusiast and gardener. He bought 17 Acacia Avenue, which is a terraced house, in a run down state and intended to do it up himself. It has been necessary since the accident for Mr Weasley to carry out essential maintenance jobs in order to make the house reasonable to live in and safer

£750 pa × (2003 – 2008) 5 years   £3,750

(b) Housework:

Since the accident either Mr or Mrs Weasley have done the Claimant's housework including cleaning, washing and ironing. Prior to the accident he used to perform all these tasks himself which used to take approximately $1\frac{1}{2}$ hours a day

10 hours a week at £5 an hour × 52 weeks = £2,600 pa

£2,600 × 5 years   £13,000

(c) Gardening:

The garden at 17 Acacia Avenue is relatively low maintenance. Allowance is made for the fact that little gardening is done in the winter months

2 hours a week × 39 weeks × £7.50 = £585 pa

£585 × 5 years	£2,925
Total	£19,675
Deduct 25% as services voluntarily performed	£14,756
Interest at 15% =	£2,213
Total (including interest)	**£16,969**

(4) Additional home running costs

See the care report of A Carer

Because of the accident the Claimant has only left the house for very short periods. During the winter he feels the cold more and it has been necessary to have the heating on the whole time. A Carer has estimated that the increased cost has been £434 pa.

December 2003 – September 2008

4.75 years × £434 =	£2,061
Interest at 15%	£309

Total (including interest)	**£2,370**

(5) Transport

Since the accident the Claimant has been dependent on others for all his transport needs. He has been driven around by Mr & Mrs Weasley who also take him into the countryside once a week.

The best estimate is that he has required 2,000 miles of additional transport a year at 17.26 pence a mile (see AA Motoring Costs 2006)

2,000 miles × 17.26 p × 4.75 years	£1,639
Interest at 15%	£245
Total (including interest)	**£1,885**

(6) Miscellaneous

(a) Hospital visits of Mr and Mrs Weasley. During the 3 months the Claimant spent in hospital they visited him every day at a cost of £5 a trip (including car parking and petrol).

£5 × 91 days =	£455
(b) Thermal Clothing £100 pa × 5 years	£500
(c) Clothing damaged in accident	£250
(d) Grab rail on stairs as Claimant is unsteady on his feet and has fallen. Cost including installation	£500
Total	£1,705
Interest at 15%	£255
Total including interest	**£1,960**

SUMMARY OF PRE-TRIAL LOSS (INCLUDING INTEREST)

(1) Loss of earnings	£65,084
(2) Care	£80,794
(3) Services	£16,969
(4) Additional home running costs	£2,370
(5) Transport	£1,885
(6) Miscellaneous	£1,960
Total	**£169,062**

C.   Future loss

(1) Loss of earnings

The Claimant repeats the matters previously set out. He worked as a clerk and if the accident had not happened he would, at the time of trial, have been in receipt of £265.22 a week net (£13,792 pa net).

He had a good work record and would have continued in this employment until the age of 65. His CV is attached marked 'RW 1'. Promotion was possible, but unlikely. It is clear from his appraisals that he was regarded by his managers as a steady and reliable worker, see 'RW2' attached. He did not have a pension.

The appropriate multiplier for a 35-year-old is 20.53

£13,792 × 20.53   **£283,149**

(2) Care

The Claimant relies on the report of A. Carer

The Claimant will require 24-hour care for the rest of his life. He is not safe to be left on his own. He is now aggressive and occasionally violent. His life expectancy has not been reduced. The appropriate multiplier is 27.51.

It is hoped to move the Claimant into single-storey accommodation as the stairs in his present home are steep, unsuitable and dangerous and he has fallen on the stairs on several occasions.

The Claimant requires care in all aspects of daily living. He sleeps heavily but is prone to wake up in a disorientated state and wander around. The care package includes the resident carer sleeping overnight on sleeping rates to cover any problems which may arise during the night. The carer also needs to provide facilitation, supervision and companionship. The total hours costed are 21 hours a day.

The Claimant will need a case manager.

Mr and Mrs Weasley have for 5 years provided significant levels of care on a daily basis at all hours of the day and night. This has caused great strain on the family relationships and it is not reasonable to expect this to continue. Mr and Mrs Weasley will continue to assist their son in whatever way they can, but they are now 72 and 69 respectively and they do feel able to continue as carers. Commercial rates are claimed.

Days

Monday – Friday:

14 hours a day × 5 days × £8.77 an hour =	£613.90 a week	

Saturday and Sunday:

14 hours a day × 2 days × £9.65 an hour =	£270.20 a week	

Nights

Monday – Friday:

7 hours a night × 5 nights × £9.65 an hour =	£337.75 a week	

Saturday and Sunday:

7 hours a night × 2 nights × £10.60 an hour =	£148.40 a week	
Total weekly cost	£1,370.25	
Annual cost = £1,370.25 × 58 weeks to allow for holidays		£79,474.50 p a
ENIC at 12.8% above £4,615.01 × 4 carers =	£18,460	
Therefore	£79,474.50	
Deduct	£18,460.00	
Total	£61,014.50 × 12.8%	£7,809.85 p a
Total annual future cost of care		£87,284.35 p a
Total cost of future care	£87,284.35 × 27.51	**£2,401,192**

[Given the Court of Appeal decision in *Thompstone v Tameside and Glossop Acute Services NHS Trust* [2008] EWCA Civ 5 the Claimant will now consider claiming on a periodical payments basis]

(3) Accommodation

The Claimant's present accommodation at 17 Acacia Avenue is unsuitable. The stairs are steep and have a bend at the top and bottom. The Claimant has fallen on occasions on the stairs. He has found a suitable property at 25 Privet Drive which is a bungalow. It is planned to have the property adapted to house carers.

The Claimant relies on the accommodation report of Mr House dated

(i) Roberts v Johnson:

Cost of bungalow at 25 Privet Drive =	£300,000	
Minus value of 17 Acacia Avenue =	£200,000	
£100,000 × 2.5 % × lifetime multiplier of 27.51 =		£68,775

(ii) Ancillary costs

Legal fees	
Removal expenses	£5,000

(iii) Cost of adaptation

See itemised architect's report	£24,000

(iv) Additional expenditure

Supervision fees	
Engineer's fees	£9,000

(v) Fitting out

Floor coverings	
Curtains	£3,500

(vi) Increased running costs

Annual energy/heating expenses agreed by care experts	£525 pa	
Telephone	£100 pa	
Water	£60 pa	
Maintenance costs	£1,500 pa	
House insurance (building and contents)	£400 pa	
Council tax (Band D) Additional cost	£250 pa	
Total	£2,835 pa	
£2,835 pa × 27.51 =		£77,990
Total		**£188,265**

(4) Transport

When the Claimant leaves his house he will need to travel by car driven by family or carers.

He will need a motor car which is reliable. A new car has the added advantages of reliability, low running costs and warranty.

(i) Cost of Vauxhall Astra 1.6i Club	
F & F page 275	£14,350

Deduct value of existing car   £7,000

                                                                £7,350

(ii) Depreciation £2,500 pa on the basis of
changing the car every 4 years

£2,500 × 27.51   £68,775

(iii) Additional mileage 3,000 miles pa

at 19.88 p per mile (AA motoring costs   £16,406
2006) × 27.51

Total   **£92,351**

(5) Equipment

(i) Mobile phone for carers

Rental per month £10 × 12 =   £120 pa

£120 × 27.51   £3,301

(ii) Thermal clothing

£100 pa × 27.51   £2,751

(iii) Computer: the Claimant is able to play some
computer games and there is evidence that these
have had a therapeutic value.

Capital cost   £1,250

Replace every 3 years (Table 27 Ogden tables)

3	£1250 × .9286 =	1161
6	£1250 × .8623 =	1078
9	£1250 × .8007 =	1001
12	£1250 × .7436 =	929
15	£1250 × .6905 =	863
18	£1250 × .6412 =	801
21	£1250 × .5954 =	744
24	£1250 × .5529 =	691
27	£1250 × .5134 =	642

                                                   £7,910

Total   **£15,212**

(6) Services

Had the accident not occurred the Claimant would have continued doing
his own decorating and DIY.

(a) Decorating and DIY

The Claimant was an accomplished decorator and did most of the jobs around the house himself. He was in the process of doing up his house. He is now unable to do any jobs. In the future he will have to pay for the jobs

to be done by others. The cost of these jobs is conservatively estimated at £750 pa.

(b) Housework

When he has the means to do so he will pay for a cleaner to do the housework. The cost of a home help is currently in the region of £7.50 per hour

5 hours a week at £7.50 an hour × 52 weeks = £1,950 pa

(c) Gardening

The Claimant plans to move to a bungalow at 25 Privet Drive which has a larger garden which will require additional maintenance. It is likely that he will spend considerable periods of time in the garden in the summer months.

4 hours a week × 39 weeks × £7.50 = £1,170 pa

Total cost = £3,870 pa

£3,870 × 27.51   **£106,463**

(7) Holidays

It will be impossible for the Claimant to take holidays alone and he will need a carer with him. An allowance is made to cover 2 weeks' holiday abroad and one week in this country, which is similar to the holidays he had before the accident. The additional cost is likely to be £2,000 pa.

£2,000 × 27.51   **£55,020**

(8) Therapies and medical review

(i) Psychological/psychiatric

The Claimant will need to see a neuro-psychologist, a behavioural psychologist and a psychiatrist annually to review his condition and assess progress or deterioration and to assess the following year's counselling and therapy requirements

Estimated at £750 pa × 27.51   £20,632

(ii) Chiropody:

The Claimant's co-ordination is now poor. He is unable to cut his toenails and this is a task which cannot be performed by a carer.

Cost £250 pa × 27.51   £6,877

(iii) Medical review

The Claimant's condition is likely to deteriorate. He needs open access to his GP and hospital if necessary.

Overall cost £250 pa × 27.51	£6.877
Total	**£34,386**

(9) Case management

It is essential that a case manager be appointed. This is recommended by the medical experts.

(i) First 12 months

Meet Claimant and parents, discuss requirements and make assessment of needs. Draft care plan, advertise, interview and appoint carers.

Set care regime in place. Attend to contracts, time sheets, wages etc

Cost

20 visits × 2 hours at £100	£4,000

Travel:

£50 × 20 visits	£1,000
Total	£5,000
VAT	£875
Total	£5,875

(ii) Annual cost

Visits to monitor the care regime. Arrange training for care workers if required. Assist when needed.

Visits

5 visits × 2 hours at £100	£1,000

Administrative time:

1.5 hours a week × £50 per hour × 52 weeks	£3,900

Travel:

£50 × 5 visits	£250
Total	£5,150
VAT	£901
Total	£6,051 p.a.

(i) £5,875

(ii) £6,051 pa × 26.51 (balance of life multiplier) = £160,412

(iii) recruitment and advertising costs = £7,500

Total	**£173,787**

(10) Court of Protection

The probable receivership costs are set out in a statement from

(a) Appointment of receiver

Costs	800	
Fees/disbursements	750	
		1,550

(b) Replacement of the receiver during the Claimant's lifetime

Costs	1,500	
PGO fees	800	
		2,300

(c) Annual receivership costs

In the first years after appointment there are additional set up costs.

First 5 years £10,000 p.a. including disbursements

		50,000
Fifth Year and subsequent years	5,500	
Fees/disbursements	700	
Subsequent annual cost	6,200	
Life multiplier 27.51 – 5 years = 22.51		139,562

(d) Annual accounts:

Accounts (including VAT)	587.50	
PGO annual fee	105.00	
Total	692.50	
£692.50 p.a. x 27.51		19,050

(e) Legal costs:

Cost of will:	5,000
Conveyancing fees:	1,500

(f) Initial employment costs:

Annual employment costs £250.00 p.a. x 27.51 =	6,877	
Payroll costs £250 p.a. x 27.51	6,877	
Total		13,755

(g) Contingency fund:

	20,000

The relevant provisions of the Mental Capacity Act 2005 came into force in October 2007. The Claimant will provide details about the additional costs to which this will inevitably give rise when they become available.

Total cost   **£252,717**

SUMMARY OF FUTURE LOSS

1.	Loss of earnings	£283,149
2.	Care	£2,401,192
3.	Accommodation	£188,265
4.	Transport	£92,351
5.	Equipment	£15,212
6.	Services	£106,463
7.	Holidays	£55,020
8.	Therapies & medial review	£34,386
9.	Case management	£173,787
10.	Court of Protection	£252,717
	TOTAL	**£3,602,542**

OVERALL SUMMARY (INCLUSIVE OF INTEREST)

(A)	General damages	£185,500
(B)	Pre-trial loss	£169,062
(C)	Future loss	£3,602,542
	OVERALL TOTAL	**£3,957,104**

APPENDIX 2

DRAFT SCHEDULE FOR LAW REFORM/FATAL ACCIDENTS ACT CLAIM

FACTS

The draft schedule set out below is for a claim in respect of mesothelioma. The Deceased was married to the Claimant and they had one dependent son. The Deceased was born on 1.1.50 and died on 1.1.2005, aged 55. He suffered from symptoms of mesothelioma for about 18 months prior to his death. He was employed at the time and intended to work to age 65. He received his full income until the date of death. The Claimant was born in 1955 and her life expectancy therefore exceeded that of the Deceased. Their son was born on 1.1.92 and was therefore 13 when his father died. He intends to go to university.

For simplicity there is no claim for dependency on pension.

IN THE COUNTY COURT Case No:

Between:

JANE SMITH

(Executrix of the estate of

JOHN SMITH

(Deceased)

Claimant

and

SHIPBUILDERS & CO

Defendants

Schedule of Loss (for Deceased Claim)

Deceased's date of birth: 1.1.50

Date of death:	1.1.05 (aged 55)
Claimant's date of birth:	1.5.55 (now aged 52)
Son's date of birth:	1.1.92 (now aged 16)
Date of Schedule:	1.1.08

All multipliers are based upon a discount rate of 2.5%.

LAW REFORM ACT CLAIM

Pain, suffering and loss of amenity

1.1 The Deceased died from malignant mesothelioma.

1.2 The Deceased developed breathlessness and chest pain in June 2003. His condition deteriorated and he became increasingly disabled by breathlessness. He was admitted to hospital on several occasions for aspiration of pleural fluid, biopsy and talc pleurodesis.

1.3 The Deceased lost his appetite and lost weight. He suffered from severe chest pain and fatigue. He became bed-bound and required night time care. He required morphine. He underwent chemotherapy and suffered marked side effects.

1.4 The Deceased suffered from a painful and debilitating terminal illness. He suffered from a substantial loss of life expectancy. He required much nursing care. He was advised of the diagnosis in December 2003 and suffered much anxiety and distress as a result.

1.5 Interest at 2% p.a. from the date of service:

£

Loss of earnings

2.1 Prior to the development of his illness the Deceased was working as an electrician. His net income was £24,000.00 per annum. He was unable to work from about January 2004. His income would have increased by about 3% in April of 2004.

2.2 Past loss

1.1.04 – 31.3.04

3 months x £2,000.00 per month = £6,000.00

1.4.04 – 1.1.05

9 months x £2,060.00 per month = £18,540.00

Total loss of earnings: **£24,540.00**

2.3 Interest at full rate from the mid point of loss: £

Cost of care

3.1   The Claimant relies upon the report from the care expert.

3.2   The Deceased became bed bound and required extensive nursing care from about July 2004. Throughout his illness the Deceased was cared for by members of his family. For about 3 months he required an average of about 2 hours of care per day. For the next month this increased to about 4 hours per day and during the 5th month he required about 8 hours of care per day.

3.3   During the last month of his life the Deceased required full time care. This was provided by his family during the day. A nurse was employed to care for him at night at a commercial rate of £14.00 per hour.

3.4   The commercial rate for domestic care is about £8.00 per hour. It is accepted that this should be discounted for tax/national insurance and the fact that care was provided gratuitously by the Claimant's family. The Claimant contends that the severity of the Deceased's condition necessitated a high level of care and she therefore contends for a discount of 20%.

3.5   <u>Past loss</u>

<u>1.7.04 – 30.9.04</u>

92 days x 2 hours per day x £8.00 x 80% = £1,177.60

<u>1.10.04 – 31.10.04</u>

31 days x 4 hours per day x £8.00 x 80% = £793.60

<u>1.11.04 – 30.11.04</u>

30 days x 8 hours per day x £8.00 x 80% = £1,536.00

<u>1.12.04 – 1.1.05</u>

32 days x 14 hours per day x £8.00 x 80% = £2,867.20

32 nights x 10 hours per night x £14.00 = £4,480.00

Total cost of care: **£10,854.40**

3.6   Interest at full rate from the mid point of loss: **£**

Services

4.1   The Claimant relies upon the report from the care expert.

4.2   The Deceased was a qualified electrician and was able to undertake plumbing and general building work. He carried out domestic DIY, decorating and household maintenance. He became completely incapacitated by his condition and was unable to complete a number of DIY/decorating projects during the last year of his life. As a result he had to employ professionals.

4.3   Past loss

Cost of labour for work undertaken: **£1,000.00**

4.4   Interest at full rate from the date of payment: £

Miscellaneous

5.1   During the course of his illness the Claimant incurred travelling expenses getting to and from hospital for treatment and consultation. These costs are set out in a separate schedule.

£350.00

5.2   Interest at half rate from the mid point of loss: £

Total Law Reform Act Claim (inclusive of   £
interest):

FATAL ACCIDENTS ACT CLAIM

Dependency on income

6.1   The Claimant relies upon the report from Dr. Smith on the Deceased's life expectancy in the absence of his mesothelioma. The Claimant has a normal life expectancy.

6.2   The Deceased was aged 55 when he died. He had a normal life expectancy. He intended to retire at age 65 (2015). The Deceased's son was aged 16 at the date of death. He intends to go to university (to 2013).

6.3   The Claimant claims a dependency of 75% of the joint family income less her residual income until her son completes university and ceases to be dependent (2013). Thereafter she claims dependency of 66.67% for the balance of the Deceased's anticipated life expectancy.

6.4   The appropriate multiplier from the date of death until the date the Deceased's son is expected to leave university (July 2013) is a fixed period of 8½ years. The appropriate multiplier for this period is about 7.67 (the mid point between 8 years and 9 years in Ogden table 28). Discount for the risk that the Deceased would not have survived to the date of trial is 0.99: 0.99 x 7.67 = 7.59

6.5 The appropriate multiplier from the date of death to the Deceased's anticipated retirement at age 65 (January 2015) is 8.56 (Ogden table 9). Discount for the risk that the Deceased would not have survived to the date of trial is 0.99: 0.99 x 8.56 = 8.47

6.6 The appropriate lifetime multiplier for the Deceased at the date of his death is 19.7 (Ogden table 1). Discount for the risk that Deceased would not have survived to the date of trial in any event is 0.99: 0.99 x 19.7 = 19.50. The balance of the multiplier after the Deceased would have reached aged 65 is therefore 19.50 – 8.47 = 11.03

6.7 At the date of death the Deceased would have had a net income of £24,720.00 per annum. It is not anticipated that this would have increased between the date of death and trial. The Claimant had an income of £6,000.00 per annum. At retirement the Deceased would have had occupational and state pensions amounting to £12,000.00 per annum net. The Claimant would have retired at the same time as the Deceased but did not have her own pension arrangements.

6.8 Past loss to the date of trial

Joint income: £24,720.00 + £6,000.00 = £30,720.00

Dependency of 75% = £23,040.00

Less Claimant's continuing income of £6,000.00 = £17,040.00

Past loss from the date of death to trial is 3 years

Past loss is therefore 3 x £17,040.00 =   **£51,120.00**

6.9 Interest at half rate from the date of death: £

6.10 Future loss

Period 1: to July 2013

Multiplier of 7.59 less past loss period of 3 years is 4.59

Multiplicand is £17,040.00

4.59 x £17,040.00 = £78,213.60

Period 2: July 2013 to January 2015

Multiplier for period from July 2013 to January 2015 is 8.47 – 7.59 = 0.88

Joint income: £24,720.00 + £6,000.00 = £30,720.00

Dependency of 66.67% = £20,481.02

Less Claimant's continuing income of £6,000.00 = £14,481.02

0.88 x £14,481.02 = £12,743.30

<u>Period 3: from January 2015 for the balance of the Deceased's life expectancy</u>

Multiplier for the period is 11.03

Dependency of 66.67% x £12,000.00 = £8,000.00

11.03 x 8,000.00 = £88,240.00

Total future dependency on earnings: **£179,196.90**

Dependency on services

7.1 The Claimant relies upon the report from the care expert.

7.2 It is estimated that the value of the Deceased's services other than gardening was about £1,500.00 per annum. Since his death the Claimant has also employed a gardener for 26 weeks per annum @ £30.00 per week.

7.3 At the date of death the Deceased was aged 55 with a lifetime multiplier of about 19.7. It is accepted that the Deceased would not have been able to manage DIY, decorating and gardening for the rest of his life. The Claimant therefore contends for a multiplier of 15.

7.4 <u>Past loss</u>

From the date of death to the date of the schedule the Claimant has had to pay for various building works and decorating that would otherwise have been undertaken by the Deceased.

<u>Building/Decorating</u>

Bathroom suite replaced: £1,500.00 labour

Decorating: £750.00 labour

<u>Gardening</u>

3 years x 26 weeks x £30.00 per week = £2,340.00

Total past loss: **£4,590.00**

7.5 Interest at full rate from the date of payment: **£**

7.6 <u>Future loss</u>

Annual estimated value of services: £1,500.00

Annual cost of gardening: £780.00

Balance of services multiplier is 15 – 3 years = 12

12 x (£1,500.00 + £780.00) = **£27,360.00**

Bereavement

8.1 Award: **£10,000.00**

8.2 Interest a full rate from the date of death (18%): **£1,800.00**

Funeral expenses

9.1   Funeral expenses including memorial: **£3,000.00**

9.2   Interest at full rate from date of payment: **£**

Total Fatal Accidents Act Claim (inclusive of   **£**
interest)

APPENDIX 3

OGDEN TABLES (6TH EDITION)

Introduction

"When it comes to the explanatory notes we must make sure that they are readily comprehensible. We must assume the most stupid circuit judge in the country and before him are the two most stupid advocates. All three of them must be able to understand what we are saying."[1]

Sir Michael Ogden QC,
on his explanatory notes to the
First Edition of the Ogden Tables.

1. This is the second edition published since Sir Michael Ogden's death. The new multipliers provided by the Government Actuary's Department use mortality rates from the latest available population projections, which take account of data following the last National Census. In general, such figures have added about 1% for most younger ages to the previous figures. There are, however, other matters here, which are discussed below and described in detail in the Explanatory Notes.

The purpose of the Ogden Tables

2. The Tables are designed to help in the calculation of future pecuniary losses.

3. The number of cases that actually fall into the multitrack, that is are worth more than £15,000, is small, and estimated by some to be only some 5% of the total claims notified. I express it as 'claims notified' for the practice of insurers has changed and now many cases are settled early without the need for the issue of proceedings.

4. When the Tables were first produced, it was on the basis that the appropriate discount rate should be chosen with regard to the yields on Index Linked Government Stock (ILGS). This was the argument presented to the House of Lords in **Wells v Wells [1999] 1 AC 345** and accepted by them in their speeches. When Lord Chancellor Irvine set the discount rate, he elected not to follow that course, but gave his own reasoning for selecting the discount rate that he chose. This was something that he was entitled to do under the powers granted to him in

---

[1]   Memoirs of Sir Michael Ogden QC, 'Variety in the Spice of Legal Life', p. 182; The Book Guild, 2002

the Damages Act 1996. He is also required under the Act to keep the discount rate he chooses under constant review, which it is said that both Lord Chancellor Irvine and his successor Lord Falconer constantly did and do.

Mortality

5.   For the most part, the new multipliers provided by the Government Actuary's Department use mortality rates from the latest available population projections, which take account of data following the last National Census. In general, such figures have had most effect on the multipliers at younger ages for loss of pension; there has been very little change in the multipliers for loss of earnings and increases of between 0% and 4% for multipliers for pecuniary loss for life compared to those in the Fifth Edition.

Contingencies other than Mortality

6.   This is the most significant contribution to this edition of the Ogden Tables. It is based on two recent and interesting pieces of research which consider the impact of contingencies other than mortality on working life. This research was carried out, in two separate exercises, by Professor Richard Verrall, Professor Steven Haberman and Mr Zoltan Butt of City University, London and by Dr Victoria Wass of Cardiff University.

7.   The findings of these two pieces of research have been combined to produce the tables which are set out in Section B of this edition of the Ogden Tables and which replace the Section B tables which were introduced in the Second Edition.

8.   The Ogden Working Party thinks that these tables are likely to prove useful to lawyers when it comes to assessing the appropriate discount to the working life multiplier for contingencies other than mortality.

9.   The research demonstrates that people without disabilities spend more time out of employment than earlier research had suggested. It is therefore appropriate to apply a higher discount for contingencies other than mortality than was indicated in the Section B tables introduced in the Second Edition of the Ogden Tables. The effect of this is that some claims for loss of earnings are likely to come down.

10.   the research also demonstrates that the factors, other than gender, which have the most effect on a person's future employment status are: (i) whether the person was employed or unemployed at the outset, (ii) whether the person is disabled or not, and (iii) the educational attainment of the person. Interestingly the research has shown that the effect of factors previously thought important, such as occupation, industrial

sector, geographic location and levels of economic activity, are relatively insignificant once educational attainment has been taken into account.

11. Accordingly, the discount to be applied to a working life multiplier (or at least a starting point) can be determined from the tables by looking up the discount factor to be applied to a person of the claimant's gender, age, educational attainment and employment status at the time of injury.

12. The tables now included at Section B may also assist those having to deal with the question of a disabled claimant's residual earnings capacity. Again, unsurprisingly to me, the research has demonstrated that disabled people are more likely to be out of employment than people without disabilities, therefore justifying a higher discount for contingencies other than mortality.

13. Both pieces of research have used the published Labour Force Survey definition of 'disabled'. This means that the range of disabilities covered by 'disabled' is very wide as it includes all people who have said that they have a condition that (a) substantially limits (or will limit due to progressive illness) their ability to carry out day-to-day activities *s* (b) affects either the amount or the type of paid work they might do.

14. There will be situations when it will be appropriate to use the factors as set out in the Section B tables to calculate a claimant's residual earning capacity on a multiplier/multiplicand basis. However, in many cases it will be appropriate to increase or reduce the discount in the tables to take account of the nature of a particular claimant's disabilities. There will also be some cases when the *Smith v. Manchester Corporation* or *Blamire* approach remains applicable. There may be still cases where a precise mathematical approach is inapplicable.

15. My view is that the findings of this research provide a very useful starting point for lawyers grappling with loss of earnings calculations and provide a basis for a more scientific approach than that which has been taken to date. There are fully worked examples in the Explanatory Notes but, clearly, they cannot cover every factual situation.

16. It also provides yet another justification for the importance of education, if such was ever needed, when faced with the unexpected hazards and problems of life visited on those who are the subject of these tables.

Variable future losses or expenses

17. The tables do not provide an immediate answer when the annual future loss or expense is likely to change at given points in time in the future, for example where a claimant's lost earnings would have increased on a sliding scale or changed due to promotion; or the claimant's future

care needs are likely to change, perhaps because it is anticipated that a family carer will not be able to continue to provide help. In such situations it is usually necessary to split the overall multiplier, whether for working life or whole of life, into segments, and then to apply those smaller segmented multipliers to the multiplicand appropriate for each period. The Explanatory Notes now include some guidance on how to use the multipliers in such cases (see paragraphs 22 to 24).

Final remarks

18.   We are conscious with each Edition of the Tables that we produce that we are being prescriptive about the way in which calculations are made.

19.   When we make suggestions for the method of calculations, each change which is put forward is the result of long and careful debate by the whole Working Party, assisted by others from outside the Working Party, who put forward proposals which we consider.

20.   The figures for the Tables themselves are produced by the Government Actuary's Department according to long established principles.

21.   All other matters are the subject of careful and detailed analysis by all the members of the Working Party.

22.   However, if anyone wishes to put forward further improvements, they are invited to do so. We travel like that Pilgrim on the Golden Journey to Samarkand, conscious of our failures and hoping for enlightenment. If you consider that you can assist us in that process, do not hesitate to write to the Government Actuary or myself.

23.   I am grateful to those members of the Working Party (listed inside the front cover) who give up their time and mental energy to attend the meetings.

1 March 2007

Robin de Wilde QC

Table 1 Multipliers for pecuniary loss for life (males)

Age at date of trial	Multiplier calculated with allowance for projected mortality from the 2004-based population projections and rate of return of											Age at date of trial
	0.0%	0.5%	1.0%	1.5%	2.0%	2.5%	3.0%	3.5%	4.0%	4.5%	5.0%	
0	86.63	69.86	57.39	47.98	40.76	35.15	30.72	27.17	24.28	21.91	19.94	0
1	85.96	69.49	57.21	47.91	40.76	35.19	30.77	27.24	24.36	21.99	20.01	1
2	84.86	68.78	56.74	47.60	40.55	35.05	30.68	27.17	24.32	21.96	19.99	2
3	83.76	68.05	56.26	47.28	40.34	34.90	30.58	27.10	24.27	21.93	19.97	3
4	82.65	67.32	55.77	46.95	40.12	34.75	30.48	27.03	24.22	21.89	19.94	4
5	81.53	66.58	55.27	46.61	39.89	34.59	30.37	26.95	24.16	21.85	19.91	5
6	80.42	65.83	54.77	46.27	39.65	34.43	30.25	26.87	24.10	21.81	19.88	6
7	79.30	65.08	54.26	45.92	39.41	34.26	30.13	26.79	24.04	21.76	19.85	7
8	78.18	64.32	53.74	45.56	39.16	34.08	30.01	26.70	23.98	21.71	19.81	8
9	77.06	63.56	53.22	45.20	38.91	33.91	29.88	26.61	23.91	21.66	19.78	9
10	75.95	62.79	52.69	44.83	38.65	33.72	29.75	26.51	23.84	21.61	19.74	10
11	74.83	62.02	52.16	44.46	38.39	33.53	29.61	26.41	23.77	21.56	19.70	11
12	73.71	61.25	51.62	44.08	38.11	33.34	29.47	26.31	23.69	21.50	19.65	12
13	72.59	60.47	51.07	43.69	37.84	33.14	29.33	26.20	23.61	21.44	19.61	13
14	71.48	59.69	50.52	43.30	37.56	32.93	29.18	26.09	23.52	21.38	19.56	14
15	70.36	58.90	49.96	42.90	37.27	32.72	29.02	25.97	23.44	21.31	19.51	15
16	69.25	58.12	49.40	42.50	36.97	32.51	28.86	25.85	23.35	21.24	19.45	16
17	68.14	57.33	48.83	42.09	36.68	32.29	28.70	25.73	23.26	21.17	19.40	17
18	67.04	56.55	48.27	41.68	36.38	32.07	28.54	25.61	23.16	21.10	19.34	18
19	65.95	55.77	47.71	41.27	36.08	31.85	28.37	25.49	23.07	21.03	19.29	19
20	64.87	54.99	47.14	40.86	35.78	31.63	28.21	25.36	22.98	20.96	19.23	20
21	63.79	54.21	46.58	40.44	35.47	31.40	28.04	25.23	22.88	20.88	19.17	21
22	62.71	53.42	46.00	40.02	35.16	31.16	27.86	25.10	22.77	20.80	19.11	22
23	61.63	52.63	45.42	39.59	34.83	30.92	27.68	24.96	22.67	20.72	19.05	23
24	60.55	51.84	44.83	39.15	34.51	30.67	27.49	24.81	22.55	20.63	18.98	24
25	59.47	51.03	44.23	38.70	34.17	30.42	27.29	24.66	22.44	20.54	18.90	25
26	58.38	50.23	43.63	38.25	33.82	30.15	27.09	24.50	22.31	20.44	18.83	26
27	57.31	49.42	43.03	37.79	33.47	29.89	26.88	24.34	22.19	20.34	18.75	27
28	56.24	48.62	42.42	37.33	33.12	29.61	26.67	24.18	22.06	20.24	18.67	28
29	55.17	47.82	41.81	36.86	32.76	29.33	26.45	24.01	21.92	20.13	18.58	29
30	54.10	47.00	41.19	36.39	32.39	29.05	26.23	23.83	21.78	20.02	18.49	30
31	53.03	46.19	40.56	35.90	32.02	28.75	26.00	23.65	21.64	19.90	18.40	31
32	51.97	45.37	39.93	35.41	31.64	28.46	25.76	23.46	21.48	19.78	18.30	32
33	50.91	44.55	39.30	34.92	31.25	28.15	25.52	23.26	21.33	19.65	18.19	33
34	49.85	43.73	38.66	34.42	30.85	27.83	25.27	23.06	21.17	19.52	18.08	34
35	48.78	42.90	38.01	33.91	30.45	27.51	25.01	22.86	21.00	19.38	17.97	35

Age at date of trial	Multiplier calculated with allowance for projected mortality from the 2004-based population projections and rate of return of											Age at date of trial
	0.0%	0.5%	1.0%	1.5%	2.0%	2.5%	3.0%	3.5%	4.0%	4.5%	5.0%	
36	47.73	42.08	37.36	33.39	30.04	27.18	24.74	22.64	20.82	19.24	17.85	36
37	46.67	41.24	36.70	32.87	29.62	26.85	24.47	22.42	20.64	19.09	17.73	37
38	45.62	40.41	36.04	32.34	29.19	26.50	24.19	22.19	20.45	18.93	17.60	38
39	44.56	39.57	35.37	31.80	28.76	26.15	23.90	21.95	20.26	18.77	17.46	39
40	43.52	38.74	34.70	31.26	28.32	25.79	23.61	21.71	20.05	18.60	17.32	40
41	42.48	37.90	34.02	30.71	27.87	25.42	23.30	21.46	19.84	18.43	17.17	41
42	41.44	37.06	33.34	30.15	27.41	25.05	22.99	21.20	19.63	18.24	17.02	42
43	40.40	36.22	32.65	29.59	26.95	24.67	22.68	20.93	19.41	18.06	16.86	43
44	39.37	35.38	31.97	29.03	26.49	24.28	22.35	20.66	19.18	17.86	16.69	44
45	38.35	34.55	31.28	28.46	26.01	23.88	22.02	20.38	18.94	17.66	16.52	45
46	37.34	33.71	30.59	27.89	25.54	23.49	21.69	20.10	18.70	17.46	16.35	46
47	36.34	32.89	29.90	27.32	25.06	23.08	21.35	19.81	18.45	17.25	16.17	47
48	35.34	32.06	29.22	26.74	24.58	22.68	21.00	19.52	18.20	17.03	15.98	48
49	34.37	31.25	28.54	26.17	24.09	22.27	20.65	19.22	17.95	16.81	15.79	49
50	33.40	30.44	27.86	25.60	23.61	21.86	20.30	18.92	17.69	16.59	15.60	50
51	32.44	29.63	27.18	25.02	23.12	21.44	19.95	18.62	17.43	16.36	15.40	51
52	31.49	28.84	26.50	24.45	22.63	21.02	19.58	18.30	17.16	16.12	15.19	52
53	30.55	28.04	25.82	23.87	22.13	20.59	19.21	17.98	16.88	15.88	14.98	53
54	29.61	27.23	25.13	23.28	21.62	20.15	18.83	17.65	16.59	15.63	14.76	54
55	28.66	26.42	24.44	22.67	21.10	19.70	18.44	17.31	16.29	15.36	14.52	55
56	27.71	25.60	23.73	22.06	20.57	19.23	18.03	16.95	15.97	15.08	14.28	56
57	26.76	24.78	23.02	21.44	20.03	18.76	17.62	16.58	15.65	14.79	14.02	57
58	25.82	23.96	22.31	20.82	19.48	18.28	17.19	16.21	15.31	14.50	13.75	58
59	24.89	23.15	21.59	20.19	18.93	17.79	16.76	15.82	14.97	14.19	13.48	59
60	23.97	22.35	20.89	19.57	18.38	17.30	16.33	15.44	14.62	13.88	13.20	60
61	23.08	21.56	20.19	18.96	17.84	16.82	15.90	15.05	14.28	13.57	12.92	61
62	22.20	20.79	19.51	18.35	17.30	16.34	15.47	14.67	13.93	13.26	12.64	62
63	21.34	20.03	18.83	17.75	16.76	15.86	15.03	14.28	13.58	12.94	12.36	63
64	20.50	19.27	18.16	17.15	16.22	15.37	14.60	13.88	13.23	12.62	12.06	64
65	19.66	18.52	17.49	16.54	15.68	14.88	14.16	13.48	12.86	12.29	11.76	65
66	18.82	17.77	16.81	15.94	15.13	14.39	13.70	13.07	12.49	11.95	11.45	66
67	17.99	17.02	16.14	15.32	14.57	13.88	13.24	12.65	12.11	11.60	11.13	67
68	17.16	16.27	15.45	14.70	14.01	13.36	12.77	12.22	11.71	11.23	10.79	68
69	16.33	15.51	14.76	14.07	13.43	12.84	12.29	11.77	11.30	10.85	10.44	69
70	15.50	14.75	14.07	13.43	12.85	12.30	11.79	11.32	10.87	10.46	10.08	70
71	14.67	14.00	13.38	12.80	12.26	11.76	11.29	10.85	10.44	10.06	9.70	71
72	13.86	13.25	12.69	12.16	11.67	11.21	10.78	10.38	10.00	9.65	9.32	72
73	13.07	12.52	12.01	11.53	11.09	10.67	10.28	9.91	9.56	9.24	8.94	73

Age at date of trial	Multiplier calculated with allowance for projected mortality from the 2004-based population projections and rate of return of											Age at date of trial
	0.0%	0.5%	1.0%	1.5%	2.0%	2.5%	3.0%	3.5%	4.0%	4.5%	5.0%	
74	12.31	11.81	11.35	10.92	10.51	10.13	9.78	9.44	9.13	8.83	8.55	74
75	11.57	11.13	10.71	10.32	9.95	9.61	9.29	8.98	8.70	8.42	8.17	75
76	10.86	10.47	10.09	9.74	9.41	9.10	8.81	8.53	8.27	8.03	7.79	76
77	10.19	9.84	9.50	9.19	8.89	8.61	8.35	8.10	7.86	7.64	7.42	77
78	9.55	9.24	8.94	8.66	8.39	8.14	7.90	7.68	7.46	7.26	7.06	78
79	8.95	8.67	8.40	8.15	7.91	7.69	7.47	7.27	7.08	6.89	6.71	79
80	8.38	8.13	7.89	7.67	7.45	7.25	7.06	6.88	6.70	6.53	6.38	80
81	7.83	7.61	7.40	7.20	7.01	6.83	6.66	6.49	6.34	6.19	6.04	81
82	7.31	7.12	6.93	6.75	6.58	6.42	6.27	6.12	5.98	5.85	5.72	82
83	6.81	6.64	6.47	6.32	6.17	6.02	5.89	5.75	5.63	5.51	5.39	83
84	6.32	6.17	6.03	5.89	5.76	5.63	5.51	5.39	5.28	5.17	5.07	84
85	5.87	5.73	5.61	5.49	5.37	5.26	5.15	5.05	4.95	4.85	4.76	85
86	5.44	5.33	5.22	5.11	5.01	4.91	4.81	4.72	4.64	4.55	4.47	86
87	5.05	4.95	4.85	4.76	4.67	4.58	4.50	4.42	4.34	4.27	4.19	87
88	4.68	4.60	4.51	4.43	4.35	4.27	4.20	4.13	4.06	4.00	3.93	88
89	4.35	4.28	4.20	4.13	4.06	4.00	3.93	3.87	3.81	3.75	3.69	89
90	4.05	3.99	3.92	3.86	3.80	3.74	3.68	3.63	3.57	3.52	3.47	90
91	3.76	3.71	3.65	3.59	3.54	3.49	3.44	3.39	3.34	3.30	3.25	91
92	3.49	3.44	3.39	3.34	3.30	3.25	3.21	3.16	3.12	3.08	3.04	92
93	3.26	3.21	3.17	3.12	3.08	3.04	3.00	2.96	2.93	2.89	2.86	93
94	3.06	3.02	2.98	2.94	2.91	2.87	2.83	2.80	2.77	2.73	2.70	94
95	2.88	2.85	2.81	2.78	2.75	2.71	2.68	2.65	2.62	2.59	2.56	95
96	2.71	2.68	2.65	2.62	2.59	2.56	2.53	2.51	2.48	2.45	2.43	96
97	2.55	2.52	2.49	2.46	2.44	2.41	2.39	2.36	2.34	2.32	2.29	97
98	2.38	2.36	2.33	2.31	2.29	2.26	2.24	2.22	2.20	2.18	2.16	98
99	2.22	2.20	2.18	2.15	2.13	2.12	2.10	2.08	2.06	2.04	2.02	99
100	2.06	2.04	2.02	2.01	1.99	1.97	1.95	1.94	1.92	1.90	1.89	100

Table 2 Multipliers for pecuniary loss for life (females)

Age at date of trial	Multiplier calculated with allowance for projected mortality from the 2004-based population projections and rate of return of											Age at date of trial
	0.0%	0.5%	1.0%	1.5%	2.0%	2.5%	3.0%	3.5%	4.0%	4.5%	5.0%	
0	90.15	72.21	58.98	49.06	41.51	35.67	31.09	27.43	24.48	22.06	20.05	0
1	89.44	71.83	58.79	48.99	41.50	35.70	31.14	27.50	24.55	22.13	20.11	1
2	88.36	71.13	58.34	48.70	41.32	35.58	31.06	27.44	24.51	22.10	20.10	2
3	87.27	70.43	57.88	48.40	41.12	35.45	30.97	27.38	24.47	22.08	20.08	3
4	86.17	69.72	57.42	48.09	40.92	35.32	30.88	27.32	24.43	22.05	20.06	4
5	85.07	69.00	56.95	47.78	40.71	35.18	30.79	27.26	24.38	22.01	20.04	5
6	83.97	68.28	56.47	47.46	40.49	35.03	30.69	27.19	24.34	21.98	20.01	6
7	82.87	67.55	55.99	47.14	40.28	34.88	30.59	27.12	24.29	21.95	19.99	7
8	81.77	66.82	55.50	46.81	40.05	34.73	30.48	27.04	24.23	21.91	19.96	8
9	80.67	66.08	55.00	46.47	39.82	34.57	30.37	26.97	24.18	21.87	19.93	9
10	79.57	65.34	54.50	46.13	39.59	34.41	30.26	26.89	24.12	21.83	19.90	10
11	78.47	64.60	53.99	45.78	39.35	34.24	30.14	26.80	24.06	21.79	19.87	11
12	77.36	63.85	53.48	45.43	39.10	34.07	30.02	26.72	24.00	21.74	19.84	12
13	76.26	63.10	52.96	45.07	38.85	33.89	29.89	26.63	23.94	21.69	19.80	13
14	75.16	62.34	52.44	44.71	38.60	33.71	29.76	26.53	23.87	21.64	19.77	14
15	74.06	61.58	51.91	44.34	38.34	33.53	29.63	26.44	23.80	21.59	19.73	15
16	72.97	60.82	51.38	43.97	38.07	33.34	29.49	26.34	23.73	21.54	19.69	16
17	71.88	60.06	50.85	43.59	37.80	33.15	29.36	26.24	23.65	21.48	19.65	17
18	70.79	59.30	50.31	43.21	37.53	32.95	29.21	26.14	23.57	21.43	19.60	18
19	69.70	58.53	49.77	42.82	37.25	32.75	29.07	26.03	23.50	21.37	19.56	19
20	68.61	57.76	49.22	42.42	36.97	32.54	28.91	25.92	23.41	21.30	19.51	20
21	67.52	56.98	48.66	42.02	36.68	32.33	28.76	25.80	23.33	21.24	19.46	21
22	66.43	56.20	48.10	41.62	36.38	32.11	28.60	25.68	23.23	21.17	19.41	22
23	65.34	55.42	47.53	41.20	36.08	31.89	28.43	25.55	23.14	21.10	19.36	23
24	64.25	54.63	46.96	40.78	35.77	31.66	28.26	25.42	23.04	21.02	19.30	24
25	63.16	53.84	46.38	40.36	35.45	31.42	28.08	25.29	22.94	20.94	19.24	25
26	62.08	53.05	45.79	39.92	35.13	31.18	27.90	25.15	22.83	20.86	19.17	26
27	60.99	52.25	45.20	39.48	34.80	30.93	27.71	25.01	22.72	20.78	19.10	27
28	59.91	51.45	44.61	39.04	34.46	30.67	27.51	24.86	22.61	20.69	19.03	28
29	58.83	50.64	44.01	38.58	34.12	30.41	27.31	24.70	22.49	20.59	18.96	29
30	57.74	49.83	43.40	38.12	33.77	30.15	27.11	24.54	22.36	20.49	18.88	30
31	56.66	49.02	42.78	37.66	33.41	29.87	26.89	24.38	22.23	20.39	18.80	31
32	55.58	48.20	42.16	37.18	33.05	29.59	26.68	24.21	22.10	20.28	18.71	32
33	54.50	47.38	41.54	36.70	32.68	29.30	26.45	24.03	21.96	20.17	18.63	33
34	53.43	46.56	40.91	36.22	32.30	29.01	26.22	23.85	21.81	20.06	18.53	34
35	52.35	45.74	40.27	35.73	31.92	28.71	25.98	23.66	21.66	19.93	18.43	35

Age at date of trial	Multiplier calculated with allowance for projected mortality from the 2004-based population projections and rate of return of											Age at date of trial
	0.0%	0.5%	1.0%	1.5%	2.0%	2.5%	3.0%	3.5%	4.0%	4.5%	5.0%	
36	51.28	44.91	39.63	35.22	31.52	28.40	25.74	23.46	21.50	19.81	18.33	36
37	50.21	44.08	38.98	34.72	31.13	28.08	25.49	23.26	21.34	19.67	18.22	37
38	49.14	43.25	38.33	34.20	30.72	27.76	25.23	23.05	21.17	19.54	18.11	38
39	48.07	42.41	37.67	33.68	30.30	27.43	24.96	22.84	21.00	19.39	17.99	39
40	47.01	41.58	37.01	33.16	29.89	27.09	24.69	22.61	20.82	19.25	17.87	40
41	45.95	40.74	36.35	32.63	29.46	26.74	24.41	22.39	20.63	19.09	17.74	41
42	44.90	39.90	35.68	32.09	29.02	26.39	24.12	22.15	20.44	18.93	17.61	42
43	43.85	39.06	35.00	31.55	28.59	26.04	23.83	21.91	20.24	18.77	17.47	43
44	42.80	38.22	34.33	31.00	28.14	25.67	23.53	21.66	20.03	18.59	17.33	44
45	41.77	37.39	33.65	30.45	27.69	25.30	23.23	21.41	19.82	18.42	17.18	45
46	40.74	36.55	32.97	29.90	27.24	24.93	22.92	21.15	19.61	18.24	17.03	46
47	39.71	35.72	32.29	29.34	26.77	24.55	22.60	20.89	19.38	18.05	16.87	47
48	38.70	34.89	31.61	28.77	26.31	24.16	22.28	20.62	19.16	17.86	16.70	48
49	37.69	34.06	30.93	28.21	25.84	23.77	21.95	20.34	18.92	17.66	16.53	49
50	36.69	33.23	30.24	27.64	25.36	23.37	21.61	20.06	18.68	17.46	16.36	50
51	35.69	32.41	29.56	27.07	24.88	22.96	21.27	19.77	18.44	17.25	16.18	51
52	34.70	31.59	28.87	26.49	24.40	22.55	20.92	19.47	18.18	17.03	15.99	52
53	33.71	30.76	28.17	25.90	23.90	22.13	20.56	19.17	17.92	16.80	15.80	53
54	32.73	29.93	27.47	25.31	23.39	21.70	20.19	18.85	17.64	16.56	15.59	54
55	31.74	29.09	26.76	24.70	22.88	21.26	19.81	18.52	17.36	16.32	15.38	55
56	30.75	28.25	26.05	24.09	22.36	20.81	19.42	18.18	17.07	16.06	15.15	56
57	29.77	27.42	25.33	23.48	21.82	20.35	19.03	17.84	16.77	15.80	14.92	57
58	28.80	26.58	24.61	22.86	21.29	19.88	18.62	17.48	16.46	15.52	14.68	58
59	27.83	25.75	23.89	22.23	20.75	19.41	18.21	17.12	16.14	15.24	14.43	59
60	26.88	24.93	23.18	21.61	20.20	18.94	17.79	16.76	15.81	14.96	14.18	60
61	25.94	24.11	22.47	20.99	19.66	18.46	17.37	16.38	15.49	14.67	13.92	61
62	25.02	23.30	21.76	20.37	19.11	17.98	16.95	16.01	15.15	14.37	13.65	62
63	24.10	22.49	21.05	19.75	18.56	17.49	16.51	15.62	14.81	14.06	13.38	63
64	23.18	21.69	20.34	19.12	18.01	17.00	16.07	15.23	14.46	13.75	13.10	64
65	22.28	20.89	19.63	18.49	17.45	16.50	15.63	14.83	14.10	13.42	12.80	65
66	21.38	20.09	18.92	17.85	16.88	15.99	15.17	14.42	13.73	13.09	12.50	66
67	20.48	19.29	18.20	17.21	16.30	15.47	14.70	13.99	13.34	12.74	12.18	67
68	19.58	18.48	17.47	16.55	15.71	14.93	14.22	13.55	12.94	12.38	11.85	68
69	18.66	17.66	16.73	15.88	15.10	14.38	13.71	13.10	12.52	11.99	11.50	69
70	17.74	16.82	15.97	15.19	14.47	13.81	13.19	12.62	12.09	11.59	11.13	70
71	16.82	15.98	15.21	14.50	13.84	13.22	12.65	12.13	11.63	11.17	10.74	71
72	15.90	15.14	14.44	13.79	13.19	12.63	12.11	11.62	11.17	10.74	10.34	72
73	14.99	14.31	13.67	13.09	12.54	12.03	11.55	11.11	10.69	10.30	9.93	73

Age at date of trial	Multiplier calculated with allowance for projected mortality from the 2004-based population projections and rate of return of											Age at date of trial
	0.0%	0.5%	1.0%	1.5%	2.0%	2.5%	3.0%	3.5%	4.0%	4.5%	5.0%	
74	14.10	13.49	12.92	12.39	11.89	11.43	11.00	10.59	10.21	9.85	9.51	74
75	13.24	12.69	12.18	11.71	11.26	10.84	10.45	10.08	9.73	9.40	9.10	75
76	12.42	11.93	11.47	11.05	10.64	10.27	9.91	9.58	9.26	8.96	8.68	76
77	11.64	11.20	10.79	10.41	10.05	9.71	9.39	9.09	8.80	8.53	8.28	77
78	10.89	10.51	10.14	9.80	9.48	9.17	8.88	8.61	8.35	8.11	7.88	78
79	10.19	9.84	9.52	9.21	8.93	8.65	8.39	8.15	7.92	7.70	7.48	79
80	9.51	9.21	8.92	8.65	8.39	8.15	7.92	7.70	7.49	7.29	7.10	80
81	8.87	8.60	8.35	8.11	7.88	7.66	7.46	7.26	7.07	6.89	6.72	81
82	8.26	8.02	7.80	7.58	7.38	7.19	7.01	6.83	6.66	6.50	6.35	82
83	7.67	7.46	7.27	7.08	6.90	6.73	6.57	6.41	6.26	6.12	5.98	83
84	7.10	6.92	6.75	6.59	6.43	6.28	6.14	6.00	5.87	5.74	5.62	84
85	6.57	6.41	6.26	6.12	5.98	5.85	5.73	5.60	5.49	5.38	5.27	85
86	6.07	5.93	5.80	5.68	5.56	5.44	5.33	5.23	5.12	5.02	4.93	86
87	5.60	5.48	5.37	5.26	5.16	5.06	4.96	4.86	4.77	4.69	4.60	87
88	5.17	5.06	4.97	4.87	4.78	4.69	4.61	4.53	4.45	4.37	4.30	88
89	4.77	4.68	4.60	4.51	4.43	4.36	4.28	4.21	4.14	4.08	4.01	89
90	4.41	4.33	4.26	4.19	4.12	4.05	3.99	3.92	3.86	3.80	3.75	90
91	4.08	4.01	3.95	3.89	3.83	3.77	3.71	3.66	3.60	3.55	3.50	91
92	3.79	3.73	3.67	3.61	3.56	3.51	3.46	3.41	3.36	3.32	3.27	92
93	3.53	3.47	3.42	3.38	3.33	3.28	3.24	3.20	3.15	3.11	3.07	93
94	3.30	3.25	3.21	3.17	3.12	3.08	3.04	3.00	2.97	2.93	2.90	94
95	3.08	3.04	3.01	2.97	2.93	2.89	2.86	2.82	2.79	2.76	2.73	95
96	2.89	2.85	2.82	2.78	2.75	2.72	2.69	2.66	2.63	2.60	2.57	96
97	2.70	2.67	2.64	2.61	2.58	2.55	2.53	2.50	2.47	2.45	2.42	97
98	2.53	2.50	2.48	2.45	2.42	2.40	2.37	2.35	2.33	2.30	2.28	98
99	2.37	2.34	2.32	2.30	2.27	2.25	2.23	2.21	2.19	2.17	2.15	99
100	2.21	2.19	2.17	2.15	2.13	2.11	2.09	2.07	2.05	2.03	2.02	100

Table 3 Multipliers for loss of earnings to pension age 50 (males)

Age at date of trial	Multiplier calculated with allowance for projected mortality from the 2004-based population projections and rate of return of											Age at date of trial
	0.0%	0.5%	1.0%	1.5%	2.0%	2.5%	3.0%	3.5%	4.0%	4.5%	5.0%	
16	33.58	30.90	28.52	26.39	24.48	22.77	21.24	19.86	18.61	17.48	16.46	16
17	32.59	30.06	27.80	25.78	23.96	22.33	20.86	19.54	18.34	17.25	16.26	17
18	31.59	29.21	27.08	25.16	23.44	21.88	20.48	19.21	18.05	17.00	16.05	18
19	30.60	28.37	26.36	24.54	22.91	21.43	20.09	18.87	17.76	16.76	15.83	19
20	29.62	27.52	25.63	23.92	22.37	20.96	19.68	18.52	17.46	16.50	15.61	20
21	28.63	26.67	24.89	23.28	21.81	20.48	19.27	18.16	17.15	16.22	15.37	21
22	27.65	25.81	24.15	22.63	21.25	19.99	18.84	17.79	16.83	15.94	15.13	22
23	26.66	24.95	23.39	21.98	20.68	19.49	18.40	17.41	16.49	15.64	14.87	23
24	25.67	24.09	22.64	21.31	20.09	18.98	17.95	17.01	16.14	15.33	14.59	24
25	24.68	23.21	21.87	20.63	19.49	18.45	17.48	16.59	15.77	15.01	14.30	25
26	23.70	22.34	21.09	19.94	18.88	17.91	17.00	16.17	15.39	14.67	14.00	26
27	22.71	21.46	20.31	19.25	18.26	17.35	16.51	15.72	14.99	14.32	13.69	27
28	21.72	20.58	19.52	18.54	17.63	16.78	16.00	15.27	14.58	13.95	13.36	28
29	20.74	19.69	18.72	17.82	16.98	16.20	15.47	14.79	14.16	13.56	13.01	29
30	19.75	18.80	17.92	17.10	16.33	15.61	14.93	14.31	13.72	13.16	12.64	30
31	18.77	17.91	17.11	16.36	15.66	15.00	14.38	13.80	13.25	12.74	12.26	31
32	17.78	17.01	16.29	15.61	14.97	14.37	13.81	13.28	12.78	12.30	11.86	32
33	16.80	16.11	15.46	14.85	14.27	13.73	13.22	12.74	12.28	11.85	11.44	33
34	15.81	15.20	14.62	14.08	13.56	13.08	12.61	12.18	11.76	11.37	11.00	34
35	14.83	14.29	13.78	13.30	12.84	12.40	11.99	11.60	11.22	10.87	10.53	35
36	13.84	13.37	12.93	12.50	12.10	11.71	11.35	11.00	10.67	10.35	10.05	36
37	12.86	12.45	12.07	11.70	11.34	11.01	10.69	10.38	10.08	9.80	9.53	37
38	11.87	11.53	11.19	10.88	10.57	10.28	10.00	9.74	9.48	9.23	9.00	38
39	10.89	10.60	10.32	10.05	9.79	9.54	9.30	9.07	8.85	8.64	8.43	39
40	9.90	9.66	9.43	9.20	8.99	8.78	8.58	8.38	8.20	8.02	7.84	40
41	8.92	8.72	8.53	8.35	8.17	8.00	7.83	7.67	7.52	7.37	7.22	41
42	7.93	7.77	7.62	7.48	7.33	7.20	7.06	6.93	6.81	6.69	6.57	42
43	6.94	6.82	6.71	6.59	6.48	6.38	6.27	6.17	6.07	5.98	5.88	43
44	5.95	5.87	5.78	5.70	5.61	5.53	5.46	5.38	5.31	5.23	5.16	44
45	4.97	4.90	4.84	4.79	4.73	4.67	4.62	4.56	4.51	4.46	4.41	45
46	3.98	3.94	3.90	3.86	3.82	3.79	3.75	3.72	3.68	3.65	3.61	46
47	2.99	2.96	2.94	2.92	2.90	2.88	2.86	2.84	2.82	2.80	2.78	47
48	1.99	1.98	1.97	1.96	1.95	1.94	1.94	1.93	1.92	1.91	1.90	48
49	1.00	1.00	0.99	0.99	0.99	0.99	0.98	0.98	0.98	0.98	0.97	49

Table 4 Multipliers for loss of earnings to pension age 50 (females)

Age at date of trial	Multiplier calculated with allowance for projected mortality from the 2004-based population projections and rate of return of											Age at date of trial
	0.0%	0.5%	1.0%	1.5%	2.0%	2.5%	3.0%	3.5%	4.0%	4.5%	5.0%	
16	33.79	31.09	28.68	26.54	24.61	22.89	21.34	19.95	18.69	17.56	16.53	16
17	32.80	30.25	27.97	25.93	24.10	22.45	20.97	19.64	18.43	17.33	16.33	17
18	31.80	29.40	27.25	25.32	23.58	22.01	20.59	19.31	18.15	17.09	16.13	18
19	30.81	28.55	26.52	24.69	23.04	21.55	20.20	18.97	17.86	16.84	15.91	19
20	29.81	27.70	25.79	24.06	22.50	21.08	19.79	18.62	17.55	16.58	15.69	20
21	28.82	26.84	25.04	23.42	21.94	20.60	19.38	18.26	17.24	16.30	15.45	21
22	27.82	25.97	24.29	22.77	21.37	20.11	18.95	17.88	16.91	16.02	15.20	22
23	26.83	25.11	23.54	22.10	20.80	19.60	18.50	17.50	16.57	15.72	14.94	23
24	25.83	24.23	22.77	21.43	20.21	19.08	18.05	17.10	16.22	15.41	14.66	24
25	24.84	23.36	22.00	20.75	19.60	18.55	17.58	16.68	15.85	15.08	14.37	25
26	23.84	22.48	21.22	20.06	18.99	18.00	17.09	16.25	15.47	14.74	14.07	26
27	22.85	21.59	20.43	19.36	18.37	17.45	16.60	15.81	15.07	14.39	13.75	27
28	21.85	20.70	19.63	18.65	17.73	16.88	16.08	15.35	14.66	14.02	13.42	28
29	20.86	19.81	18.83	17.92	17.08	16.29	15.55	14.87	14.23	13.63	13.07	29
30	19.87	18.91	18.02	17.19	16.41	15.69	15.01	14.38	13.78	13.23	12.70	30
31	18.87	18.01	17.20	16.44	15.74	15.07	14.45	13.87	13.32	12.80	12.32	31
32	17.88	17.10	16.37	15.69	15.05	14.44	13.88	13.34	12.84	12.36	11.91	32
33	16.89	16.19	15.54	14.92	14.34	13.80	13.28	12.80	12.34	11.90	11.49	33
34	15.89	15.28	14.70	14.15	13.63	13.14	12.67	12.23	11.82	11.42	11.04	34
35	14.90	14.36	13.85	13.36	12.90	12.46	12.04	11.65	11.27	10.92	10.58	35
36	13.91	13.44	12.99	12.56	12.15	11.76	11.40	11.04	10.71	10.39	10.09	36
37	12.92	12.51	12.12	11.75	11.39	11.05	10.73	10.42	10.12	9.84	9.57	37
38	11.92	11.57	11.24	10.92	10.62	10.32	10.04	9.77	9.52	9.27	9.03	38
39	10.93	10.64	10.36	10.08	9.82	9.58	9.34	9.10	8.88	8.67	8.46	39
40	9.94	9.70	9.46	9.24	9.02	8.81	8.61	8.41	8.23	8.04	7.87	40
41	8.95	8.75	8.56	8.37	8.20	8.02	7.86	7.70	7.54	7.39	7.24	41
42	7.95	7.80	7.65	7.50	7.36	7.22	7.09	6.96	6.83	6.71	6.59	42
43	6.96	6.84	6.73	6.61	6.50	6.39	6.29	6.19	6.09	5.99	5.90	43
44	5.97	5.88	5.80	5.71	5.63	5.55	5.47	5.40	5.32	5.25	5.18	44
45	4.98	4.92	4.86	4.80	4.74	4.68	4.63	4.57	4.52	4.47	4.42	45
46	3.98	3.95	3.91	3.87	3.83	3.79	3.76	3.72	3.69	3.65	3.62	46
47	2.99	2.97	2.95	2.93	2.90	2.88	2.86	2.84	2.82	2.80	2.78	47
48	2.00	1.99	1.98	1.97	1.96	1.95	1.94	1.93	1.92	1.91	1.90	48
49	1.00	1.00	0.99	0.99	0.99	0.99	0.98	0.98	0.98	0.98	0.97	49

Table 5 Multipliers for loss of earnings to pension age 55 (males)

Age at date of trial	Multiplier calculated with allowance for projected mortality from the 2004-based population projections and rate of return of											Age at date of trial
	0.0%	0.5%	1.0%	1.5%	2.0%	2.5%	3.0%	3.5%	4.0%	4.5%	5.0%	
16	38.37	34.90	31.85	29.17	26.81	24.72	22.87	21.22	19.75	18.44	17.27	16
17	37.37	34.07	31.16	28.60	26.34	24.33	22.54	20.95	19.53	18.25	17.11	17
18	36.38	33.24	30.48	28.03	25.86	23.93	22.21	20.67	19.29	18.06	16.94	18
19	35.39	32.42	29.79	27.45	25.37	23.52	21.87	20.38	19.05	17.85	16.77	19
20	34.41	31.59	29.09	26.87	24.88	23.11	21.52	20.09	18.80	17.64	16.59	20
21	33.42	30.76	28.39	26.27	24.38	22.68	21.16	19.79	18.54	17.42	16.41	21
22	32.43	29.92	27.68	25.67	23.87	22.25	20.79	19.47	18.28	17.19	16.21	22
23	31.45	29.08	26.97	25.06	23.35	21.80	20.41	19.14	18.00	16.95	16.00	23
24	30.46	28.24	26.24	24.44	22.82	21.35	20.02	18.81	17.71	16.70	15.79	24
25	29.47	27.39	25.51	23.81	22.27	20.88	19.61	18.46	17.40	16.44	15.56	25
26	28.49	26.54	24.77	23.17	21.72	20.40	19.19	18.09	17.09	16.17	15.32	26
27	27.50	25.68	24.03	22.53	21.16	19.91	18.76	17.72	16.76	15.88	15.07	27
28	26.52	24.82	23.28	21.87	20.58	19.40	18.32	17.33	16.42	15.58	14.81	28
29	25.53	23.96	22.52	21.20	20.00	18.89	17.87	16.93	16.07	15.27	14.54	29
30	24.55	23.09	21.76	20.53	19.40	18.36	17.40	16.52	15.70	14.95	14.25	30
31	23.57	22.22	20.98	19.84	18.79	17.82	16.92	16.09	15.32	14.61	13.95	31
32	22.59	21.35	20.21	19.15	18.17	17.27	16.43	15.65	14.93	14.26	13.63	32
33	21.60	20.47	19.42	18.45	17.54	16.70	15.92	15.20	14.52	13.89	13.30	33
34	20.62	19.59	18.63	17.73	16.90	16.12	15.40	14.72	14.09	13.50	12.95	34
35	19.64	18.70	17.82	17.01	16.24	15.53	14.86	14.24	13.65	13.10	12.59	35
36	18.66	17.81	17.01	16.27	15.57	14.92	14.31	13.73	13.19	12.68	12.21	36
37	17.68	16.91	16.20	15.52	14.89	14.30	13.74	13.21	12.71	12.25	11.80	37
38	16.70	16.02	15.37	14.77	14.20	13.66	13.15	12.67	12.22	11.79	11.38	38
39	15.72	15.11	14.54	14.00	13.49	13.00	12.55	12.11	11.70	11.31	10.94	39
40	14.74	14.20	13.70	13.22	12.76	12.33	11.92	11.53	11.16	10.81	10.48	40
41	13.76	13.29	12.85	12.43	12.03	11.64	11.28	10.94	10.61	10.29	9.99	41
42	12.78	12.37	11.99	11.62	11.27	10.94	10.62	10.32	10.03	9.75	9.48	42
43	11.80	11.45	11.12	10.81	10.51	10.22	9.94	9.68	9.42	9.18	8.95	43
44	10.82	10.53	10.25	9.98	9.73	9.48	9.24	9.02	8.80	8.59	8.39	44
45	9.84	9.60	9.37	9.15	8.93	8.73	8.53	8.33	8.15	7.97	7.80	45
46	8.86	8.67	8.48	8.30	8.12	7.95	7.79	7.63	7.47	7.32	7.18	46
47	7.88	7.73	7.58	7.43	7.29	7.16	7.03	6.90	6.77	6.65	6.53	47
48	6.91	6.79	6.67	6.56	6.45	6.34	6.24	6.14	6.04	5.95	5.85	48
49	5.93	5.84	5.75	5.67	5.59	5.51	5.43	5.36	5.28	5.21	5.14	49
50	4.95	4.89	4.83	4.77	4.71	4.65	4.60	4.55	4.49	4.44	4.39	50
51	3.96	3.93	3.89	3.85	3.81	3.78	3.74	3.70	3.67	3.64	3.60	51

Age at date of trial	Multiplier calculated with allowance for projected mortality from the 2004-based population projections and rate of return of											Age at date of trial
	0.0%	0.5%	1.0%	1.5%	2.0%	2.5%	3.0%	3.5%	4.0%	4.5%	5.0%	
52	2.98	2.96	2.94	2.91	2.89	2.87	2.85	2.83	2.81	2.79	2.77	52
53	1.99	1.98	1.97	1.96	1.95	1.94	1.93	1.92	1.91	1.91	1.90	53
54	1.00	0.99	0.99	0.99	0.99	0.99	0.98	0.98	0.98	0.98	0.97	54

Table 6 Multipliers for loss of earnings to pension age 55 (females)

Age at date of trial	Multiplier calculated with allowance for projected mortality from the 2004-based population projections and rate of return of											Age at date of trial
	0.0%	0.5%	1.0%	1.5%	2.0%	2.5%	3.0%	3.5%	4.0%	4.5%	5.0%	
16	38.67	35.16	32.08	29.37	26.98	24.87	23.00	21.34	19.86	18.54	17.35	16
17	37.68	34.33	31.40	28.81	26.52	24.49	22.68	21.08	19.64	18.35	17.20	17
18	36.68	33.51	30.71	28.23	26.04	24.09	22.35	20.80	19.41	18.16	17.04	18
19	35.69	32.68	30.02	27.66	25.56	23.68	22.01	20.51	19.17	17.96	16.87	19
20	34.69	31.84	29.32	27.07	25.06	23.27	21.66	20.22	18.92	17.75	16.69	20
21	33.70	31.01	28.61	26.47	24.56	22.84	21.30	19.91	18.66	17.53	16.50	21
22	32.70	30.16	27.90	25.86	24.04	22.40	20.93	19.60	18.39	17.30	16.30	22
23	31.71	29.32	27.17	25.25	23.52	21.96	20.54	19.27	18.11	17.06	16.10	23
24	30.71	28.47	26.44	24.62	22.98	21.50	20.15	18.93	17.82	16.80	15.88	24
25	29.72	27.61	25.71	23.99	22.44	21.02	19.74	18.58	17.51	16.54	15.65	25
26	28.72	26.75	24.97	23.35	21.88	20.54	19.32	18.21	17.20	16.27	15.41	26
27	27.73	25.89	24.22	22.70	21.31	20.05	18.89	17.84	16.87	15.98	15.16	27
28	26.73	25.02	23.46	22.03	20.73	19.54	18.45	17.45	16.53	15.68	14.90	28
29	25.74	24.15	22.69	21.36	20.14	19.02	17.99	17.05	16.17	15.37	14.62	29
30	24.75	23.27	21.92	20.68	19.54	18.49	17.52	16.63	15.81	15.04	14.34	30
31	23.75	22.39	21.14	19.99	18.93	17.95	17.04	16.20	15.42	14.70	14.03	31
32	22.76	21.51	20.35	19.29	18.30	17.39	16.54	15.76	15.03	14.35	13.71	32
33	21.77	20.62	19.56	18.58	17.66	16.82	16.03	15.30	14.61	13.98	13.38	33
34	20.78	19.73	18.76	17.86	17.02	16.23	15.50	14.82	14.18	13.59	13.03	34
35	19.79	18.84	17.95	17.12	16.35	15.63	14.96	14.33	13.74	13.18	12.66	35
36	18.79	17.94	17.13	16.38	15.68	15.02	14.40	13.82	13.27	12.76	12.28	36
37	17.80	17.03	16.31	15.63	14.99	14.39	13.82	13.29	12.79	12.32	11.87	37
38	16.81	16.12	15.47	14.86	14.29	13.74	13.23	12.75	12.29	11.86	11.45	38
39	15.82	15.21	14.63	14.09	13.57	13.08	12.62	12.18	11.77	11.38	11.00	39
40	14.83	14.30	13.78	13.30	12.84	12.41	11.99	11.60	11.23	10.87	10.54	40
41	13.85	13.38	12.93	12.50	12.10	11.71	11.35	11.00	10.67	10.35	10.05	41
42	12.86	12.45	12.06	11.69	11.34	11.01	10.68	10.38	10.08	9.80	9.53	42
43	11.87	11.52	11.19	10.87	10.57	10.28	10.00	9.73	9.48	9.23	9.00	43
44	10.88	10.59	10.31	10.04	9.78	9.54	9.30	9.07	8.85	8.64	8.43	44
45	9.90	9.66	9.42	9.20	8.98	8.77	8.57	8.38	8.19	8.01	7.84	45
46	8.91	8.72	8.53	8.34	8.17	7.99	7.83	7.67	7.51	7.36	7.22	46
47	7.93	7.77	7.62	7.47	7.33	7.19	7.06	6.93	6.81	6.68	6.57	47
48	6.94	6.82	6.70	6.59	6.48	6.37	6.27	6.17	6.07	5.98	5.88	48
49	5.95	5.87	5.78	5.70	5.61	5.53	5.46	5.38	5.31	5.23	5.16	49
50	4.97	4.90	4.84	4.79	4.73	4.67	4.62	4.56	4.51	4.46	4.41	50
51	3.98	3.94	3.90	3.86	3.82	3.79	3.75	3.72	3.68	3.65	3.61	51

52	2.99	2.96	2.94	2.92	2.90	2.88	2.86	2.84	2.82	2.80	2.78	52
53	1.99	1.98	1.97	1.96	1.95	1.95	1.94	1.93	1.92	1.91	1.90	53
54	1.00	1.00	0.99	0.99	0.99	0.99	0.98	0.98	0.98	0.98	0.97	54

Table 7 Multipliers for loss of earnings to pension age 60 (males)

Age at date of trial	Multiplier calculated with allowance for projected mortality from the 2004-based population projections and rate of return of											Age at date of trial
	0.0%	0.5%	1.0%	1.5%	2.0%	2.5%	3.0%	3.5%	4.0%	4.5%	5.0%	
16	43.07	38.71	34.96	31.70	28.87	26.41	24.25	22.35	20.68	19.20	17.89	16
17	42.07	37.90	34.30	31.17	28.44	26.05	23.96	22.12	20.49	19.04	17.76	17
18	41.07	37.10	33.64	30.63	28.00	25.70	23.67	21.88	20.29	18.88	17.63	18
19	40.08	36.29	32.98	30.10	27.56	25.34	23.37	21.63	20.09	18.72	17.49	19
20	39.10	35.48	32.32	29.55	27.12	24.97	23.07	21.38	19.88	18.55	17.35	20
21	38.11	34.67	31.65	29.00	26.66	24.59	22.76	21.12	19.67	18.37	17.20	21
22	37.12	33.85	30.98	28.44	26.19	24.20	22.43	20.85	19.44	18.18	17.04	22
23	36.14	33.03	30.29	27.87	25.72	23.81	22.10	20.58	19.21	17.98	16.88	23
24	35.15	32.21	29.60	27.29	25.23	23.40	21.76	20.29	18.97	17.78	16.71	24
25	34.16	31.38	28.91	26.70	24.74	22.98	21.41	19.99	18.72	17.56	16.52	25
26	33.18	30.55	28.20	26.11	24.23	22.55	21.04	19.68	18.45	17.34	16.33	26
27	32.19	29.71	27.49	25.50	23.72	22.12	20.67	19.36	18.18	17.11	16.13	27
28	31.21	28.87	26.78	24.89	23.20	21.67	20.29	19.04	17.90	16.87	15.93	28
29	30.23	28.03	26.05	24.27	22.67	21.21	19.89	18.70	17.61	16.61	15.71	29
30	29.24	27.18	25.33	23.65	22.12	20.74	19.49	18.35	17.30	16.35	15.48	30
31	28.26	26.33	24.59	23.01	21.57	20.26	19.07	17.98	16.99	16.08	15.24	31
32	27.28	25.48	23.85	22.36	21.01	19.77	18.64	17.61	16.66	15.79	14.99	32
33	26.30	24.63	23.10	21.71	20.43	19.27	18.20	17.22	16.32	15.49	14.72	33
34	25.32	23.77	22.34	21.04	19.85	18.76	17.75	16.82	15.97	15.18	14.45	34
35	24.34	22.90	21.58	20.37	19.26	18.23	17.28	16.41	15.60	14.85	14.16	35
36	23.36	22.03	20.81	19.69	18.65	17.69	16.80	15.98	15.22	14.51	13.86	36
37	22.39	21.16	20.04	18.99	18.03	17.14	16.31	15.54	14.82	14.16	13.54	37
38	21.41	20.29	19.25	18.29	17.40	16.57	15.80	15.08	14.41	13.79	13.21	38
39	20.43	19.41	18.46	17.58	16.76	15.99	15.28	14.61	13.99	13.40	12.86	39
40	19.45	18.53	17.66	16.85	16.10	15.40	14.74	14.12	13.54	13.00	12.49	40
41	18.48	17.64	16.86	16.12	15.43	14.79	14.18	13.62	13.08	12.58	12.11	41
42	17.50	16.75	16.04	15.38	14.75	14.17	13.62	13.10	12.61	12.14	11.71	42
43	16.53	15.86	15.22	14.63	14.06	13.53	13.03	12.56	12.11	11.69	11.29	43
44	15.56	14.96	14.40	13.86	13.36	12.88	12.43	12.00	11.60	11.21	10.85	44
45	14.59	14.06	13.56	13.09	12.64	12.22	11.81	11.43	11.06	10.72	10.39	45
46	13.62	13.16	12.72	12.31	11.91	11.54	11.18	10.84	10.51	10.20	9.90	46
47	12.65	12.26	11.88	11.52	11.17	10.84	10.53	10.23	9.94	9.66	9.40	47
48	11.69	11.35	11.02	10.71	10.42	10.13	9.86	9.60	9.34	9.10	8.87	48
49	10.72	10.44	10.16	9.90	9.65	9.40	9.17	8.95	8.73	8.52	8.32	49
50	9.76	9.52	9.30	9.08	8.86	8.66	8.46	8.27	8.09	7.91	7.74	50
51	8.80	8.61	8.42	8.24	8.07	7.90	7.73	7.58	7.42	7.28	7.13	51

Age at date of trial	Multiplier calculated with allowance for projected mortality from the 2004-based population projections and rate of return of											Age at date of trial
	0.0%	0.5%	1.0%	1.5%	2.0%	2.5%	3.0%	3.5%	4.0%	4.5%	5.0%	
52	7.83	7.68	7.53	7.39	7.25	7.11	6.98	6.86	6.73	6.61	6.50	52
53	6.87	6.75	6.63	6.52	6.41	6.31	6.21	6.11	6.01	5.92	5.82	53
54	5.90	5.81	5.72	5.64	5.56	5.48	5.41	5.33	5.26	5.19	5.12	54
55	4.92	4.86	4.80	4.75	4.69	4.63	4.58	4.53	4.47	4.42	4.37	55
56	3.95	3.91	3.87	3.83	3.80	3.76	3.72	3.69	3.65	3.62	3.59	56
57	2.97	2.95	2.92	2.90	2.88	2.86	2.84	2.82	2.80	2.78	2.76	57
58	1.98	1.97	1.96	1.96	1.95	1.94	1.93	1.92	1.91	1.90	1.89	58
59	1.00	0.99	0.99	0.99	0.99	0.98	0.98	0.98	0.98	0.97	0.97	59

Table 8 Multipliers for loss of earnings to pension age 60 (females)

Age at date of trial	Multiplier calculated with allowance for projected mortality from the 2004-based population projections and rate of return of											Age at date of trial
	0.0%	0.5%	1.0%	1.5%	2.0%	2.5%	3.0%	3.5%	4.0%	4.5%	5.0%	
16	43.49	39.07	35.26	31.97	29.10	26.60	24.42	22.50	20.81	19.32	17.99	16
17	42.49	38.27	34.62	31.44	28.68	26.26	24.14	22.27	20.63	19.16	17.87	17
18	41.50	37.46	33.96	30.91	28.24	25.91	23.85	22.04	20.43	19.01	17.74	18
19	40.50	36.65	33.30	30.37	27.80	25.55	23.56	21.80	20.23	18.84	17.60	19
20	39.51	35.84	32.63	29.82	27.35	25.18	23.25	21.55	20.03	18.67	17.46	20
21	38.51	35.02	31.96	29.27	26.89	24.80	22.94	21.29	19.81	18.49	17.31	21
22	37.51	34.20	31.28	28.70	26.43	24.41	22.62	21.02	19.59	18.31	17.16	22
23	36.52	33.37	30.59	28.13	25.95	24.01	22.28	20.74	19.35	18.11	16.99	23
24	35.52	32.54	29.89	27.55	25.46	23.60	21.94	20.45	19.11	17.91	16.82	24
25	34.53	31.70	29.19	26.96	24.96	23.18	21.59	20.15	18.86	17.69	16.64	25
26	33.53	30.86	28.48	26.36	24.46	22.75	21.22	19.84	18.60	17.47	16.45	26
27	32.54	30.02	27.77	25.75	23.94	22.31	20.85	19.52	18.33	17.24	16.25	27
28	31.54	29.17	27.04	25.13	23.42	21.86	20.46	19.19	18.04	17.00	16.04	28
29	30.55	28.32	26.32	24.51	22.88	21.40	20.07	18.85	17.75	16.74	15.83	29
30	29.56	27.47	25.58	23.87	22.33	20.93	19.66	18.50	17.44	16.48	15.60	30
31	28.56	26.61	24.84	23.23	21.77	20.45	19.24	18.14	17.13	16.20	15.36	31
32	27.57	25.74	24.09	22.58	21.21	19.95	18.81	17.76	16.80	15.92	15.10	32
33	26.58	24.88	23.33	21.92	20.63	19.45	18.36	17.37	16.46	15.61	14.84	33
34	25.59	24.01	22.57	21.25	20.04	18.93	17.91	16.97	16.10	15.30	14.56	34
35	24.60	23.14	21.80	20.57	19.44	18.39	17.44	16.55	15.73	14.97	14.27	35
36	23.61	22.26	21.02	19.88	18.82	17.85	16.95	16.12	15.35	14.63	13.97	36
37	22.62	21.38	20.23	19.18	18.20	17.29	16.45	15.67	14.95	14.28	13.65	37
38	21.63	20.49	19.44	18.47	17.56	16.72	15.94	15.21	14.53	13.90	13.31	38
39	20.64	19.60	18.64	17.75	16.91	16.14	15.41	14.74	14.11	13.51	12.96	39
40	19.65	18.71	17.83	17.02	16.25	15.54	14.87	14.24	13.66	13.11	12.59	40
41	18.67	17.81	17.02	16.27	15.58	14.92	14.31	13.74	13.20	12.69	12.21	41
42	17.68	16.92	16.20	15.52	14.89	14.30	13.74	13.21	12.71	12.25	11.80	42
43	16.70	16.01	15.37	14.77	14.19	13.66	13.15	12.67	12.22	11.79	11.38	43
44	15.71	15.11	14.54	14.00	13.48	13.00	12.54	12.11	11.70	11.31	10.94	44
45	14.73	14.20	13.69	13.22	12.76	12.33	11.92	11.53	11.16	10.81	10.48	45
46	13.76	13.29	12.85	12.43	12.02	11.64	11.28	10.93	10.60	10.29	9.99	46
47	12.78	12.37	11.99	11.62	11.27	10.94	10.62	10.32	10.03	9.75	9.48	47
48	11.80	11.46	11.13	10.81	10.51	10.22	9.94	9.68	9.43	9.18	8.95	48
49	10.82	10.53	10.25	9.99	9.73	9.48	9.25	9.02	8.80	8.59	8.39	49
50	9.85	9.61	9.37	9.15	8.94	8.73	8.53	8.34	8.15	7.97	7.80	50
51	8.87	8.67	8.49	8.30	8.13	7.96	7.79	7.63	7.48	7.33	7.19	51

Age at date of trial	Multiplier calculated with allowance for projected mortality from the 2004-based population projections and rate of return of											Age at date of trial
	0.0%	0.5%	1.0%	1.5%	2.0%	2.5%	3.0%	3.5%	4.0%	4.5%	5.0%	
52	7.89	7.74	7.59	7.44	7.30	7.16	7.03	6.90	6.78	6.66	6.54	52
53	6.91	6.79	6.68	6.56	6.46	6.35	6.25	6.15	6.05	5.95	5.86	53
54	5.93	5.84	5.76	5.67	5.59	5.51	5.44	5.36	5.29	5.22	5.14	54
55	4.95	4.89	4.83	4.77	4.71	4.66	4.60	4.55	4.50	4.44	4.39	55
56	3.96	3.93	3.89	3.85	3.81	3.78	3.74	3.70	3.67	3.64	3.60	56
57	2.98	2.96	2.93	2.91	2.89	2.87	2.85	2.83	2.81	2.79	2.77	57
58	1.99	1.98	1.97	1.96	1.95	1.94	1.93	1.92	1.91	1.90	1.90	58
59	1.00	0.99	0.99	0.99	0.99	0.99	0.98	0.98	0.98	0.98	0.97	59

Table 9 Multipliers for loss of earnings to pension age 65 (males)

Age at date of trial	Multiplier calculated with allowance for projected mortality from the 2004-based population projections and rate of return of											Age at date of trial
	0.0%	0.5%	1.0%	1.5%	2.0%	2.5%	3.0%	3.5%	4.0%	4.5%	5.0%	
16	47.63	42.33	37.83	33.99	30.69	27.86	25.40	23.27	21.42	19.79	18.36	16
17	46.62	41.54	37.20	33.49	30.29	27.54	25.15	23.07	21.25	19.66	18.26	17
18	45.63	40.75	36.57	32.98	29.89	27.22	24.89	22.86	21.09	19.53	18.15	18
19	44.64	39.96	35.94	32.48	29.49	26.89	24.63	22.66	20.92	19.39	18.04	19
20	43.65	39.16	35.31	31.97	29.08	26.56	24.37	22.44	20.74	19.25	17.92	20
21	42.66	38.37	34.66	31.45	28.66	26.23	24.09	22.22	20.56	19.10	17.80	21
22	41.67	37.57	34.02	30.93	28.24	25.88	23.81	21.99	20.37	18.95	17.67	22
23	40.69	36.77	33.36	30.40	27.80	25.52	23.52	21.75	20.18	18.78	17.54	23
24	39.70	35.96	32.70	29.86	27.36	25.16	23.22	21.50	19.97	18.62	17.40	24
25	38.71	35.15	32.04	29.31	26.90	24.78	22.91	21.24	19.76	18.44	17.25	25
26	37.72	34.33	31.36	28.75	26.44	24.40	22.59	20.98	19.54	18.25	17.10	26
27	36.73	33.51	30.68	28.18	25.97	24.01	22.26	20.71	19.31	18.06	16.94	27
28	35.75	32.69	30.00	27.61	25.49	23.61	21.93	20.42	19.08	17.86	16.77	28
29	34.76	31.87	29.31	27.03	25.01	23.20	21.58	20.13	18.83	17.66	16.60	29
30	33.78	31.04	28.61	26.45	24.51	22.78	21.23	19.83	18.57	17.44	16.41	30
31	32.80	30.21	27.91	25.85	24.01	22.35	20.86	19.52	18.31	17.21	16.22	31
32	31.82	29.38	27.20	25.25	23.49	21.91	20.49	19.20	18.04	16.98	16.02	32
33	30.84	28.54	26.49	24.63	22.97	21.46	20.10	18.87	17.75	16.73	15.80	33
34	29.86	27.70	25.76	24.01	22.43	21.00	19.71	18.53	17.45	16.48	15.58	34
35	28.88	26.86	25.04	23.39	21.89	20.53	19.30	18.17	17.15	16.21	15.35	35
36	27.90	26.01	24.30	22.75	21.34	20.05	18.88	17.81	16.83	15.93	15.11	36
37	26.93	25.16	23.56	22.10	20.77	19.56	18.45	17.43	16.50	15.64	14.85	37
38	25.95	24.31	22.81	21.45	20.20	19.05	18.00	17.04	16.16	15.34	14.59	38
39	24.98	23.45	22.06	20.78	19.61	18.54	17.55	16.64	15.80	15.02	14.31	39
40	24.00	22.59	21.30	20.11	19.02	18.01	17.08	16.22	15.43	14.70	14.01	40
41	23.03	21.73	20.53	19.43	18.41	17.47	16.60	15.79	15.05	14.35	13.71	41
42	22.06	20.86	19.76	18.74	17.79	16.92	16.10	15.35	14.65	14.00	13.39	42
43	21.09	19.99	18.98	18.04	17.16	16.35	15.60	14.89	14.24	13.62	13.05	43
44	20.12	19.12	18.19	17.33	16.52	15.77	15.07	14.42	13.81	13.24	12.70	44
45	19.16	18.25	17.40	16.61	15.88	15.19	14.54	13.94	13.37	12.84	12.34	45
46	18.20	17.38	16.61	15.89	15.22	14.58	13.99	13.44	12.91	12.42	11.96	46
47	17.24	16.50	15.81	15.16	14.55	13.97	13.43	12.92	12.44	11.99	11.56	47
48	16.29	15.63	15.00	14.42	13.87	13.35	12.86	12.39	11.95	11.54	11.15	48
49	15.33	14.75	14.20	13.67	13.18	12.71	12.27	11.85	11.45	11.07	10.71	49
50	14.39	13.87	13.38	12.92	12.48	12.06	11.66	11.29	10.93	10.59	10.26	50
51	13.44	12.99	12.56	12.15	11.76	11.40	11.04	10.71	10.39	10.08	9.79	51

Age at date of trial	Multiplier calculated with allowance for projected mortality from the 2004-based population projections and rate of return of											Age at date of trial
	0.0%	0.5%	1.0%	1.5%	2.0%	2.5%	3.0%	3.5%	4.0%	4.5%	5.0%	
52	12.49	12.10	11.73	11.38	11.04	10.71	10.41	10.11	9.83	9.56	9.30	52
53	11.55	11.21	10.89	10.59	10.30	10.02	9.75	9.49	9.24	9.01	8.78	53
54	10.60	10.32	10.05	9.79	9.54	9.30	9.07	8.85	8.63	8.43	8.23	54
55	9.65	9.41	9.19	8.97	8.76	8.56	8.37	8.18	8.00	7.83	7.66	55
56	8.69	8.50	8.32	8.14	7.97	7.81	7.65	7.49	7.34	7.20	7.06	56
57	7.74	7.59	7.44	7.30	7.16	7.03	6.90	6.78	6.66	6.54	6.42	57
58	6.78	6.67	6.56	6.45	6.34	6.24	6.14	6.04	5.94	5.85	5.76	58
59	5.83	5.74	5.66	5.58	5.50	5.42	5.35	5.27	5.20	5.13	5.06	59
60	4.87	4.81	4.75	4.70	4.64	4.59	4.53	4.48	4.43	4.38	4.33	60
61	3.91	3.87	3.84	3.80	3.76	3.73	3.69	3.66	3.62	3.59	3.56	61
62	2.95	2.93	2.90	2.88	2.86	2.84	2.82	2.80	2.78	2.76	2.74	62
63	1.98	1.97	1.96	1.95	1.94	1.93	1.92	1.91	1.90	1.89	1.88	63
64	0.99	0.99	0.99	0.99	0.98	0.98	0.98	0.98	0.97	0.97	0.97	64

Table 10 Multipliers for loss of earnings to pension age 65 (females)

Age at date of trial	Multiplier calculated with allowance for projected mortality from the 2004-based population projections and rate of return of											Age at date of trial
	0.0%	0.5%	1.0%	1.5%	2.0%	2.5%	3.0%	3.5%	4.0%	4.5%	5.0%	
16	48.22	42.83	38.24	34.34	30.99	28.11	25.62	23.46	21.58	19.93	18.48	16
17	47.22	42.04	37.62	33.84	30.60	27.80	25.37	23.26	21.42	19.80	18.38	17
18	46.22	41.25	37.00	33.35	30.20	27.48	25.12	23.06	21.26	19.68	18.28	18
19	45.23	40.46	36.37	32.84	29.80	27.16	24.86	22.86	21.09	19.54	18.17	19
20	44.23	39.66	35.73	32.33	29.39	26.83	24.60	22.64	20.92	19.40	18.06	20
21	43.23	38.86	35.08	31.81	28.97	26.49	24.32	22.42	20.74	19.26	17.94	21
22	42.23	38.05	34.43	31.29	28.54	26.15	24.04	22.19	20.55	19.10	17.81	22
23	41.24	37.24	33.77	30.75	28.11	25.79	23.75	21.95	20.36	18.94	17.68	23
24	40.24	36.43	33.11	30.21	27.66	25.43	23.45	21.71	20.16	18.78	17.54	24
25	39.24	35.61	32.44	29.66	27.21	25.05	23.14	21.45	19.95	18.60	17.40	25
26	38.25	34.79	31.76	29.10	26.75	24.67	22.83	21.19	19.73	18.42	17.25	26
27	37.25	33.97	31.08	28.53	26.28	24.28	22.50	20.92	19.50	18.23	17.09	27
28	36.25	33.14	30.39	27.95	25.80	23.88	22.16	20.63	19.26	18.03	16.92	28
29	35.26	32.31	29.69	27.37	25.31	23.46	21.82	20.34	19.02	17.82	16.75	29
30	34.26	31.47	28.99	26.78	24.81	23.04	21.46	20.04	18.76	17.61	16.56	30
31	33.27	30.63	28.28	26.18	24.30	22.61	21.10	19.73	18.50	17.38	16.37	31
32	32.28	29.79	27.56	25.57	23.78	22.17	20.72	19.41	18.22	17.15	16.17	32
33	31.28	28.94	26.84	24.95	23.25	21.72	20.33	19.08	17.94	16.90	15.96	33
34	30.29	28.09	26.11	24.33	22.71	21.26	19.93	18.73	17.64	16.65	15.74	34
35	29.30	27.24	25.38	23.69	22.17	20.78	19.52	18.38	17.33	16.38	15.51	35
36	28.31	26.38	24.63	23.05	21.61	20.30	19.10	18.01	17.01	16.10	15.26	36
37	27.32	25.52	23.88	22.39	21.04	19.80	18.67	17.63	16.68	15.81	15.01	37
38	26.33	24.66	23.13	21.73	20.46	19.29	18.22	17.24	16.34	15.51	14.74	38
39	25.34	23.79	22.36	21.06	19.87	18.77	17.76	16.84	15.98	15.19	14.46	39
40	24.36	22.92	21.60	20.38	19.27	18.24	17.29	16.42	15.61	14.86	14.17	40
41	23.37	22.04	20.82	19.69	18.66	17.70	16.81	15.99	15.23	14.52	13.86	41
42	22.39	21.17	20.04	19.00	18.03	17.14	16.31	15.54	14.83	14.16	13.54	42
43	21.41	20.29	19.25	18.29	17.40	16.57	15.80	15.08	14.41	13.79	13.21	43
44	20.43	19.41	18.46	17.58	16.76	15.99	15.28	14.61	13.99	13.40	12.86	44
45	19.45	18.53	17.66	16.85	16.10	15.40	14.74	14.12	13.54	13.00	12.49	45
46	18.48	17.64	16.86	16.12	15.43	14.79	14.19	13.62	13.08	12.58	12.11	46
47	17.51	16.75	16.05	15.38	14.76	14.17	13.62	13.10	12.61	12.15	11.71	47
48	16.54	15.86	15.23	14.63	14.07	13.54	13.04	12.56	12.11	11.69	11.29	48
49	15.57	14.97	14.41	13.87	13.37	12.89	12.44	12.01	11.60	11.22	10.85	49
50	14.60	14.07	13.57	13.10	12.65	12.23	11.82	11.44	11.07	10.73	10.39	50

Age at date of trial	Multiplier calculated with allowance for projected mortality from the 2004-based population projections and rate of return of											Age at date of trial
	0.0%	0.5%	1.0%	1.5%	2.0%	2.5%	3.0%	3.5%	4.0%	4.5%	5.0%	
51	13.64	13.17	12.74	12.32	11.93	11.55	11.19	10.85	10.52	10.21	9.91	51
52	12.67	12.27	11.89	11.53	11.18	10.85	10.54	10.24	9.95	9.67	9.41	52
53	11.70	11.36	11.04	10.73	10.43	10.14	9.87	9.61	9.35	9.11	8.88	53
54	10.73	10.45	10.17	9.91	9.66	9.41	9.18	8.95	8.74	8.53	8.33	54
55	9.77	9.53	9.30	9.08	8.87	8.66	8.47	8.28	8.09	7.92	7.74	55
56	8.80	8.61	8.42	8.24	8.06	7.90	7.73	7.58	7.42	7.28	7.13	56
57	7.83	7.68	7.53	7.38	7.25	7.11	6.98	6.85	6.73	6.61	6.49	57
58	6.86	6.74	6.63	6.52	6.41	6.30	6.20	6.10	6.01	5.91	5.82	58
59	5.89	5.80	5.72	5.64	5.56	5.48	5.40	5.33	5.25	5.18	5.11	59
60	4.92	4.86	4.80	4.74	4.68	4.63	4.57	4.52	4.47	4.42	4.37	60
61	3.94	3.91	3.87	3.83	3.79	3.76	3.72	3.69	3.65	3.62	3.59	61
62	2.97	2.94	2.92	2.90	2.88	2.86	2.84	2.82	2.80	2.78	2.76	62
63	1.98	1.97	1.96	1.96	1.95	1.94	1.93	1.92	1.91	1.90	1.89	63
64	1.00	0.99	0.99	0.99	0.99	0.98	0.98	0.98	0.98	0.97	0.97	64

Table 11 Multipliers for loss of earnings to pension age 70 (males)

Age at date of trial	Multiplier calculated with allowance for projected mortality from the 2004-based population projections and rate of return of											Age at date of trial
	0.0%	0.5%	1.0%	1.5%	2.0%	2.5%	3.0%	3.5%	4.0%	4.5%	5.0%	
16	52.01	45.72	40.46	36.02	32.27	29.09	26.36	24.02	22.00	20.25	18.72	16
17	51.00	44.94	39.85	35.55	31.91	28.80	26.14	23.84	21.86	20.14	18.63	17
18	50.00	44.16	39.24	35.08	31.54	28.51	25.91	23.66	21.72	20.02	18.54	18
19	49.01	43.39	38.64	34.60	31.16	28.22	25.68	23.48	21.57	19.91	18.45	19
20	48.01	42.61	38.03	34.13	30.79	27.92	25.44	23.29	21.42	19.79	18.35	20
21	47.02	41.83	37.41	33.64	30.40	27.61	25.20	23.10	21.27	19.67	18.25	21
22	46.03	41.05	36.79	33.14	30.01	27.30	24.95	22.90	21.11	19.54	18.15	22
23	45.04	40.26	36.16	32.64	29.61	26.98	24.69	22.69	20.94	19.40	18.04	23
24	44.05	39.47	35.53	32.13	29.20	26.65	24.42	22.48	20.77	19.26	17.93	24
25	43.06	38.67	34.89	31.62	28.78	26.31	24.15	22.25	20.59	19.11	17.80	25
26	42.06	37.87	34.24	31.09	28.35	25.96	23.87	22.02	20.40	18.96	17.68	26
27	41.07	37.06	33.59	30.56	27.92	25.61	23.58	21.79	20.20	18.80	17.54	27
28	40.09	36.26	32.93	30.02	27.48	25.25	23.28	21.54	20.00	18.63	17.41	28
29	39.10	35.45	32.27	29.48	27.03	24.88	22.97	21.29	19.79	18.46	17.26	29
30	38.12	34.64	31.60	28.93	26.58	24.50	22.66	21.03	19.57	18.27	17.11	30
31	37.13	33.83	30.92	28.37	26.11	24.11	22.34	20.76	19.35	18.08	16.95	31
32	36.15	33.01	30.24	27.80	25.64	23.72	22.01	20.48	19.11	17.89	16.78	32
33	35.17	32.19	29.56	27.23	25.16	23.31	21.67	20.19	18.87	17.68	16.61	33
34	34.19	31.37	28.87	26.64	24.66	22.90	21.32	19.90	18.62	17.47	16.43	34
35	33.21	30.54	28.17	26.05	24.16	22.47	20.96	19.59	18.36	17.25	16.24	35
36	32.23	29.71	27.46	25.46	23.66	22.04	20.59	19.27	18.09	17.02	16.04	36
37	31.25	28.88	26.75	24.85	23.14	21.60	20.21	18.95	17.81	16.77	15.83	37
38	30.27	28.04	26.04	24.23	22.61	21.14	19.81	18.61	17.52	16.52	15.62	38
39	29.30	27.20	25.31	23.61	22.07	20.68	19.41	18.26	17.22	16.26	15.39	39
40	28.32	26.36	24.59	22.98	21.52	20.20	19.00	17.90	16.90	15.99	15.15	40
41	27.35	25.51	23.85	22.34	20.97	19.72	18.58	17.53	16.58	15.70	14.90	41
42	26.38	24.67	23.11	21.70	20.40	19.22	18.14	17.15	16.24	15.41	14.64	42
43	25.41	23.82	22.37	21.04	19.83	18.72	17.70	16.76	15.90	15.10	14.37	43
44	24.45	22.97	21.62	20.38	19.24	18.20	17.24	16.35	15.54	14.78	14.08	44
45	23.49	22.12	20.87	19.71	18.65	17.67	16.77	15.94	15.17	14.45	13.79	45
46	22.53	21.27	20.11	19.04	18.05	17.14	16.29	15.51	14.78	14.11	13.48	46
47	21.58	20.42	19.35	18.36	17.44	16.59	15.80	15.07	14.39	13.75	13.16	47
48	20.63	19.57	18.59	17.67	16.83	16.04	15.30	14.62	13.98	13.39	12.83	48
49	19.69	18.72	17.82	16.98	16.20	15.47	14.79	14.16	13.57	13.01	12.49	49
50	18.76	17.88	17.06	16.29	15.57	14.90	14.27	13.69	13.14	12.62	12.13	50
51	17.83	17.03	16.28	15.59	14.93	14.32	13.74	13.20	12.69	12.21	11.76	51

Age at date of trial	Multiplier calculated with allowance for projected mortality from the 2004-based population projections and rate of return of											Age at date of trial
	0.0%	0.5%	1.0%	1.5%	2.0%	2.5%	3.0%	3.5%	4.0%	4.5%	5.0%	
52	16.90	16.18	15.51	14.87	14.28	13.72	13.19	12.70	12.23	11.79	11.37	52
53	15.97	15.32	14.72	14.15	13.62	13.11	12.63	12.18	11.75	11.35	10.96	53
54	15.03	14.46	13.93	13.42	12.94	12.48	12.05	11.64	11.25	10.89	10.54	54
55	14.10	13.60	13.12	12.67	12.24	11.84	11.45	11.09	10.74	10.40	10.09	55
56	13.17	12.73	12.31	11.91	11.54	11.18	10.84	10.51	10.20	9.90	9.62	56
57	12.23	11.85	11.49	11.15	10.82	10.50	10.20	9.91	9.64	9.38	9.12	57
58	11.30	10.97	10.66	10.37	10.08	9.81	9.55	9.30	9.06	8.83	8.61	58
59	10.37	10.09	9.83	9.58	9.34	9.11	8.88	8.67	8.46	8.26	8.07	59
60	9.44	9.21	9.00	8.79	8.58	8.39	8.20	8.02	7.84	7.67	7.51	60
61	8.52	8.33	8.15	7.98	7.82	7.65	7.50	7.35	7.20	7.06	6.92	61
62	7.60	7.45	7.31	7.17	7.03	6.91	6.78	6.66	6.54	6.42	6.31	62
63	6.67	6.56	6.45	6.34	6.24	6.14	6.04	5.94	5.85	5.76	5.67	63
64	5.75	5.66	5.58	5.50	5.42	5.35	5.27	5.20	5.13	5.06	4.99	64
65	4.81	4.75	4.70	4.64	4.58	4.53	4.48	4.43	4.38	4.33	4.28	65
66	3.87	3.83	3.80	3.76	3.72	3.69	3.65	3.62	3.59	3.55	3.52	66
67	2.92	2.90	2.88	2.86	2.84	2.82	2.80	2.78	2.76	2.74	2.72	67
68	1.96	1.95	1.94	1.93	1.92	1.92	1.91	1.90	1.89	1.88	1.87	68
69	0.99	0.99	0.98	0.98	0.98	0.98	0.98	0.97	0.97	0.97	0.97	69

Table 12 Multipliers for loss of earnings to pension age 70 (females)

Age at date of trial	Multiplier calculated with allowance for projected mortality from the 2004-based population projections and rate of return of											Age at date of trial
	0.0%	0.5%	1.0%	1.5%	2.0%	2.5%	3.0%	3.5%	4.0%	4.5%	5.0%	
16	52.83	46.39	41.01	36.48	32.65	29.40	26.62	24.24	22.19	20.41	18.85	16
17	51.83	45.62	40.41	36.02	32.29	29.12	26.41	24.08	22.06	20.30	18.77	17
18	50.83	44.85	39.81	35.55	31.93	28.84	26.19	23.90	21.92	20.20	18.69	18
19	49.83	44.07	39.21	35.08	31.56	28.55	25.96	23.72	21.78	20.09	18.60	19
20	48.83	43.29	38.59	34.60	31.19	28.26	25.73	23.54	21.64	19.97	18.51	20
21	47.83	42.50	37.98	34.11	30.80	27.95	25.49	23.35	21.48	19.85	18.42	21
22	46.83	41.71	37.35	33.62	30.41	27.64	25.24	23.15	21.33	19.72	18.31	22
23	45.83	40.92	36.72	33.12	30.01	27.32	24.99	22.95	21.16	19.59	18.21	23
24	44.83	40.12	36.09	32.61	29.60	26.99	24.72	22.74	20.99	19.45	18.10	24
25	43.83	39.32	35.44	32.09	29.19	26.66	24.45	22.52	20.81	19.31	17.98	25
26	42.83	38.52	34.79	31.57	28.76	26.32	24.17	22.29	20.63	19.16	17.85	26
27	41.83	37.71	34.14	31.04	28.33	25.96	23.89	22.05	20.44	19.00	17.73	27
28	40.83	36.90	33.48	30.50	27.89	25.60	23.59	21.81	20.24	18.84	17.59	28
29	39.83	36.08	32.81	29.95	27.44	25.23	23.29	21.56	20.03	18.67	17.45	29
30	38.83	35.26	32.14	29.39	26.98	24.86	22.97	21.30	19.82	18.49	17.30	30
31	37.84	34.44	31.46	28.83	26.52	24.47	22.65	21.03	19.59	18.30	17.14	31
32	36.84	33.61	30.77	28.26	26.04	24.07	22.32	20.76	19.36	18.11	16.98	32
33	35.85	32.78	30.08	27.68	25.56	23.67	21.98	20.47	19.12	17.90	16.81	33
34	34.85	31.95	29.38	27.10	25.07	23.25	21.63	20.18	18.87	17.69	16.63	34
35	33.86	31.12	28.68	26.50	24.56	22.83	21.27	19.87	18.61	17.47	16.44	35
36	32.87	30.28	27.97	25.90	24.05	22.39	20.90	19.56	18.34	17.24	16.25	36
37	31.88	29.43	27.25	25.29	23.53	21.95	20.52	19.23	18.06	17.00	16.04	37
38	30.89	28.59	26.52	24.67	23.00	21.49	20.13	18.89	17.77	16.75	15.82	38
39	29.90	27.74	25.80	24.04	22.46	21.03	19.73	18.55	17.47	16.49	15.60	39
40	28.91	26.89	25.06	23.41	21.91	20.55	19.32	18.19	17.16	16.22	15.36	40
41	27.93	26.03	24.32	22.76	21.35	20.06	18.89	17.82	16.84	15.94	15.12	41
42	26.94	25.18	23.57	22.11	20.78	19.57	18.46	17.44	16.51	15.65	14.86	42
43	25.96	24.32	22.82	21.46	20.21	19.06	18.01	17.05	16.16	15.34	14.59	43
44	24.99	23.46	22.07	20.79	19.62	18.54	17.55	16.64	15.80	15.03	14.31	44
45	24.01	22.60	21.31	20.12	19.02	18.01	17.09	16.23	15.43	14.70	14.02	45
46	23.04	21.74	20.54	19.44	18.42	17.48	16.61	15.80	15.05	14.36	13.71	46
47	22.07	20.88	19.77	18.75	17.80	16.93	16.11	15.36	14.66	14.00	13.39	47
48	21.11	20.01	19.00	18.05	17.18	16.36	15.61	14.90	14.25	13.63	13.06	48
49	20.15	19.15	18.22	17.35	16.54	15.79	15.09	14.44	13.82	13.25	12.72	49
50	19.19	18.28	17.43	16.64	15.90	15.21	14.56	13.95	13.39	12.85	12.35	50

Age at date of trial	Multiplier calculated with allowance for projected mortality from the 2004-based population projections and rate of return of											Age at date of trial
	0.0%	0.5%	1.0%	1.5%	2.0%	2.5%	3.0%	3.5%	4.0%	4.5%	5.0%	
51	18.23	17.41	16.64	15.92	15.24	14.61	14.02	13.46	12.93	12.44	11.98	51
52	17.27	16.53	15.84	15.19	14.57	14.00	13.46	12.94	12.46	12.01	11.58	52
53	16.32	15.66	15.03	14.45	13.89	13.37	12.88	12.41	11.97	11.56	11.16	53
54	15.36	14.77	14.22	13.69	13.20	12.73	12.29	11.87	11.47	11.09	10.73	54
55	14.40	13.89	13.40	12.93	12.49	12.07	11.68	11.30	10.94	10.60	10.27	55
56	13.45	13.00	12.57	12.16	11.77	11.40	11.05	10.71	10.39	10.09	9.80	56
57	12.49	12.10	11.73	11.38	11.04	10.71	10.40	10.11	9.83	9.56	9.30	57
58	11.54	11.21	10.89	10.58	10.29	10.01	9.74	9.48	9.24	9.00	8.77	58
59	10.59	10.31	10.04	9.78	9.53	9.29	9.06	8.84	8.63	8.42	8.23	59
60	9.64	9.41	9.18	8.97	8.76	8.56	8.36	8.18	7.99	7.82	7.65	60
61	8.69	8.50	8.32	8.14	7.97	7.80	7.64	7.49	7.34	7.19	7.05	61
62	7.74	7.59	7.44	7.30	7.17	7.03	6.90	6.78	6.66	6.54	6.42	62
63	6.79	6.67	6.56	6.45	6.35	6.24	6.14	6.04	5.95	5.85	5.76	63
64	5.84	5.75	5.67	5.59	5.51	5.43	5.35	5.28	5.21	5.14	5.07	64
65	4.88	4.82	4.76	4.70	4.65	4.59	4.54	4.49	4.43	4.38	4.33	65
66	3.92	3.88	3.84	3.80	3.77	3.73	3.70	3.66	3.63	3.59	3.56	66
67	2.95	2.93	2.91	2.89	2.87	2.84	2.82	2.80	2.78	2.77	2.75	67
68	1.98	1.97	1.96	1.95	1.94	1.93	1.92	1.91	1.90	1.89	1.88	68
69	0.99	0.99	0.99	0.99	0.98	0.98	0.98	0.98	0.97	0.97	0.97	69

Table 13 Multipliers for loss of earnings to pension age 75 (males)

Age at date of trial	Multiplier calculated with allowance for projected mortality from the 2004-based population projections and rate of return of											Age at date of trial
	0.0%	0.5%	1.0%	1.5%	2.0%	2.5%	3.0%	3.5%	4.0%	4.5%	5.0%	
16	56.16	48.85	42.82	37.81	33.63	30.11	27.14	24.61	22.45	20.59	18.98	16
17	55.14	48.08	42.23	37.36	33.29	29.85	26.94	24.46	22.33	20.50	18.91	17
18	54.13	47.31	41.65	36.91	32.94	29.58	26.73	24.30	22.21	20.40	18.83	18
19	53.13	46.54	41.06	36.46	32.59	29.32	26.53	24.14	22.08	20.30	18.75	19
20	52.13	45.78	40.47	36.01	32.24	29.04	26.31	23.97	21.95	20.20	18.67	20
21	51.13	45.01	39.88	35.55	31.88	28.77	26.10	23.80	21.82	20.09	18.59	21
22	50.14	44.24	39.28	35.08	31.52	28.48	25.87	23.62	21.68	19.98	18.50	22
23	49.14	43.46	38.67	34.61	31.15	28.19	25.64	23.44	21.53	19.87	18.41	23
24	48.14	42.68	38.06	34.12	30.77	27.89	25.40	23.25	21.38	19.75	18.31	24
25	47.14	41.89	37.44	33.63	30.38	27.58	25.15	23.05	21.22	19.62	18.21	25
26	46.15	41.10	36.81	33.14	29.98	27.26	24.90	22.85	21.06	19.49	18.10	26
27	45.15	40.31	36.18	32.63	29.58	26.94	24.64	22.64	20.89	19.35	17.99	27
28	44.16	39.52	35.54	32.12	29.17	26.61	24.37	22.42	20.71	19.20	17.87	28
29	43.17	38.73	34.91	31.61	28.75	26.27	24.10	22.20	20.53	19.06	17.75	29
30	42.18	37.93	34.26	31.09	28.33	25.92	23.82	21.97	20.34	18.90	17.62	30
31	41.19	37.12	33.61	30.56	27.90	25.57	23.53	21.73	20.15	18.74	17.49	31
32	40.20	36.32	32.95	30.02	27.46	25.21	23.23	21.49	19.94	18.57	17.35	32
33	39.21	35.51	32.29	29.48	27.01	24.84	22.93	21.24	19.73	18.40	17.20	33
34	38.23	34.70	31.62	28.92	26.55	24.46	22.61	20.97	19.52	18.22	17.05	34
35	37.24	33.89	30.95	28.37	26.09	24.08	22.29	20.71	19.29	18.03	16.89	35
36	36.26	33.07	30.27	27.80	25.62	23.68	21.96	20.43	19.06	17.83	16.72	36
37	35.28	32.25	29.58	27.23	25.13	23.28	21.62	20.14	18.81	17.62	16.55	37
38	34.30	31.43	28.89	26.64	24.64	22.86	21.27	19.84	18.56	17.41	16.37	38
39	33.32	30.61	28.20	26.06	24.15	22.44	20.91	19.54	18.30	17.18	16.17	39
40	32.34	29.78	27.50	25.46	23.64	22.01	20.54	19.22	18.03	16.95	15.97	40
41	31.37	28.95	26.79	24.86	23.12	21.57	20.16	18.90	17.75	16.71	15.77	41
42	30.40	28.12	26.08	24.25	22.60	21.12	19.77	18.56	17.46	16.46	15.55	42
43	29.43	27.29	25.36	23.63	22.07	20.66	19.38	18.22	17.16	16.20	15.32	43
44	28.46	26.45	24.64	23.01	21.53	20.19	18.97	17.86	16.85	15.93	15.09	44
45	27.50	25.62	23.92	22.38	20.98	19.71	18.55	17.50	16.53	15.65	14.84	45
46	26.55	24.79	23.19	21.75	20.43	19.23	18.13	17.13	16.21	15.36	14.59	46
47	25.60	23.96	22.47	21.11	19.87	18.74	17.70	16.75	15.87	15.07	14.33	47
48	24.66	23.13	21.74	20.47	19.31	18.24	17.26	16.36	15.53	14.76	14.05	48
49	23.72	22.31	21.01	19.82	18.73	17.73	16.81	15.96	15.17	14.45	13.77	49
50	22.79	21.48	20.28	19.18	18.16	17.22	16.35	15.55	14.81	14.12	13.48	50
51	21.87	20.66	19.55	18.52	17.58	16.70	15.89	15.13	14.44	13.79	13.18	51

Age at date of trial	Multiplier calculated with allowance for projected mortality from the 2004-based population projections and rate of return of											Age at date of trial
	0.0%	0.5%	1.0%	1.5%	2.0%	2.5%	3.0%	3.5%	4.0%	4.5%	5.0%	
52	20.95	19.84	18.82	17.87	16.99	16.17	15.41	14.71	14.05	13.44	12.87	52
53	20.04	19.02	18.07	17.20	16.38	15.63	14.92	14.27	13.65	13.08	12.54	53
54	19.12	18.19	17.32	16.52	15.77	15.07	14.42	13.81	13.24	12.70	12.20	54
55	18.20	17.35	16.57	15.83	15.14	14.50	13.90	13.33	12.81	12.31	11.84	55
56	17.27	16.51	15.80	15.13	14.50	13.92	13.36	12.84	12.36	11.90	11.46	56
57	16.35	15.67	15.03	14.42	13.85	13.32	12.81	12.34	11.89	11.47	11.07	57
58	15.44	14.82	14.25	13.70	13.19	12.71	12.25	11.82	11.41	11.02	10.66	58
59	14.52	13.98	13.47	12.98	12.52	12.09	11.68	11.29	10.92	10.56	10.23	59
60	13.62	13.14	12.69	12.26	11.85	11.46	11.09	10.74	10.41	10.09	9.79	60
61	12.72	12.30	11.91	11.53	11.17	10.82	10.50	10.19	9.89	9.60	9.33	61
62	11.83	11.47	11.12	10.79	10.48	10.18	9.89	9.62	9.35	9.10	8.86	62
63	10.95	10.64	10.34	10.06	9.78	9.52	9.27	9.03	8.80	8.58	8.37	63
64	10.06	9.80	9.55	9.31	9.08	8.85	8.64	8.43	8.23	8.04	7.86	64
65	9.18	8.96	8.75	8.55	8.35	8.16	7.98	7.81	7.64	7.48	7.32	65
66	8.29	8.11	7.94	7.77	7.61	7.46	7.31	7.16	7.02	6.89	6.75	66
67	7.40	7.26	7.12	6.99	6.86	6.73	6.61	6.49	6.38	6.27	6.16	67
68	6.50	6.40	6.29	6.19	6.09	5.99	5.89	5.80	5.71	5.62	5.54	68
69	5.61	5.52	5.45	5.37	5.29	5.22	5.15	5.08	5.01	4.94	4.88	69
70	4.70	4.64	4.59	4.53	4.48	4.43	4.38	4.33	4.28	4.23	4.18	70
71	3.79	3.75	3.72	3.68	3.65	3.61	3.58	3.55	3.51	3.48	3.45	71
72	2.87	2.85	2.83	2.81	2.79	2.77	2.75	2.73	2.71	2.69	2.67	72
73	1.94	1.93	1.92	1.91	1.90	1.89	1.88	1.87	1.86	1.85	1.85	73
74	0.98	0.98	0.98	0.97	0.97	0.97	0.97	0.97	0.96	0.96	0.96	74

Table 14 Multipliers for loss of earnings to pension age 75 (females)

Age at date of trial	Multiplier calculated with allowance for projected mortality from the 2004-based population projections and rate of return of											Age at date of trial
	0.0%	0.5%	1.0%	1.5%	2.0%	2.5%	3.0%	3.5%	4.0%	4.5%	5.0%	
16	57.27	49.74	43.54	38.39	34.10	30.50	27.46	24.88	22.67	20.78	19.14	16
17	56.27	48.99	42.97	37.96	33.77	30.25	27.27	24.73	22.56	20.69	19.07	17
18	55.26	48.22	42.39	37.52	33.44	30.00	27.08	24.58	22.45	20.60	19.00	18
19	54.26	47.46	41.81	37.08	33.10	29.74	26.88	24.43	22.33	20.51	18.93	19
20	53.25	46.69	41.22	36.63	32.75	29.47	26.67	24.27	22.20	20.41	18.85	20
21	52.25	45.92	40.62	36.17	32.40	29.19	26.45	24.10	22.07	20.31	18.77	21
22	51.24	45.15	40.02	35.70	32.04	28.91	26.23	23.93	21.94	20.20	18.69	22
23	50.24	44.37	39.42	35.23	31.67	28.62	26.01	23.75	21.80	20.09	18.60	23
24	49.23	43.58	38.81	34.75	31.29	28.33	25.77	23.57	21.65	19.98	18.51	24
25	48.23	42.79	38.19	34.26	30.91	28.02	25.53	23.38	21.50	19.86	18.41	25
26	47.22	42.00	37.56	33.77	30.52	27.71	25.29	23.18	21.34	19.73	18.31	26
27	46.22	41.21	36.93	33.27	30.12	27.39	25.03	22.97	21.18	19.60	18.20	27
28	45.22	40.41	36.30	32.76	29.71	27.07	24.77	22.76	21.01	19.46	18.09	28
29	44.22	39.61	35.65	32.25	29.30	26.73	24.50	22.55	20.83	19.31	17.97	29
30	43.21	38.80	35.01	31.72	28.87	26.39	24.22	22.32	20.64	19.16	17.85	30
31	42.21	38.00	34.35	31.19	28.44	26.04	23.94	22.09	20.45	19.01	17.72	31
32	41.21	37.18	33.69	30.65	28.00	25.68	23.64	21.85	20.26	18.84	17.59	32
33	40.21	36.37	33.03	30.11	27.56	25.32	23.34	21.60	20.05	18.67	17.45	33
34	39.22	35.55	32.36	29.56	27.10	24.94	23.03	21.34	19.84	18.50	17.30	34
35	38.22	34.73	31.68	29.00	26.64	24.56	22.71	21.07	19.62	18.31	17.14	35
36	37.22	33.91	31.00	28.43	26.17	24.16	22.38	20.80	19.39	18.12	16.98	36
37	36.23	33.08	30.31	27.86	25.69	23.76	22.05	20.52	19.15	17.92	16.81	37
38	35.24	32.25	29.61	27.27	25.20	23.35	21.70	20.22	18.90	17.71	16.64	38
39	34.24	31.42	28.91	26.68	24.70	22.93	21.35	19.92	18.64	17.49	16.45	39
40	33.26	30.58	28.21	26.09	24.19	22.50	20.98	19.61	18.38	17.27	16.26	40
41	32.27	29.75	27.49	25.48	23.68	22.06	20.61	19.29	18.10	17.03	16.05	41
42	31.28	28.91	26.78	24.87	23.16	21.61	20.22	18.96	17.82	16.78	15.84	42
43	30.30	28.07	26.06	24.25	22.63	21.16	19.83	18.62	17.53	16.53	15.62	43
44	29.33	27.23	25.34	23.63	22.09	20.69	19.42	18.27	17.22	16.27	15.39	44
45	28.35	26.38	24.61	23.00	21.54	20.22	19.01	17.91	16.91	16.00	15.16	45
46	27.38	25.54	23.88	22.36	20.99	19.73	18.59	17.55	16.59	15.71	14.91	46
47	26.42	24.70	23.14	21.72	20.43	19.24	18.16	17.17	16.26	15.42	14.65	47
48	25.45	23.86	22.40	21.07	19.85	18.74	17.72	16.78	15.91	15.12	14.38	48
49	24.50	23.01	21.66	20.42	19.28	18.23	17.27	16.38	15.56	14.80	14.10	49
50	23.54	22.17	20.91	19.75	18.69	17.71	16.80	15.97	15.19	14.48	13.81	50

Age at date of trial	Multiplier calculated with allowance for projected mortality from the 2004-based population projections and rate of return of											Age at date of trial
	0.0%	0.5%	1.0%	1.5%	2.0%	2.5%	3.0%	3.5%	4.0%	4.5%	5.0%	
51	22.59	21.33	20.16	19.09	18.09	17.18	16.33	15.54	14.81	14.14	13.51	51
52	21.64	20.48	19.40	18.41	17.49	16.63	15.84	15.11	14.42	13.79	13.19	52
53	20.69	19.63	18.64	17.72	16.87	16.08	15.34	14.66	14.02	13.42	12.86	53
54	19.74	18.77	17.87	17.02	16.24	15.51	14.83	14.19	13.59	13.04	12.51	54
55	18.79	17.91	17.09	16.32	15.60	14.93	14.30	13.71	13.16	12.64	12.15	55
56	17.85	17.05	16.30	15.60	14.95	14.33	13.75	13.21	12.70	12.22	11.77	56
57	16.90	16.18	15.51	14.88	14.28	13.72	13.20	12.70	12.23	11.79	11.37	57
58	15.96	15.32	14.72	14.15	13.61	13.10	12.63	12.17	11.75	11.34	10.96	58
59	15.02	14.45	13.92	13.41	12.93	12.47	12.04	11.63	11.25	10.88	10.53	59
60	14.09	13.59	13.11	12.66	12.23	11.83	11.44	11.08	10.73	10.40	10.08	60
61	13.16	12.72	12.31	11.91	11.53	11.17	10.83	10.51	10.19	9.90	9.61	61
62	12.23	11.86	11.49	11.15	10.82	10.50	10.20	9.92	9.64	9.38	9.13	62
63	11.31	10.99	10.68	10.38	10.09	9.82	9.56	9.31	9.07	8.84	8.62	63
64	10.39	10.11	9.85	9.60	9.35	9.12	8.90	8.68	8.48	8.28	8.08	64
65	9.46	9.23	9.02	8.80	8.60	8.41	8.22	8.03	7.86	7.69	7.53	65
66	8.54	8.35	8.17	8.00	7.83	7.67	7.51	7.36	7.22	7.08	6.94	66
67	7.61	7.46	7.32	7.18	7.05	6.92	6.79	6.67	6.55	6.43	6.32	67
68	6.68	6.56	6.45	6.35	6.24	6.14	6.04	5.95	5.85	5.76	5.67	68
69	5.74	5.66	5.58	5.50	5.42	5.34	5.27	5.20	5.13	5.06	4.99	69
70	4.81	4.75	4.69	4.63	4.58	4.52	4.47	4.42	4.37	4.32	4.27	70
71	3.86	3.83	3.79	3.75	3.72	3.68	3.65	3.61	3.58	3.55	3.51	71
72	2.91	2.89	2.87	2.85	2.83	2.81	2.79	2.77	2.75	2.73	2.71	72
73	1.96	1.95	1.94	1.93	1.92	1.91	1.90	1.89	1.88	1.87	1.87	73
74	0.99	0.99	0.98	0.98	0.98	0.98	0.97	0.97	0.97	0.97	0.96	74

Table 15 Multipliers for loss of pension commencing age 50 (males)

Age at date of trial	Multiplier calculated with allowance for projected mortality from the 2004-based population projections and rate of return of											Age at date of trial
	0.0%	0.5%	1.0%	1.5%	2.0%	2.5%	3.0%	3.5%	4.0%	4.5%	5.0%	
0	37.30	26.17	18.48	13.13	9.38	6.75	4.87	3.54	2.58	1.90	1.40	0
1	37.37	26.36	18.71	13.36	9.60	6.94	5.04	3.68	2.70	1.99	1.47	1
2	37.27	26.42	18.85	13.54	9.77	7.10	5.18	3.80	2.80	2.08	1.54	2
3	37.16	26.49	19.00	13.71	9.95	7.26	5.33	3.93	2.91	2.17	1.62	3
4	37.04	26.54	19.14	13.88	10.13	7.43	5.48	4.06	3.02	2.26	1.70	4
5	36.93	26.60	19.28	14.05	10.30	7.60	5.63	4.19	3.14	2.36	1.78	5
6	36.81	26.66	19.42	14.23	10.49	7.77	5.79	4.33	3.26	2.46	1.87	6
7	36.70	26.71	19.56	14.41	10.67	7.95	5.95	4.47	3.38	2.57	1.96	7
8	36.58	26.77	19.70	14.59	10.86	8.13	6.12	4.62	3.51	2.68	2.05	8
9	36.47	26.82	19.85	14.77	11.05	8.31	6.29	4.78	3.65	2.79	2.15	9
10	36.35	26.88	19.99	14.95	11.25	8.50	6.46	4.93	3.78	2.92	2.26	10
11	36.24	26.93	20.14	15.14	11.45	8.70	6.64	5.10	3.93	3.04	2.36	11
12	36.12	26.99	20.28	15.33	11.65	8.90	6.83	5.27	4.08	3.17	2.48	12
13	36.01	27.04	20.43	15.52	11.85	9.10	7.02	5.44	4.24	3.31	2.60	13
14	35.89	27.10	20.58	15.71	12.06	9.31	7.22	5.62	4.40	3.45	2.72	14
15	35.78	27.15	20.73	15.91	12.27	9.52	7.42	5.81	4.56	3.60	2.86	15
16	35.66	27.21	20.88	16.11	12.49	9.74	7.62	6.00	4.74	3.76	3.00	16
17	35.55	27.27	21.03	16.31	12.71	9.96	7.84	6.20	4.92	3.92	3.14	17
18	35.45	27.33	21.19	16.52	12.94	10.19	8.06	6.40	5.11	4.09	3.29	18
19	35.35	27.40	21.35	16.73	13.17	10.42	8.29	6.62	5.31	4.27	3.45	19
20	35.25	27.47	21.52	16.95	13.41	10.67	8.52	6.84	5.51	4.46	3.62	20
21	35.16	27.54	21.68	17.17	13.66	10.92	8.77	7.07	5.73	4.66	3.80	21
22	35.07	27.61	21.85	17.39	13.90	11.17	9.02	7.31	5.95	4.86	3.99	22
23	34.98	27.68	22.02	17.61	14.16	11.43	9.27	7.55	6.18	5.07	4.18	23
24	34.88	27.75	22.20	17.84	14.41	11.70	9.54	7.81	6.42	5.30	4.39	24
25	34.78	27.82	22.36	18.07	14.67	11.97	9.81	8.07	6.67	5.53	4.60	25
26	34.69	27.89	22.54	18.30	14.94	12.25	10.09	8.34	6.92	5.77	4.83	26
27	34.60	27.96	22.71	18.54	15.21	12.53	10.37	8.62	7.19	6.02	5.06	27
28	34.51	28.04	22.90	18.79	15.49	12.83	10.67	8.91	7.47	6.29	5.31	28
29	34.43	28.12	23.08	19.04	15.78	13.13	10.98	9.21	7.76	6.57	5.57	29
30	34.35	28.20	23.27	19.29	16.07	13.44	11.29	9.53	8.07	6.86	5.85	30
31	34.27	28.28	23.45	19.54	16.36	13.76	11.62	9.85	8.38	7.16	6.13	31
32	34.19	28.36	23.64	19.80	16.66	14.08	11.95	10.18	8.71	7.47	6.44	32
33	34.11	28.44	23.84	20.07	16.97	14.42	12.30	10.53	9.05	7.81	6.75	33
34	34.03	28.53	24.03	20.34	17.29	14.76	12.65	10.89	9.40	8.15	7.09	34
35	33.96	28.61	24.23	20.61	17.61	15.11	13.02	11.26	9.77	8.51	7.44	35

Age at date of trial	Multiplier calculated with allowance for projected mortality from the 2004-based population projections and rate of return of											Age at date of trial
	0.0%	0.5%	1.0%	1.5%	2.0%	2.5%	3.0%	3.5%	4.0%	4.5%	5.0%	
36	33.88	28.70	24.43	20.89	17.94	15.47	13.39	11.64	10.16	8.89	7.81	36
37	33.81	28.79	24.63	21.17	18.27	15.84	13.78	12.04	10.56	9.28	8.19	37
38	33.74	28.88	24.84	21.46	18.62	16.22	14.19	12.45	10.97	9.70	8.60	38
39	33.68	28.98	25.05	21.75	18.97	16.61	14.60	12.88	11.40	10.13	9.03	39
40	33.62	29.08	25.27	22.05	19.33	17.01	15.03	13.33	11.86	10.58	9.48	40
41	33.56	29.18	25.49	22.36	19.70	17.43	15.47	13.79	12.33	11.06	9.95	41
42	33.51	29.29	25.72	22.68	20.08	17.85	15.93	14.27	12.82	11.56	10.45	42
43	33.46	29.40	25.95	23.00	20.47	18.29	16.40	14.76	13.33	12.08	10.98	43
44	33.42	29.52	26.19	23.33	20.87	18.74	16.89	15.28	13.87	12.63	11.53	44
45	33.38	29.64	26.43	23.67	21.29	19.21	17.40	15.82	14.43	13.20	12.12	45
46	33.36	29.78	26.69	24.03	21.72	19.70	17.94	16.39	15.02	13.81	12.73	46
47	33.35	29.92	26.96	24.40	22.16	20.21	18.49	16.98	15.64	14.45	13.39	47
48	33.35	30.08	27.25	24.78	22.62	20.73	19.07	17.59	16.29	15.12	14.08	48
49	33.37	30.25	27.54	25.18	23.11	21.28	19.67	18.24	16.97	15.83	14.82	49
50	33.40	30.44	27.86	25.60	23.61	21.86	20.30	18.92	17.69	16.59	15.60	50

Table 16 Multipliers for loss of pension commencing age 50 (females)

Age at date of trial	Multiplier calculated with allowance for projected mortality from the 2004-based population projections and rate of return of											Age at date of trial
	0.0%	0.5%	1.0%	1.5%	2.0%	2.5%	3.0%	3.5%	4.0%	4.5%	5.0%	
0	40.61	28.35	19.93	14.10	10.03	7.18	5.17	3.75	2.73	1.99	1.47	0
1	40.68	28.55	20.17	14.34	10.26	7.39	5.34	3.89	2.84	2.09	1.54	1
2	40.59	28.64	20.34	14.54	10.45	7.56	5.50	4.02	2.96	2.18	1.62	2
3	40.49	28.72	20.50	14.73	10.64	7.74	5.66	4.16	3.07	2.28	1.70	3
4	40.39	28.80	20.66	14.92	10.84	7.92	5.82	4.30	3.19	2.38	1.78	4
5	40.29	28.87	20.83	15.12	11.04	8.10	5.98	4.44	3.31	2.48	1.87	5
6	40.19	28.95	20.99	15.31	11.24	8.29	6.15	4.59	3.44	2.59	1.96	6
7	40.09	29.03	21.16	15.51	11.44	8.49	6.33	4.74	3.57	2.71	2.06	7
8	39.98	29.11	21.32	15.72	11.65	8.69	6.51	4.90	3.71	2.82	2.16	8
9	39.88	29.18	21.49	15.92	11.86	8.89	6.70	5.07	3.86	2.95	2.26	9
10	39.78	29.26	21.66	16.13	12.08	9.10	6.89	5.24	4.01	3.08	2.37	10
11	39.68	29.34	21.83	16.34	12.30	9.31	7.08	5.42	4.16	3.21	2.49	11
12	39.58	29.42	22.00	16.55	12.52	9.52	7.28	5.60	4.32	3.35	2.61	12
13	39.47	29.49	22.17	16.77	12.75	9.75	7.49	5.79	4.49	3.50	2.74	13
14	39.37	29.57	22.35	16.98	12.98	9.97	7.70	5.98	4.66	3.65	2.87	14
15	39.27	29.65	22.52	17.20	13.22	10.21	7.92	6.18	4.84	3.81	3.01	15
16	39.17	29.73	22.70	17.43	13.46	10.45	8.15	6.39	5.03	3.98	3.16	16
17	39.08	29.81	22.88	17.66	13.70	10.69	8.38	6.60	5.23	4.15	3.32	17
18	38.98	29.90	23.06	17.89	13.96	10.94	8.62	6.83	5.43	4.34	3.48	18
19	38.89	29.98	23.25	18.13	14.21	11.20	8.87	7.06	5.64	4.53	3.65	19
20	38.79	30.06	23.43	18.37	14.47	11.46	9.12	7.29	5.86	4.73	3.83	20
21	38.70	30.15	23.62	18.61	14.74	11.73	9.38	7.54	6.09	4.93	4.02	21
22	38.61	30.23	23.81	18.85	15.01	12.01	9.65	7.79	6.32	5.15	4.21	22
23	38.51	30.32	24.00	19.10	15.28	12.29	9.93	8.06	6.57	5.38	4.42	23
24	38.42	30.40	24.19	19.35	15.56	12.58	10.21	8.33	6.82	5.61	4.64	24
25	38.33	30.48	24.38	19.60	15.85	12.87	10.50	8.61	7.09	5.86	4.86	25
26	38.23	30.57	24.58	19.86	16.14	13.17	10.80	8.90	7.36	6.12	5.10	26
27	38.14	30.66	24.77	20.13	16.43	13.48	11.11	9.20	7.65	6.39	5.35	27
28	38.05	30.74	24.97	20.39	16.73	13.80	11.43	9.51	7.95	6.67	5.61	28
29	37.97	30.83	25.17	20.66	17.04	14.12	11.76	9.83	8.26	6.96	5.89	29
30	37.88	30.92	25.38	20.93	17.36	14.46	12.10	10.17	8.58	7.27	6.18	30
31	37.79	31.01	25.58	21.21	17.67	14.80	12.44	10.51	8.91	7.59	6.48	31
32	37.70	31.10	25.79	21.49	18.00	15.15	12.80	10.86	9.26	7.92	6.80	32
33	37.62	31.19	26.00	21.78	18.33	15.50	13.17	11.23	9.62	8.27	7.14	33
34	37.53	31.29	26.21	22.07	18.67	15.87	13.55	11.61	10.00	8.64	7.49	34
35	37.45	31.38	26.43	22.37	19.02	16.25	13.94	12.01	10.39	9.02	7.86	35

Age at date of trial	Multiplier calculated with allowance for projected mortality from the 2004-based population projections and rate of return of											Age at date of trial
	0.0%	0.5%	1.0%	1.5%	2.0%	2.5%	3.0%	3.5%	4.0%	4.5%	5.0%	
36	37.37	31.47	26.64	22.67	19.37	16.63	14.34	12.42	10.79	9.42	8.24	36
37	37.29	31.57	26.87	22.97	19.73	17.03	14.76	12.84	11.22	9.83	8.65	37
38	37.21	31.67	27.09	23.28	20.10	17.43	15.18	13.28	11.66	10.27	9.08	38
39	37.14	31.77	27.32	23.60	20.48	17.85	15.63	13.73	12.11	10.72	9.53	39
40	37.07	31.88	27.55	23.92	20.87	18.28	16.08	14.20	12.59	11.20	10.00	40
41	37.01	31.99	27.79	24.25	21.26	18.72	16.55	14.69	13.09	11.70	10.50	41
42	36.94	32.10	28.03	24.59	21.67	19.17	17.04	15.20	13.61	12.22	11.02	42
43	36.89	32.22	28.28	24.93	22.08	19.64	17.54	15.72	14.15	12.77	11.57	43
44	36.83	32.34	28.53	25.29	22.51	20.12	18.06	16.27	14.71	13.35	12.15	44
45	36.79	32.47	28.80	25.65	22.95	20.62	18.60	16.84	15.30	13.95	12.76	45
46	36.75	32.61	29.07	26.03	23.40	21.13	19.16	17.43	15.92	14.58	13.40	46
47	36.72	32.75	29.35	26.41	23.87	21.66	19.74	18.05	16.56	15.25	14.08	47
48	36.70	32.90	29.63	26.81	24.35	22.21	20.34	18.69	17.24	15.95	14.80	48
49	36.69	33.06	29.93	27.22	24.85	22.78	20.96	19.36	17.94	16.68	15.56	49
50	36.69	33.23	30.24	27.64	25.36	23.37	21.61	20.06	18.68	17.46	16.36	50

Table 17 Multipliers for loss of pension commencing age 55 (males)

Age at date of trial	Multiplier calculated with allowance for projected mortality from the 2004-based population projections and rate of return of											Age at date of trial
	0.0%	0.5%	1.0%	1.5%	2.0%	2.5%	3.0%	3.5%	4.0%	4.5%	5.0%	
0	32.51	22.49	15.64	10.94	7.69	5.43	3.86	2.75	1.97	1.42	1.03	0
1	32.56	22.64	15.83	11.13	7.86	5.59	3.99	2.86	2.06	1.49	1.08	1
2	32.45	22.68	15.94	11.27	8.00	5.71	4.10	2.95	2.14	1.55	1.13	2
3	32.35	22.73	16.06	11.40	8.14	5.84	4.21	3.05	2.22	1.62	1.19	3
4	32.23	22.77	16.17	11.54	8.28	5.97	4.33	3.15	2.30	1.69	1.25	4
5	32.12	22.81	16.28	11.68	8.43	6.11	4.45	3.25	2.39	1.76	1.31	5
6	32.01	22.84	16.39	11.82	8.57	6.24	4.57	3.36	2.48	1.84	1.37	6
7	31.89	22.88	16.51	11.97	8.72	6.38	4.70	3.47	2.57	1.92	1.43	7
8	31.78	22.92	16.62	12.11	8.87	6.53	4.83	3.58	2.67	2.00	1.50	8
9	31.67	22.96	16.73	12.26	9.02	6.67	4.96	3.70	2.77	2.09	1.57	9
10	31.55	23.00	16.85	12.41	9.18	6.82	5.09	3.82	2.88	2.17	1.65	10
11	31.44	23.03	16.96	12.55	9.34	6.98	5.23	3.95	2.99	2.27	1.73	11
12	31.33	23.07	17.08	12.71	9.50	7.13	5.38	4.07	3.10	2.37	1.81	12
13	31.21	23.11	17.19	12.86	9.66	7.29	5.53	4.21	3.22	2.47	1.90	13
14	31.10	23.14	17.31	13.01	9.83	7.45	5.68	4.34	3.34	2.57	1.99	14
15	30.99	23.18	17.43	13.17	9.99	7.62	5.83	4.49	3.46	2.68	2.09	15
16	30.88	23.22	17.55	13.33	10.17	7.79	6.00	4.63	3.59	2.80	2.19	16
17	30.77	23.26	17.67	13.49	10.34	7.97	6.16	4.78	3.73	2.92	2.29	17
18	30.66	23.30	17.80	13.65	10.52	8.15	6.33	4.94	3.87	3.04	2.40	18
19	30.56	23.35	17.92	13.82	10.71	8.33	6.51	5.10	4.02	3.18	2.52	19
20	30.47	23.40	18.05	13.99	10.90	8.52	6.69	5.27	4.17	3.31	2.64	20
21	30.37	23.45	18.18	14.17	11.09	8.71	6.88	5.45	4.33	3.46	2.77	21
22	30.28	23.50	18.32	14.35	11.29	8.91	7.07	5.63	4.50	3.61	2.90	22
23	30.19	23.55	18.45	14.53	11.49	9.12	7.27	5.82	4.67	3.76	3.04	23
24	30.09	23.60	18.59	14.71	11.69	9.33	7.47	6.01	4.85	3.93	3.19	24
25	29.99	23.64	18.72	14.89	11.89	9.54	7.68	6.21	5.03	4.10	3.34	25
26	29.90	23.69	18.86	15.07	12.10	9.75	7.89	6.41	5.23	4.27	3.51	26
27	29.81	23.74	19.00	15.26	12.32	9.98	8.12	6.62	5.43	4.46	3.68	27
28	29.72	23.80	19.14	15.46	12.54	10.21	8.34	6.85	5.63	4.65	3.86	28
29	29.64	23.85	19.29	15.66	12.76	10.45	8.58	7.07	5.85	4.86	4.04	29
30	29.55	23.91	19.43	15.86	12.99	10.69	8.82	7.31	6.08	5.07	4.24	30
31	29.47	23.97	19.58	16.06	13.22	10.93	9.07	7.55	6.31	5.29	4.45	31
32	29.38	24.02	19.73	16.26	13.46	11.19	9.33	7.81	6.55	5.52	4.67	32
33	29.30	24.08	19.88	16.47	13.71	11.45	9.59	8.07	6.81	5.76	4.89	33
34	29.22	24.14	20.03	16.69	13.95	11.71	9.87	8.34	7.07	6.02	5.13	34
35	29.14	24.20	20.18	16.90	14.21	11.98	10.15	8.62	7.34	6.28	5.38	35

Age at date of trial	Multiplier calculated with allowance for projected mortality from the 2004-based population projections and rate of return of											Age at date of trial
	0.0%	0.5%	1.0%	1.5%	2.0%	2.5%	3.0%	3.5%	4.0%	4.5%	5.0%	
36	29.07	24.27	20.34	17.12	14.46	12.26	10.43	8.91	7.63	6.55	5.65	36
37	28.99	24.33	20.50	17.34	14.73	12.55	10.73	9.21	7.93	6.84	5.92	37
38	28.92	24.40	20.66	17.57	15.00	12.84	11.04	9.52	8.23	7.14	6.22	38
39	28.85	24.46	20.83	17.80	15.27	13.15	11.36	9.84	8.55	7.46	6.52	39
40	28.78	24.54	21.00	18.04	15.55	13.46	11.68	10.18	8.89	7.79	6.84	40
41	28.72	24.61	21.17	18.28	15.84	13.78	12.02	10.52	9.24	8.13	7.18	41
42	28.66	24.69	21.35	18.53	16.14	14.11	12.37	10.88	9.60	8.50	7.54	42
43	28.60	24.77	21.53	18.78	16.44	14.45	12.73	11.26	9.98	8.87	7.91	43
44	28.55	24.85	21.72	19.04	16.76	14.80	13.11	11.65	10.38	9.27	8.31	44
45	28.51	24.95	21.91	19.31	17.08	15.16	13.50	12.05	10.79	9.69	8.73	45
46	28.48	25.05	22.11	19.59	17.42	15.54	13.90	12.47	11.23	10.13	9.17	46
47	28.45	25.16	22.33	19.88	17.77	15.93	14.32	12.92	11.68	10.59	9.63	47
48	28.44	25.28	22.55	20.18	18.13	16.33	14.76	13.38	12.16	11.08	10.13	48
49	28.44	25.41	22.78	20.50	18.50	16.76	15.22	13.87	12.67	11.60	10.65	49
50	28.45	25.55	23.03	20.83	18.90	17.20	15.70	14.37	13.20	12.15	11.21	50
51	28.48	25.71	23.29	21.17	19.31	17.66	16.21	14.91	13.76	12.72	11.80	51
52	28.51	25.88	23.57	21.53	19.74	18.15	16.73	15.47	14.34	13.33	12.42	52
53	28.56	26.06	23.85	21.90	20.18	18.65	17.28	16.06	14.96	13.98	13.08	53
54	28.61	26.24	24.14	22.29	20.64	19.17	17.85	16.67	15.61	14.65	13.78	54
55	28.66	26.42	24.44	22.67	21.10	19.70	18.44	17.31	16.29	15.36	14.52	55

Table 18 Multipliers for loss of pension commencing age 55 (females)

Age at date of trial	Multiplier calculated with allowance for projected mortality from the 2004-based population projections and rate of return of											Age at date of trial
	0.0%	0.5%	1.0%	1.5%	2.0%	2.5%	3.0%	3.5%	4.0%	4.5%	5.0%	
0	35.74	24.61	17.04	11.87	8.31	5.85	4.14	2.94	2.10	1.51	1.09	0
1	35.79	24.77	17.25	12.07	8.50	6.01	4.28	3.06	2.19	1.58	1.15	1
2	35.70	24.84	17.38	12.23	8.65	6.15	4.40	3.16	2.28	1.65	1.20	2
3	35.60	24.90	17.51	12.39	8.81	6.30	4.52	3.26	2.37	1.72	1.26	3
4	35.50	24.96	17.65	12.54	8.97	6.44	4.65	3.37	2.46	1.80	1.32	4
5	35.40	25.02	17.78	12.70	9.13	6.59	4.78	3.49	2.55	1.88	1.39	5
6	35.30	25.08	17.91	12.87	9.29	6.74	4.92	3.60	2.65	1.96	1.45	6
7	35.20	25.14	18.05	13.03	9.46	6.90	5.06	3.72	2.75	2.04	1.52	7
8	35.10	25.19	18.19	13.20	9.63	7.06	5.20	3.85	2.86	2.13	1.60	8
9	35.00	25.25	18.32	13.36	9.80	7.22	5.34	3.97	2.97	2.23	1.68	9
10	34.90	25.31	18.46	13.53	9.97	7.38	5.49	4.11	3.08	2.32	1.76	10
11	34.80	25.37	18.60	13.70	10.15	7.55	5.65	4.24	3.20	2.42	1.84	11
12	34.69	25.43	18.74	13.88	10.33	7.73	5.81	4.38	3.32	2.53	1.93	12
13	34.59	25.49	18.88	14.05	10.52	7.91	5.97	4.53	3.45	2.64	2.03	13
14	34.49	25.54	19.02	14.23	10.70	8.09	6.14	4.68	3.58	2.75	2.13	14
15	34.39	25.60	19.16	14.41	10.89	8.27	6.31	4.84	3.72	2.87	2.23	15
16	34.30	25.66	19.31	14.60	11.09	8.46	6.49	5.00	3.86	3.00	2.34	16
17	34.20	25.73	19.45	14.78	11.29	8.66	6.67	5.16	4.01	3.13	2.45	17
18	34.11	25.79	19.60	14.97	11.49	8.86	6.86	5.34	4.17	3.27	2.57	18
19	34.01	25.85	19.75	15.16	11.70	9.06	7.05	5.51	4.33	3.41	2.69	19
20	33.92	25.91	19.90	15.36	11.91	9.27	7.25	5.70	4.49	3.56	2.83	20
21	33.82	25.98	20.05	15.55	12.12	9.49	7.46	5.89	4.67	3.71	2.96	21
22	33.73	26.04	20.21	15.75	12.34	9.71	7.67	6.08	4.85	3.87	3.11	22
23	33.64	26.11	20.36	15.95	12.56	9.93	7.89	6.29	5.03	4.04	3.26	23
24	33.54	26.17	20.51	16.16	12.79	10.16	8.11	6.50	5.23	4.22	3.42	24
25	33.45	26.23	20.67	16.36	13.01	10.39	8.34	6.71	5.43	4.40	3.58	25
26	33.36	26.30	20.83	16.57	13.25	10.63	8.57	6.94	5.64	4.59	3.76	26
27	33.27	26.36	20.99	16.79	13.49	10.88	8.81	7.17	5.85	4.79	3.94	27
28	33.18	26.43	21.15	17.00	13.73	11.13	9.06	7.41	6.08	5.00	4.13	28
29	33.09	26.49	21.31	17.22	13.98	11.39	9.32	7.66	6.31	5.22	4.34	29
30	33.00	26.56	21.48	17.44	14.23	11.65	9.58	7.91	6.56	5.45	4.55	30
31	32.91	26.62	21.64	17.67	14.48	11.92	9.86	8.18	6.81	5.69	4.77	31
32	32.82	26.69	21.81	17.90	14.75	12.20	10.14	8.45	7.07	5.94	5.00	32
33	32.73	26.76	21.98	18.13	15.01	12.49	10.42	8.73	7.34	6.20	5.25	33
34	32.65	26.83	22.15	18.36	15.29	12.78	10.72	9.03	7.63	6.47	5.50	34
35	32.57	26.90	22.32	18.60	15.56	13.07	11.02	9.33	7.92	6.75	5.77	35

Age at date of trial	Multiplier calculated with allowance for projected mortality from the 2004-based population projections and rate of return of											Age at date of trial
	0.0%	0.5%	1.0%	1.5%	2.0%	2.5%	3.0%	3.5%	4.0%	4.5%	5.0%	
36	32.48	26.97	22.50	18.84	15.85	13.38	11.34	9.64	8.23	7.05	6.05	36
37	32.40	27.05	22.68	19.09	16.14	13.69	11.66	9.97	8.55	7.36	6.35	37
38	32.32	27.12	22.86	19.34	16.43	14.01	12.00	10.30	8.88	7.68	6.66	38
39	32.25	27.20	23.04	19.60	16.73	14.34	12.34	10.65	9.23	8.02	6.99	39
40	32.18	27.28	23.23	19.86	17.04	14.68	12.69	11.01	9.59	8.37	7.33	40
41	32.11	27.36	23.42	20.12	17.36	15.03	13.06	11.39	9.96	8.74	7.69	41
42	32.04	27.45	23.61	20.39	17.68	15.39	13.44	11.78	10.35	9.13	8.07	42
43	31.98	27.54	23.81	20.67	18.01	15.76	13.83	12.18	10.76	9.53	8.47	43
44	31.92	27.63	24.02	20.96	18.36	16.14	14.23	12.60	11.18	9.96	8.89	44
45	31.87	27.73	24.23	21.25	18.71	16.53	14.65	13.03	11.63	10.41	9.34	45
46	31.83	27.84	24.45	21.55	19.07	16.93	15.09	13.49	12.09	10.87	9.81	46
47	31.79	27.95	24.67	21.86	19.44	17.35	15.54	13.96	12.58	11.37	10.30	47
48	31.76	28.07	24.90	22.18	19.83	17.78	16.00	14.45	13.08	11.88	10.82	48
49	31.73	28.19	25.15	22.51	20.22	18.23	16.49	14.96	13.61	12.43	11.37	49
50	31.72	28.33	25.40	22.85	20.63	18.70	16.99	15.50	14.17	13.00	11.95	50
51	31.72	28.47	25.66	23.20	21.06	19.18	17.52	16.05	14.75	13.60	12.57	51
52	31.72	28.62	25.92	23.57	21.50	19.67	18.06	16.63	15.36	14.23	13.21	52
53	31.72	28.77	26.20	23.94	21.95	20.19	18.63	17.24	16.00	14.89	13.90	53
54	31.73	28.93	26.48	24.31	22.41	20.71	19.21	17.87	16.67	15.59	14.62	54
55	31.74	29.09	26.76	24.70	22.88	21.26	19.81	18.52	17.36	16.32	15.38	55

Table 19 Multipliers for loss of pension commencing age 60 (males)

Age at date of trial	Multiplier calculated with allowance for projected mortality from the 2004-based population projections and rate of return of											Age at date of trial
	0.0%	0.5%	1.0%	1.5%	2.0%	2.5%	3.0%	3.5%	4.0%	4.5%	5.0%	
0	27.80	18.95	12.98	8.94	6.18	4.29	3.00	2.10	1.48	1.04	0.74	0
1	27.83	19.07	13.13	9.09	6.32	4.41	3.09	2.18	1.54	1.09	0.78	1
2	27.72	19.10	13.22	9.19	6.42	4.51	3.18	2.25	1.60	1.14	0.82	2
3	27.62	19.12	13.31	9.30	6.53	4.61	3.27	2.32	1.66	1.19	0.86	3
4	27.51	19.15	13.39	9.41	6.64	4.71	3.35	2.40	1.72	1.24	0.90	4
5	27.40	19.17	13.48	9.52	6.76	4.81	3.45	2.48	1.79	1.29	0.94	5
6	27.28	19.19	13.56	9.63	6.87	4.92	3.54	2.55	1.85	1.35	0.98	6
7	27.17	19.21	13.65	9.74	6.98	5.03	3.63	2.64	1.92	1.40	1.03	7
8	27.06	19.24	13.74	9.85	7.10	5.14	3.73	2.72	1.99	1.46	1.08	8
9	26.95	19.26	13.82	9.97	7.22	5.25	3.83	2.81	2.07	1.53	1.13	9
10	26.84	19.28	13.91	10.08	7.34	5.36	3.94	2.90	2.14	1.59	1.18	10
11	26.73	19.30	14.00	10.20	7.46	5.48	4.04	2.99	2.22	1.66	1.24	11
12	26.62	19.32	14.09	10.31	7.58	5.60	4.15	3.09	2.31	1.73	1.30	12
13	26.51	19.34	14.17	10.43	7.71	5.72	4.26	3.19	2.39	1.80	1.36	13
14	26.40	19.36	14.26	10.55	7.84	5.85	4.38	3.29	2.48	1.88	1.43	14
15	26.29	19.38	14.35	10.67	7.97	5.97	4.50	3.40	2.57	1.96	1.49	15
16	26.18	19.40	14.44	10.79	8.10	6.10	4.62	3.50	2.67	2.04	1.56	16
17	26.08	19.43	14.53	10.92	8.24	6.24	4.74	3.62	2.77	2.13	1.64	17
18	25.97	19.45	14.63	11.05	8.38	6.37	4.87	3.73	2.87	2.22	1.72	18
19	25.87	19.48	14.72	11.18	8.52	6.52	5.00	3.85	2.98	2.31	1.80	19
20	25.78	19.51	14.82	11.31	8.66	6.66	5.14	3.98	3.09	2.41	1.89	20
21	25.68	19.54	14.92	11.44	8.81	6.81	5.28	4.11	3.21	2.51	1.98	21
22	25.59	19.57	15.02	11.58	8.96	6.96	5.43	4.24	3.33	2.62	2.07	22
23	25.50	19.60	15.13	11.72	9.12	7.12	5.57	4.38	3.46	2.73	2.17	23
24	25.40	19.63	15.23	11.86	9.27	7.27	5.73	4.52	3.59	2.85	2.27	24
25	25.30	19.65	15.33	12.00	9.43	7.43	5.88	4.67	3.72	2.97	2.38	25
26	25.21	19.68	15.43	12.14	9.59	7.60	6.04	4.82	3.86	3.10	2.50	26
27	25.12	19.71	15.53	12.29	9.75	7.77	6.21	4.98	4.01	3.23	2.62	27
28	25.03	19.75	15.64	12.43	9.92	7.94	6.38	5.14	4.16	3.37	2.74	28
29	24.95	19.79	15.75	12.59	10.09	8.12	6.56	5.31	4.32	3.52	2.87	29
30	24.86	19.82	15.86	12.74	10.27	8.31	6.74	5.49	4.48	3.67	3.01	30
31	24.77	19.85	15.97	12.89	10.45	8.49	6.92	5.66	4.65	3.82	3.16	31
32	24.69	19.89	16.08	13.05	10.63	8.68	7.12	5.85	4.82	3.99	3.31	32
33	24.61	19.93	16.20	13.21	10.81	8.88	7.31	6.04	5.01	4.16	3.47	33
34	24.52	19.96	16.31	13.37	11.00	9.08	7.52	6.24	5.20	4.34	3.64	34
35	24.44	20.00	16.43	13.54	11.19	9.28	7.73	6.45	5.40	4.53	3.81	35

Age at date of trial	Multiplier calculated with allowance for projected mortality from the 2004-based population projections and rate of return of											Age at date of trial
	0.0%	0.5%	1.0%	1.5%	2.0%	2.5%	3.0%	3.5%	4.0%	4.5%	5.0%	
36	24.36	20.04	16.54	13.70	11.39	9.49	7.94	6.66	5.60	4.72	3.99	36
37	24.28	20.08	16.66	13.87	11.59	9.71	8.16	6.88	5.82	4.93	4.19	37
38	24.21	20.12	16.78	14.05	11.79	9.93	8.39	7.11	6.04	5.14	4.39	38
39	24.13	20.17	16.91	14.22	12.00	10.16	8.62	7.34	6.27	5.37	4.60	39
40	24.06	20.21	17.03	14.40	12.22	10.39	8.87	7.59	6.51	5.60	4.83	40
41	24.00	20.26	17.16	14.59	12.44	10.63	9.12	7.84	6.76	5.84	5.06	41
42	23.93	20.31	17.30	14.77	12.66	10.88	9.38	8.10	7.02	6.10	5.31	42
43	23.87	20.36	17.43	14.97	12.89	11.13	9.64	8.38	7.29	6.37	5.57	43
44	23.81	20.42	17.57	15.17	13.13	11.40	9.92	8.66	7.58	6.65	5.85	44
45	23.76	20.48	17.72	15.37	13.37	11.67	10.21	8.96	7.88	6.94	6.14	45
46	23.72	20.55	17.87	15.58	13.63	11.95	10.51	9.26	8.19	7.25	6.44	46
47	23.68	20.63	18.03	15.80	13.89	12.24	10.82	9.59	8.52	7.58	6.77	47
48	23.66	20.72	18.20	16.03	14.16	12.55	11.14	9.92	8.86	7.93	7.11	48
49	23.64	20.81	18.37	16.27	14.45	12.86	11.48	10.28	9.22	8.29	7.47	49
50	23.64	20.91	18.56	16.52	14.74	13.20	11.84	10.65	9.60	8.67	7.86	50
51	23.64	21.03	18.76	16.78	15.06	13.54	12.21	11.04	10.00	9.08	8.26	51
52	23.66	21.15	18.97	17.06	15.38	13.90	12.60	11.45	10.42	9.51	8.70	52
53	23.68	21.29	19.19	17.34	15.72	14.28	13.01	11.88	10.87	9.96	9.16	53
54	23.71	21.42	19.41	17.63	16.06	14.67	13.43	12.32	11.33	10.44	9.64	54
55	23.74	21.56	19.63	17.93	16.41	15.07	13.86	12.78	11.81	10.94	10.15	55
56	23.77	21.70	19.86	18.23	16.78	15.48	14.31	13.26	12.32	11.46	10.69	56
57	23.80	21.84	20.09	18.54	17.15	15.90	14.78	13.76	12.84	12.01	11.26	57
58	23.84	21.99	20.34	18.86	17.54	16.34	15.26	14.29	13.40	12.60	11.86	58
59	23.89	22.16	20.60	19.20	17.95	16.81	15.78	14.84	13.99	13.22	12.51	59
60	23.97	22.35	20.89	19.57	18.38	17.30	16.33	15.44	14.62	13.88	13.20	60

Table 20 Multipliers for loss of pension commencing age 60 (females)

Age at date of trial	Multiplier calculated with allowance for projected mortality from the 2004-based population projections and rate of return of											Age at date of trial
	0.0%	0.5%	1.0%	1.5%	2.0%	2.5%	3.0%	3.5%	4.0%	4.5%	5.0%	
0	30.93	20.99	14.32	9.82	6.77	4.69	3.26	2.28	1.60	1.13	0.80	0
1	30.96	21.12	14.49	9.99	6.92	4.81	3.37	2.36	1.67	1.18	0.84	1
2	30.86	21.17	14.59	10.11	7.04	4.92	3.46	2.44	1.73	1.23	0.88	2
3	30.77	21.21	14.70	10.24	7.16	5.04	3.56	2.52	1.80	1.28	0.92	3
4	30.67	21.25	14.81	10.36	7.29	5.15	3.66	2.60	1.86	1.34	0.97	4
5	30.57	21.30	14.91	10.49	7.42	5.27	3.76	2.69	1.94	1.40	1.01	5
6	30.47	21.34	15.02	10.62	7.55	5.39	3.86	2.78	2.01	1.46	1.06	6
7	30.37	21.38	15.13	10.75	7.68	5.51	3.97	2.87	2.08	1.52	1.11	7
8	30.27	21.42	15.23	10.88	7.81	5.63	4.08	2.96	2.16	1.59	1.17	8
9	30.17	21.46	15.34	11.02	7.95	5.76	4.19	3.06	2.25	1.65	1.22	9
10	30.07	21.50	15.45	11.15	8.09	5.89	4.31	3.16	2.33	1.73	1.28	10
11	29.97	21.54	15.56	11.29	8.23	6.02	4.43	3.27	2.42	1.80	1.34	11
12	29.87	21.58	15.67	11.43	8.37	6.16	4.55	3.37	2.51	1.88	1.41	12
13	29.77	21.62	15.78	11.57	8.52	6.30	4.67	3.48	2.61	1.96	1.48	13
14	29.67	21.66	15.89	11.71	8.66	6.44	4.80	3.60	2.71	2.04	1.55	14
15	29.57	21.70	16.00	11.85	8.82	6.58	4.94	3.72	2.81	2.13	1.62	15
16	29.48	21.75	16.12	12.00	8.97	6.73	5.07	3.84	2.92	2.22	1.70	16
17	29.38	21.79	16.23	12.15	9.13	6.89	5.22	3.97	3.03	2.32	1.78	17
18	29.29	21.84	16.35	12.30	9.29	7.04	5.36	4.10	3.14	2.42	1.87	18
19	29.20	21.88	16.47	12.45	9.45	7.20	5.51	4.23	3.26	2.52	1.96	19
20	29.10	21.92	16.59	12.60	9.61	7.36	5.66	4.37	3.38	2.63	2.05	20
21	29.01	21.96	16.70	12.76	9.78	7.53	5.82	4.51	3.51	2.74	2.15	21
22	28.92	22.01	16.82	12.91	9.95	7.70	5.98	4.66	3.65	2.86	2.25	22
23	28.82	22.05	16.95	13.07	10.13	7.88	6.15	4.82	3.79	2.99	2.36	23
24	28.73	22.10	17.07	13.24	10.31	8.05	6.32	4.97	3.93	3.11	2.48	24
25	28.64	22.14	17.19	13.40	10.49	8.24	6.49	5.14	4.08	3.25	2.60	25
26	28.55	22.18	17.31	13.56	10.67	8.42	6.67	5.31	4.23	3.39	2.72	26
27	28.46	22.23	17.44	13.73	10.86	8.61	6.86	5.48	4.40	3.54	2.85	27
28	28.37	22.28	17.56	13.90	11.05	8.81	7.05	5.66	4.56	3.69	2.99	28
29	28.28	22.32	17.69	14.07	11.24	9.01	7.25	5.85	4.74	3.85	3.13	29
30	28.19	22.37	17.82	14.25	11.44	9.21	7.45	6.04	4.92	4.01	3.29	30
31	28.10	22.41	17.95	14.42	11.64	9.42	7.66	6.24	5.10	4.19	3.44	31
32	28.01	22.46	18.08	14.60	11.84	9.64	7.87	6.45	5.30	4.37	3.61	32
33	27.93	22.51	18.21	14.79	12.05	9.86	8.09	6.66	5.50	4.56	3.79	33
34	27.84	22.55	18.34	14.97	12.26	10.08	8.32	6.88	5.71	4.75	3.97	34
35	27.76	22.60	18.48	15.16	12.48	10.31	8.55	7.11	5.93	4.96	4.16	35

Age at date of trial	Multiplier calculated with allowance for projected mortality from the 2004-based population projections and rate of return of											Age at date of trial
	0.0%	0.5%	1.0%	1.5%	2.0%	2.5%	3.0%	3.5%	4.0%	4.5%	5.0%	
36	27.67	22.65	18.61	15.35	12.70	10.55	8.79	7.34	6.16	5.17	4.36	36
37	27.59	22.70	18.75	15.54	12.93	10.79	9.03	7.59	6.39	5.40	4.57	37
38	27.51	22.75	18.89	15.74	13.16	11.04	9.29	7.84	6.64	5.63	4.80	38
39	27.43	22.81	19.03	15.94	13.39	11.29	9.55	8.10	6.89	5.88	5.03	39
40	27.36	22.87	19.18	16.14	13.63	11.55	9.82	8.37	7.16	6.14	5.27	40
41	27.29	22.92	19.33	16.35	13.88	11.82	10.10	8.65	7.43	6.40	5.53	41
42	27.22	22.98	19.48	16.56	14.13	12.10	10.38	8.94	7.72	6.68	5.80	42
43	27.15	23.05	19.63	16.78	14.39	12.38	10.68	9.24	8.02	6.98	6.09	43
44	27.09	23.12	19.79	17.00	14.66	12.67	10.99	9.56	8.33	7.29	6.39	44
45	27.03	23.19	19.96	17.23	14.93	12.97	11.31	9.88	8.66	7.61	6.70	45
46	26.98	23.27	20.13	17.47	15.21	13.28	11.64	10.22	9.00	7.95	7.04	46
47	26.94	23.35	20.30	17.71	15.50	13.61	11.98	10.57	9.36	8.30	7.39	47
48	26.90	23.43	20.48	17.96	15.80	13.94	12.33	10.94	9.73	8.68	7.76	48
49	26.86	23.53	20.67	18.22	16.11	14.28	12.70	11.32	10.12	9.07	8.15	49
50	26.84	23.63	20.87	18.49	16.43	14.64	13.08	11.72	10.53	9.48	8.56	50
51	26.82	23.74	21.07	18.76	16.76	15.01	13.48	12.14	10.96	9.91	8.99	51
52	26.81	23.85	21.28	19.05	17.10	15.39	13.89	12.57	11.40	10.37	9.45	52
53	26.80	23.96	21.49	19.34	17.44	15.78	14.32	13.02	11.87	10.85	9.94	53
54	26.80	24.08	21.71	19.63	17.80	16.19	14.76	13.49	12.36	11.35	10.45	54
55	26.79	24.20	21.93	19.93	18.17	16.60	15.21	13.97	12.87	11.87	10.98	55
56	26.79	24.33	22.16	20.24	18.54	17.03	15.68	14.48	13.40	12.43	11.55	56
57	26.79	24.46	22.39	20.56	18.93	17.48	16.17	15.01	13.95	13.01	12.15	57
58	26.81	24.60	22.64	20.89	19.34	17.94	16.69	15.56	14.54	13.62	12.78	58
59	26.84	24.75	22.90	21.24	19.76	18.43	17.23	16.14	15.16	14.27	13.46	59
60	26.88	24.93	23.18	21.61	20.20	18.94	17.79	16.76	15.81	14.96	14.18	60

Table 21 Multipliers for loss of pension commencing age 65 (males)

Age at date of trial	Multiplier calculated with allowance for projected mortality from the 2004-based population projections and rate of return of											Age at date of trial
	0.0%	0.5%	1.0%	1.5%	2.0%	2.5%	3.0%	3.5%	4.0%	4.5%	5.0%	
0	23.20	15.58	10.51	7.12	4.85	3.31	2.27	1.56	1.08	0.75	0.52	0
1	23.21	15.67	10.63	7.24	4.95	3.40	2.34	1.62	1.13	0.79	0.55	1
2	23.11	15.68	10.69	7.32	5.03	3.47	2.41	1.67	1.17	0.82	0.58	2
3	23.00	15.69	10.75	7.40	5.11	3.55	2.47	1.73	1.21	0.85	0.60	3
4	22.90	15.70	10.82	7.48	5.20	3.62	2.54	1.78	1.26	0.89	0.63	4
5	22.79	15.71	10.88	7.56	5.28	3.70	2.60	1.84	1.30	0.93	0.66	5
6	22.68	15.72	10.94	7.65	5.36	3.78	2.67	1.89	1.35	0.96	0.69	6
7	22.58	15.73	11.00	7.73	5.45	3.86	2.74	1.95	1.40	1.00	0.72	7
8	22.47	15.73	11.06	7.81	5.54	3.94	2.81	2.02	1.45	1.05	0.76	8
9	22.36	15.74	11.13	7.90	5.63	4.02	2.89	2.08	1.50	1.09	0.79	9
10	22.25	15.75	11.19	7.98	5.72	4.11	2.96%	2.14	1.56	1.13	0.83	10
11	22.15	15.75	11.25	8.07	5.81	4.19	3.04	2.21	1.61	1.18	0.87	11
12	22.04	15.76	11.31	8.15	5.90	4.28	3.12	2.28	1.67	1.23	0.91	12
13	21.93	15.77	11.38	8.24	5.99	4.37	3.20	2.35	1.73	1.28	0.95	13
14	21.83	15.77	11.44	8.33	6.09	4.46	3.29	2.43	1.80	1.34	1.00	14
15	21.72	15.78	11.50	8.42	6.18	4.56	3.37	2.50	1.86	1.39	1.04	15
16	21.62	15.78	11.57	8.51	6.28	4.66	3.46	2.58	1.93	1.45	1.09	16
17	21.52	15.79	11.63	8.60	6.38	4.75	3.55	2.66	2.00	1.51	1.14	17
18	21.42	15.80	11.70	8.70	6.49	4.85	3.65	2.75	2.08	1.57	1.20	18
19	21.32	15.81	11.77	8.79	6.59	4.96	3.74	2.83	2.15	1.64	1.25	19
20	21.22	15.82	11.84	8.89	6.70	5.06	3.84	2.92	2.23	1.71	1.31	20
21	21.13	15.84	11.91	8.99	6.81	5.17	3.94	3.02	2.31	1.78	1.37	21
22	21.04	15.85	11.98	9.09	6.92	5.29	4.05	3.11	2.40	1.85	1.44	22
23	20.95	15.86	12.06	9.19	7.03	5.40	4.16	3.21	2.49	1.93	1.51	23
24	20.85	15.87	12.13	9.30	7.15	5.51	4.27	3.31	2.58	2.01	1.58	24
25	20.76	15.88	12.20	9.40	7.26	5.63	4.38	3.42	2.67	2.10	1.65	25
26	20.67	15.90	12.27	9.50	7.38	5.75	4.50	3.53	2.77	2.19	1.73	26
27	20.58	15.91	12.34	9.61	7.50	5.88	4.62	3.64	2.87	2.28	1.81	27
28	20.49	15.93	12.42	9.72	7.63	6.00	4.74	3.75	2.98	2.37	1.89	28
29	20.41	15.94	12.50	9.83	7.75	6.14	4.87	3.87	3.09	2.47	1.98	29
30	20.32	15.96	12.58	9.94	7.88	6.27	5.00	4.00	3.21	2.58	2.08	30
31	20.23	15.97	12.65	10.05	8.01	6.40	5.13	4.13	3.33	2.69	2.18	31
32	20.15	15.99	12.73	10.17	8.14	6.54	5.27	4.26	3.45	2.80	2.28	32
33	20.07	16.01	12.81	10.28	8.28	6.69	5.41	4.40	3.58	2.92	2.39	33
34	19.99	16.03	12.89	10.40	8.42	6.83	5.56	4.54	3.71	3.04	2.50	34
35	19.90	16.04	12.97	10.52	8.56	6.98	5.71	4.68	3.85	3.17	2.62	35

Age at date of trial	Multiplier calculated with allowance for projected mortality from the 2004-based population projections and rate of return of											Age at date of trial
	0.0%	0.5%	1.0%	1.5%	2.0%	2.5%	3.0%	3.5%	4.0%	4.5%	5.0%	
36	19.82	16.06	13.05	10.64	8.70	7.13	5.86	4.83	3.99	3.31	2.74	36
37	19.74	16.08	13.14	10.76	8.85	7.29	6.02	4.99	4.14	3.45	2.88	37
38	19.67	16.10	13.22	10.89	8.99	7.45	6.18	5.15	4.30	3.59	3.01	38
39	19.59	16.12	13.31	11.02	9.15	7.61	6.35	5.31	4.46	3.75	3.16	39
40	19.52	16.15	13.40	11.15	9.30	7.78	6.53	5.49	4.62	3.91	3.31	40
41	19.45	16.17	13.49	11.28	9.46	7.95	6.71	5.67	4.80	4.07	3.47	41
42	19.38	16.20	13.58	11.42	9.62	8.13	6.89	5.85	4.98	4.25	3.63	42
43	19.31	16.23	13.68	11.56	9.79	8.32	7.08	6.04	5.17	4.43	3.81	43
44	19.25	16.26	13.77	11.70	9.96	8.50	7.28	6.24	5.37	4.62	3.99	44
45	19.19	16.30	13.88	11.85	10.14	8.70	7.48	6.45	5.57	4.82	4.18	45
46	19.14	16.34	13.98	12.00	10.32	8.90	7.69	6.67	5.79	5.03	4.39	46
47	19.10	16.39	14.10	12.16	10.51	9.11	7.91	6.89	6.01	5.26	4.61	47
48	19.06	16.44	14.22	12.32	10.71	9.33	8.15	7.13	6.25	5.49	4.83	48
49	19.03	16.50	14.34	12.50	10.92	9.56	8.39	7.37	6.50	5.74	5.08	49
50	19.01	16.57	14.48	12.68	11.13	9.80	8.64	7.63	6.76	6.00	5.33	50
51	19.00	16.65	14.62	12.87	11.36	10.04	8.90	7.91	7.04	6.28	5.61	51
52	19.00	16.73	14.77	13.07	11.59	10.30	9.18	8.19	7.33	6.57	5.90	52
53	19.00	16.82	14.93	13.28	11.84	10.57	9.47	8.49	7.63	6.87	6.20	53
54	19.01	16.92	15.09	13.49	12.09	10.85	9.76	8.80	7.95	7.20	6.53	54
55	19.02	17.01	15.25	13.70	12.34	11.14	10.07	9.13	8.28	7.53	6.86	55
56	19.02	17.10	15.41	13.92	12.60	11.43	10.39	9.46	8.63	7.89	7.22	56
57	19.02	17.19	15.58	14.14	12.87	11.73	10.71	9.80	8.99	8.26	7.60	57
58	19.04	17.30	15.75	14.37	13.14	12.04	11.05	10.17	9.37	8.65	8.00	58
59	19.06	17.41	15.93	14.61	13.43	12.37	11.41	10.55	9.77	9.06	8.42	59
60	19.10	17.54	16.13	14.87	13.74	12.72	11.79	10.96	10.20	9.51	8.88	60
61	19.17	17.69	16.36	15.16	14.08	13.09	12.20	11.39	10.66	9.98	9.37	61
62	19.26	17.86	16.61	15.47	14.44	13.50	12.64	11.86	11.15	10.50	9.90	62
63	19.37	18.06	16.88	15.80	14.82	13.93	13.12	12.37	11.68	11.05	10.47	63
64	19.50	18.28	17.17	16.16	15.24	14.39	13.62	12.91	12.25	11.65	11.09	64
65	19.66	18.52	17.49	16.54	15.68	14.88	14.16	13.48	12.86	12.29	11.76	65

Table 22 Multipliers for loss of pension commencing age 65 (females)

Age at date of trial	Multiplier calculated with allowance for projected mortality from the 2004-based population projections and rate of return of											Age at date of trial
	0.0%	0.5%	1.0%	1.5%	2.0%	2.5%	3.0%	3.5%	4.0%	4.5%	5.0%	
0	26.18	17.52	11.78	7.95	5.39	3.67	2.51	1.72	1.19	0.82	0.57	0
1	26.20	17.62	11.91	8.08	5.51	3.77	2.59	1.79	1.24	0.86	0.60	1
2	26.10	17.65	11.99	8.18	5.60	3.85	2.66	1.85	1.29	0.90	0.63	2
3	26.01	17.68	12.07	8.28	5.70	3.94	2.74	1.91	1.33	0.94	0.66	3
4	25.91	17.70	12.15	8.37	5.80	4.03	2.81	1.97	1.38	0.98	0.69	4
5	25.81	17.73	12.23	8.47	5.89	4.12	2.89	2.03	1.44	1.02	0.72	5
6	25.72	17.75	12.31	8.57	5.99	4.21	2.97	2.10	1.49	1.06	0.76	6
7	25.62	17.78	12.39	8.67	6.10	4.30	3.05	2.17	1.55	1.11	0.79	7
8	25.52	17.80	12.47	8.77	6.20	4.40	3.13	2.24	1.60	1.15	0.83	8
9	25.42	17.83	12.55	8.88	6.30	4.49	3.21	2.31	1.66	1.20	0.87	9
10	25.33	17.85	12.64	8.98	6.41	4.59	3.30	2.38	1.73	1.25	0.91	10
11	25.23	17.88	12.72	9.09	6.52	4.69	3.39	2.46	1.79	1.31	0.96	11
12	25.13	17.90	12.80	9.19	6.63	4.80	3.48	2.54	1.86	1.36	1.00	12
13	25.03	17.92	12.88	9.30	6.74	4.90	3.58	2.62	1.93	1.42	1.05	13
14	24.94	17.95	12.97	9.41	6.85	5.01	3.67	2.70	2.00	1.48	1.10	14
15	24.84	17.97	13.05	9.52	6.97	5.12	3.77	2.79	2.07	1.54	1.15	15
16	24.75	18.00	13.14	9.63	7.09	5.23	3.88	2.88	2.15	1.61	1.21	16
17	24.66	18.02	13.23	9.74	7.21	5.35	3.98	2.98	2.23	1.68	1.27	17
18	24.56	18.05	13.31	9.86	7.33	5.47	4.09	3.07	2.31	1.75	1.33	18
19	24.47	18.07	13.40	9.98	7.45	5.59	4.20	3.17	2.40	1.82	1.39	19
20	24.38	18.10	13.49	10.09	7.58	5.71	4.32	3.27	2.49	1.90	1.46	20
21	24.29	18.13	13.58	10.21	7.71	5.84	4.43	3.38	2.58	1.98	1.52	21
22	24.20	18.15	13.67	10.33	7.84	5.96	4.55	3.49	2.68	2.07	1.60	22
23	24.11	18.18	13.76	10.45	7.97	6.10	4.68	3.60	2.78	2.15	1.67	23
24	24.01	18.20	13.85	10.58	8.10	6.23	4.81	3.72	2.89	2.25	1.75	24
25	23.92	18.23	13.94	10.70	8.24	6.37	4.94	3.84	2.99	2.34	1.84	25
26	23.83	18.25	14.03	10.83	8.38	6.51	5.07	3.96	3.11	2.44	1.92	26
27	23.74	18.28	14.13	10.95	8.52	6.65	5.21	4.09	3.22	2.55	2.02	27
28	23.66	18.31	14.22	11.08	8.67	6.80	5.35	4.22	3.34	2.65	2.11	28
29	23.57	18.34	14.31	11.21	8.81	6.95	5.50	4.36	3.47	2.77	2.21	29
30	23.48	18.36	14.41	11.35	8.96	7.10	5.65	4.50	3.60	2.88	2.32	30
31	23.39	18.39	14.50	11.48	9.11	7.26	5.80	4.65	3.73	3.01	2.43	31
32	23.30	18.41	14.60	11.61	9.27	7.42	5.96	4.80	3.87	3.14	2.55	32
33	23.22	18.44	14.70	11.75	9.43	7.58	6.12	4.95	4.02	3.27	2.67	33
34	23.14	18.47	14.80	11.89	9.59	7.75	6.29	5.11	4.17	3.41	2.79	34
35	23.05	18.50	14.90	12.03	9.75	7.92	6.46	5.28	4.33	3.55	2.93	35

APIL Guide to Damages

Age at date of trial	Multiplier calculated with allowance for projected mortality from the 2004-based population projections and rate of return of											Age at date of trial
	0.0%	0.5%	1.0%	1.5%	2.0%	2.5%	3.0%	3.5%	4.0%	4.5%	5.0%	
36	22.97	18.53	15.00	12.18	9.92	8.10	6.64	5.45	4.49	3.71	3.07	36
37	22.89	18.56	15.10	12.32	10.09	8.28	6.82	5.63	4.66	3.86	3.21	37
38	22.81	18.59	15.20	12.47	10.26	8.47	7.00	5.81	4.83	4.03	3.37	38
39	22.73	18.62	15.31	12.62	10.44	8.65	7.20	6.00	5.02	4.20	3.53	39
40	22.65	18.66	15.42	12.78	10.62	8.85	7.40	6.20	5.21	4.38	3.70	40
41	22.58	18.70	15.53	12.93	10.80	9.05	7.60	6.40	5.40	4.57	3.88	41
42	22.51	18.73	15.64	13.09	10.99	9.25	7.81	6.61	5.61	4.77	4.07	42
43	22.44	18.77	15.75	13.26	11.19	9.46	8.03	6.83	5.82	4.98	4.26	43
44	22.37	18.82	15.87	13.42	11.39	9.68	8.26	7.06	6.05	5.19	4.47	44
45	22.31	18.86	15.99	13.60	11.59	9.91	8.49	7.29	6.28	5.42	4.69	45
46	22.26	18.91	16.12	13.77	11.80	10.14	8.73	7.54	6.52	5.66	4.92	46
47	22.21	18.97	16.25	13.95	12.02	10.38	8.98	7.79	6.78	5.91	5.16	47
48	22.16	19.03	16.38	14.14	12.24	10.62	9.24	8.06	7.04	6.17	5.41	48
49	22.12	19.09	16.52	14.34	12.47	10.88	9.51	8.33	7.32	6.44	5.68	49
50	22.08	19.16	16.67	14.54	12.71	11.14	9.79	8.62	7.61	6.73	5.97	50
51	22.06	19.23	16.82	14.74	12.96	11.42	10.08	8.92	7.91	7.03	6.26	51
52	22.03	19.31	16.98	14.96	13.21	11.70	10.38	9.23	8.23	7.35	6.58	52
53	22.01	19.40	17.13	15.18	13.47	11.99	10.69	9.56	8.56	7.69	6.91	53
54	21.99	19.48	17.30	15.40	13.74	12.29	11.02	9.90	8.91	8.04	7.26	54
55	21.97	19.56	17.46	15.62	14.01	12.60	11.35	10.24	9.27	8.40	7.63	55
56	21.96	19.65	17.63	15.85	14.29	12.91	11.69	10.61	9.64	8.79	8.02	56
57	21.94	19.74	17.80	16.09	14.58	13.24	12.05	10.99	10.04	9.19	8.43	57
58	21.94	19.84	17.98	16.34	14.88	13.58	12.42	11.38	10.45	9.61	8.86	58
59	21.94	19.95	18.17	16.60	15.19	13.93	12.81	11.80	10.89	10.06	9.32	59
60	21.96	20.07	18.38	16.87	15.52	14.31	13.22	12.23	11.35	10.54	9.81	60
61	22.00	20.20	18.60	17.16	15.87	14.70	13.65	12.70	11.83	11.05	10.33	61
62	22.05	20.36	18.84	17.47	16.23	15.12	14.11	13.19	12.35	11.59	10.89	62
63	22.11	20.52	19.09	17.79	16.62	15.55	14.59	13.71	12.90	12.16	11.49	63
64	22.19	20.70	19.35	18.13	17.02	16.01	15.09	14.25	13.48	12.77	12.12	64
65	22.28	20.89	19.63	18.49	17.45	16.50	15.63	14.83	14.10	13.42	12.80	65

Table 23 Multipliers for loss of pension commencing age 70 (males)

Age at date of trial	Multiplier calculated with allowance for projected mortality from the 2004-based population projections and rate of return of											Age at date of trial
	0.0%	0.5%	1.0%	1.5%	2.0%	2.5%	3.0%	3.5%	4.0%	4.5%	5.0%	
0	18.76	12.41	8.24	5.50	3.68	2.47	1.67	1.13	0.77	0.52	0.36	0
1	18.75	12.47	8.32	5.58	3.75	2.53	1.72	1.17	0.80	0.55	0.37	1
2	18.65	12.47	8.37	5.64	3.81	2.59	1.76	1.20	0.83	0.57	0.39	2
3	18.55	12.47	8.41	5.69	3.87	2.64	1.81	1.24	0.86	0.59	0.41	3
4	18.45	12.46	8.45	5.75	3.93	2.69	1.85	1.28	0.89	0.62	0.43	4
5	18.35	12.46	8.49	5.81	3.99	2.75	1.90	1.32	0.92	0.64	0.45	5
6	18.24	12.45	8.53	5.87	4.05	2.80	1.95	1.36	0.95	0.67	0.47	6
7	18.14	12.45	8.57	5.93	4.11	2.86	2.00	1.40	0.98	0.69	0.49	7
8	18.04	12.44	8.61	5.98	4.17	2.92	2.05	1.44	1.02	0.72	0.51	8
9	17.94	12.44	8.65	6.04	4.24	2.98	2.10	1.49	1.06	0.75	0.54	9
10	17.84	12.43	8.70	6.10	4.30	3.04	2.15	1.53	1.09	0.78	0.56	10
11	17.74	12.43	8.74	6.16	4.36	3.10	2.21	1.58	1.13	0.81	0.59	11
12	17.64	12.42	8.78	6.23	4.43	3.16	2.26	1.63	1.17	0.85	0.61	12
13	17.53	12.41	8.82	6.29	4.50	3.23	2.32	1.68	1.21	0.88	0.64	13
14	17.43	12.41	8.86	6.35	4.56	3.29	2.38	1.73	1.26	0.92	0.67	14
15	17.33	12.40	8.90	6.41	4.63	3.36	2.44	1.78	1.30	0.95	0.70	15
16	17.23	12.39	8.94	6.47	4.70	3.42	2.50	1.83	1.35	0.99	0.73	16
17	17.14	12.39	8.98	6.54	4.77	3.49	2.57	1.89	1.40	1.03	0.77	17
18	17.04	12.38	9.03	6.60	4.84	3.56	2.63	1.95	1.45	1.08	0.80	18
19	16.95	12.38	9.07	6.67	4.92	3.64	2.70	2.01	1.50	1.12	0.84	19
20	16.86	12.38	9.12	6.74	4.99	3.71	2.77	2.07	1.55	1.17	0.88	20
21	16.77	12.38	9.16	6.81	5.07	3.79	2.84	2.13	1.61	1.21	0.92	21
22	16.68	12.37	9.21	6.88	5.15	3.87	2.91	2.20	1.67	1.26	0.96	22
23	16.59	12.37	9.26	6.95	5.23	3.95	2.99	2.27	1.72	1.32	1.01	23
24	16.50	12.37	9.30	7.02	5.31	4.03	3.06	2.34	1.79	1.37	1.05	24
25	16.41	12.37	9.35	7.09	5.39	4.11	3.14	2.41	1.85	1.43	1.10	25
26	16.32	12.36	9.39	7.16	5.47	4.19	3.22	2.48	1.92	1.48	1.15	26
27	16.23	12.36	9.44	7.23	5.55	4.28	3.30	2.56	1.99	1.54	1.21	27
28	16.15	12.36	9.49	7.31	5.64	4.37	3.39	2.64	2.06	1.61	1.26	28
29	16.07	12.36	9.54	7.38	5.73	4.46	3.48	2.72	2.13	1.68	1.32	29
30	15.99	12.36	9.59	7.46	5.82	4.55	3.57	2.80	2.21	1.74	1.38	30
31	15.90	12.36	9.64	7.54	5.91	4.64	3.66	2.89	2.29	1.82	1.44	31
32	15.82	12.36	9.69	7.61	6.00	4.74	3.75	2.98	2.37	1.89	1.51	32
33	15.74	12.36	9.74	7.69	6.09	4.84	3.85	3.07	2.46	1.97	1.58	33
34	15.66	12.36	9.79	7.77	6.19	4.94	3.95	3.17	2.54	2.05	1.65	34
35	15.58	12.37	9.84	7.85	6.28	5.04	4.05	3.26	2.64	2.13	1.73	35

Age at date of trial	Multiplier calculated with allowance for projected mortality from the 2004-based population projections and rate of return of											Age at date of trial
	0.0%	0.5%	1.0%	1.5%	2.0%	2.5%	3.0%	3.5%	4.0%	4.5%	5.0%	
36	15.50	12.37	9.89	7.93	6.38	5.14	4.16	3.37	2.73	2.22	1.81	36
37	15.42	12.37	9.95	8.02	6.48	5.25	4.26	3.47	2.83	2.31	1.90	37
38	15.34	12.37	10.00	8.10	6.58	5.36	4.37	3.58	2.93	2.41	1.98	38
39	15.27	12.37	10.05	8.19	6.69	5.47	4.49	3.69	3.04	2.51	2.08	39
40	15.20	12.38	10.11	8.28	6.79	5.59	4.61	3.81	3.15	2.61	2.17	40
41	15.13	12.39	10.17	8.37	6.90	5.71	4.73	3.93	3.27	2.72	2.27	41
42	15.06	12.39	10.23	8.46	7.01	5.83	4.85	4.05	3.39	2.84	2.38	42
43	14.99	12.40	10.29	8.55	7.13	5.95	4.98	4.18	3.51	2.96	2.49	43
44	14.92	12.41	10.35	8.65	7.24	6.08	5.11	4.31	3.64	3.08	2.61	44
45	14.86	12.43	10.41	8.75	7.36	6.21	5.25	4.45	3.77	3.21	2.73	45
46	14.81	12.44	10.48	8.85	7.49	6.35	5.39	4.59	3.92	3.35	2.86	46
47	14.76	12.47	10.55	8.96	7.62	6.49	5.54	4.74	4.06	3.49	3.00	47
48	14.71	12.49	10.63	9.07	7.75	6.64	5.70	4.90	4.22	3.64	3.15	48
49	14.67	12.52	10.71	9.19	7.89	6.79	5.86	5.06	4.38	3.80	3.30	49
50	14.64	12.56	10.80	9.31	8.04	6.95	6.03	5.24	4.55	3.97	3.47	50
51	14.61	12.61	10.90	9.44	8.19	7.12	6.20	5.42	4.74	4.15	3.64	51
52	14.60	12.66	11.00	9.57	8.35	7.30	6.39	5.61	4.93	4.34	3.82	52
53	14.59	12.71	11.10	9.71	8.52	7.48	6.58	5.80	5.12	4.53	4.02	53
54	14.57	12.77	11.21	9.86	8.69	7.67	6.78	6.01	5.33	4.74	4.22	54
55	14.56	12.82	11.31	10.00	8.86	7.86	6.99	6.22	5.55	4.96	4.43	55
56	14.55	12.88	11.42	10.15	9.03	8.06	7.20	6.44	5.77	5.18	4.66	56
57	14.53	12.93	11.53	10.30	9.21	8.26	7.41	6.67	6.01	5.42	4.89	57
58	14.52	12.99	11.64	10.45	9.40	8.47	7.64	6.90	6.25	5.67	5.14	58
59	14.52	13.06	11.76	10.61	9.59	8.69	7.88	7.15	6.51	5.93	5.41	59
60	14.53	13.13	11.89	10.79	9.80	8.92	8.13	7.42	6.78	6.21	5.69	60
61	14.56	13.23	12.04	10.97	10.02	9.17	8.40	7.70	7.08	6.51	6.00	61
62	14.61	13.34	12.20	11.18	10.26	9.43	8.69	8.01	7.40	6.84	6.33	62
63	14.67	13.47	12.38	11.41	10.52	9.72	9.00	8.34	7.74	7.19	6.69	63
64	14.75	13.61	12.58	11.65	10.80	10.03	9.33	8.69	8.10	7.56	7.07	64
65	14.85	13.77	12.79	11.90	11.09	10.35	9.68	9.06	8.49	7.97	7.49	65
66	14.95	13.94	13.02	12.18	11.41	10.70	10.05.	9.45	8.90	8.40	7.93	66
67	15.07	14.12	13.26	12.46	11.73	11.06	10.45	9.88	9.35	8.86	8.41	67
68	15.20	14.32	13.51	12.77	12.08	11.45	10.86	10.32	9.82	9.35	8.92	68
69	15.34	14.53	13.78	13.09	12.45	11.86	11.31	10.80	10.33	9.89	9.47	69
70	15.50	14.75	14.07	13.43	12.85	12.30	11.79	11.32	10.87	10.46	10.08	70

Table 24 Multipliers for loss of pension commencing age 70 (females)

Age at date of trial	Multiplier calculated with allowance for projected mortality from the 2004-based population projections and rate of return of											Age at date of trial
	0.0%	0.5%	1.0%	1.5%	2.0%	2.5%	3.0%	3.5%	4.0%	4.5%	5.0%	
0	21.54	14.21	9.41	6.25	4.17	2.80	1.88	1.27	0.86	0.58	0.40	0
1	21.54	14.28	9.50	6.35	4.26	2.87	1.94	1.31	0.89	0.61	0.42	1
2	21.45	14.29	9.56	6.42	4.33	2.93	1.99	1.36	0.93	0.64	0.44	2
3	21.35	14.30	9.62	6.49	4.40	2.99	2.04	1.40	0.96	0.66	0.46	3
4	21.26	14.31	9.68	6.57	4.47	3.06	2.10	1.44	1.00	0.69	0.48	4
5	21.17	14.32	9.73	6.64	4.54	3.12	2.15	1.49	1.03	0.72	0.50	5
6	21.07	14.34	9.79	6.71	4.62	3.19	2.21	1.54	1.07	0.75	0.53	6
7	20.98	14.35	9.85	6.79	4.69	3.26	2.27	1.59	1.11	0.78	0.55	7
8	20.88	14.36	9.91	6.86	4.77	3.33	2.33	1.64	1.15	0.81	0.58	8
9	20.79	14.37	9.96	6.94	4.85	3.40	2.39	1.69	1.19	0.85	0.60	9
10	20.70	14.38	10.02	7.01	4.93	3.47	2.45	1.74	1.24	0.88	0.63	10
11	20.60	14.39	10.08	7.09	5.00	3.54	2.52	1.80	1.28	0.92	0.66	11
12	20.51	14.39	10.14	7.17	5.09	3.62	2.59	1.85	1.33	0.96	0.69	12
13	20.41	14.40	10.20	7.25	5.17	3.70	2.65	1.91	1.38	1.00	0.73	13
14	20.32	14.41	10.26	7.33	5.25	3.78	2.72	1.97	1.43	1.04	0.76	14
15	20.23	14.42	10.32	7.41	5.33	3.86	2.80	2.03	1.48	1.08	0.80	15
16	20.14	14.43	10.38	7.49	5.42	3.94	2.87	2.10	1.54	1.13	0.83	16
17	20.05	14.44	10.44	7.57	5.51	4.02	2.95	2.16	1.59	1.18	0.87	17
18	19.96	14.45	10.50	7.66	5.60	4.11	3.02	2.23	1.65	1.23	0.91	18
19	19.87	14.46	10.56	7.74	5.69	4.20	3.10	2.30	1.71	1.28	0.96	19
20	19.78	14.47	10.62	7.82	5.78	4.28	3.19	2.37	1.78	1.33	1.00	20
21	19.69	14.48	10.69	7.91	5.87	4.38	3.27	2.45	1.84	1.39	1.05	21
22	19.60	14.49	10.75	8.00	5.97	4.47	3.36	2.53	1.91	1.45	1.10	22
23	19.52	14.50	10.81	8.09	6.07	4.56	3.44	2.61	1.98	1.51	1.15	23
24	19.43	14.51	10.87	8.17	6.16	4.66	3.54	2.69	2.05	1.57	1.20	24
25	19.34	14.52	10.94	8.26	6.26	4.76	3.63	2.77	2.13	1.63	1.26	25
26	19.25	14.53	11.00	8.35	6.36	4.86	3.72	2.86	2.20	1.70	1.32	26
27	19.17	14.54	11.07	8.45	6.47	4.97	3.82	2.95	2.29	1.77	1.38	27
28	19.08	14.55	11.13	8.54	6.57	5.07	3.92	3.05	2.37	1.85	1.44	28
29	18.99	14.56	11.20	8.63	6.68	5.18	4.03	3.14	2.46	1.92	1.51	29
30	18.91	14.57	11.26	8.73	6.79	5.29	4.13	3.24	2.55	2.01	1.58	30
31	18.82	14.58	11.33	8.82	6.89	5.40	4.24	3.34	2.64	2.09	1.66	31
32	18.74	14.59	11.39	8.92	7.01	5.52	4.36	3.45	2.74	2.18	1.73	32
33	18.66	14.60	11.46	9.02	7.12	5.64	4.47	3.56	2.84	2.27	1.82	33
34	18.57	14.61	11.53	9.12	7.24	5.76	4.59	3.67	2.94	2.36	1.90	34
35	18.49	14.62	11.60	9.22	7.35	5.88	4.71	3.79	3.05	2.46	1.99	35

APIL Guide to Damages

Age at date of trial	Multiplier calculated with allowance for projected mortality from the 2004-based population projections and rate of return of											Age at date of trial
	0.0%	0.5%	1.0%	1.5%	2.0%	2.5%	3.0%	3.5%	4.0%	4.5%	5.0%	
36	18.41	14.63	11.67	9.32	7.47	6.00	4.84	3.90	3.16	2.56	2.08	36
37	18.33	14.65	11.74	9.43	7.59	6.13	4.96	4.03	3.28	2.67	2.18	37
38	18.25	14.66	11.81	9.53	7.72	6.26	5.10	4.16	3.40	2.78	2.29	38
39	18.17	14.67	11.88	9.64	7.84	6.40	5.23	4.29	3.52	2.90	2.39	39
40	18.10	14.69	11.95	9.75	7.97	6.54	5.37	4.43	3.65	3.02	2.51	40
41	18.03	14.70	12.03	9.86	8.11	6.68	5.52	4.57	3.79	3.15	2.62	41
42	17.95	14.72	12.10	9.98	8.24	6.83	5.67	4.71	3.93	3.28	2.75	42
43	17.88	14.74	12.18	10.09	8.38	6.97	5.82	4.86	4.08	3.42	2.88	43
44	17.82	14.76	12.26	10.21	8.52	7.13	5.98	5.02	4.23	3.57	3.02	44
45	17.75	14.79	12.35	10.33	8.67	7.29	6.14	5.19	4.39	3.72	3.16	45
46	17.70	14.81	12.43	10.46	8.82	7.45	6.31	5.36	4.55	3.88	3.31	46
47	17.64	14.84	12.52	10.59	8.97	7.62	6.49	5.53	4.73	4.05	3.47	47
48	17.59	14.88	12.61	10.72	9.13	7.79	6.67	5.71	4.91	4.22	3.64	48
49	17.54	14.91	12.71	10.86	9.29	7.97	6.86	5.91	5.10	4.41	3.82	49
50	17.50	14.96	12.81	11.00	9.46	8.16	7.05	6.10	5.29	4.60	4.01	50
51	17.46	15.00	12.92	11.15	9.64	8.35	7.25	6.31	5.50	4.80	4.20	51
52	17.43	15.05	13.03	11.30	9.82	8.55	7.47	6.53	5.72	5.02	4.41	52
53	17.40	15.10	13.14	11.45	10.01	8.76	7.68	6.75	5.94	5.24	4.63	53
54	17.37	15.15	13.25	11.61	10.20	8.97	7.91	6.98	6.18	5.47	4.86	54
55	17.33	15.20	13.36	11.77	10.39	9.19	8.14	7.22	6.42	5.72	5.10	55
56	17.30	15.26	13.48	11.93	10.58	9.41	8.38	7.47	6.67	5.97	5.36	56
57	17.28	15.31	13.60	12.10	10.79	9.63	8.62	7.73	6.94	6.24	5.62	57
58	17.26	15.37	13.72	12.27	11.00	9.87	8.88	8.00	7.22	6.52	5.91	58
59	17.24	15.44	13.85	12.45	11.22	10.12	9.15	8.28	7.51	6.82	6.21	59
60	17.24	15.52	14.00	12.65	11.45	10.38	9.43	8.58	7.82	7.14	6.52	60
61	17.25	15.61	14.15	12.85	11.69	10.66	9.73	8.90	8.15	7.47	6.87	61
62	17.27	15.71	14.31	13.07	11.95	10.95	10.04	9.23	8.49	7.83	7.23	62
63	17.31	15.82	14.49	13.29	12.22	11.25	10.37	9.58	8.86	8.21	7.62	63
64	17.35	15.94	14.68	13.53	12.50	11.57	10.72	9.95	9.25	8.61	8.03	64
65	17.40	16.07	14.87	13.79	12.80	11.90	11.09	10.34	9.66	9.04	8.47	65
66	17.46	16.21	15.08	14.05	13.11	12.26	11.47	10.76	10.10	9.49	8.94	66
67	17.53	16.36	15.30	14.32	13.44	12.62	11.88	11.19	10.56	9.98	9.44	67
68	17.60	16.51	15.52	14.61	13.77	13.00	12.30	11.64	11.04	10.48	9.97	68
69	17.67	16.66	15.74	14.90	14.12	13.40	12.73	12.12	11.55	11.02	10.53	69
70	17.74	16.82	15.97	15.19	14.47	13.81	13.19	12.62	12.09	11.59	11.13	70

Table 25 Multipliers for loss of pension commencing age 75 (males)

Age at date of trial	Multiplier calculated with allowance for projected mortality from the 2004-based population projections and rate of return of											Age at date of trial
	0.0%	0.5%	1.0%	1.5%	2.0%	2.5%	3.0%	3.5%	4.0%	4.5%	5.0%	
0	14.52	9.46	6.18	4.06	2.67	1.76	1.17	0.78	0.52	0.35	0.23	0
1	14.50	9.49	6.24	4.11	2.72	1.81	1.20	0.80	0.54	0.36	0.24	1
2	14.41	9.48	6.26	4.15	2.76	1.84	1.23	0.83	0.56	0.38	0.26	2
3	14.31	9.47	6.29	4.19	2.80	1.88	1.26	0.85	0.58	0.39	0.27	3
4	14.22	9.46	6.31	4.23	2.84	1.91	1.29	0.88	0.60	0.41	0.28	4
5	14.12	9.44	6.33	4.26	2.88	1.95	1.33	0.90	0.62	0.42	0.29	5
6	14.03	9.43	6.36	4.30	2.92	1.99	1.36	0.93	0.64	0.44	0.30	6
7	13.93	9.41	6.38	4.34	2.96	2.03	1.39	0.96	0.66	0.46	0.32	7
8	13.84	9.40	6.40	4.38	3.00	2.06	1.42	0.99	0.68	0.48	0.33	8
9	13.74	9.38	6.42	4.41	3.04	2.10	1.46	1.01	0.71	0.49	0.35	9
10	13.65	9.36	6.45	4.45	3.08	2.14	1.49	1.04	0.73	0.51	0.36	10
11	13.56	9.35	6.47	4.49	3.13	2.18	1.53	1.07	0.76	0.53	0.38	11
12	13.46	9.33	6.49	4.53	3.17	2.22	1.57	1.11	0.78	0.56	0.40	12
13	13.37	9.32	6.51	4.57	3.21	2.27	1.60	1.14	0.81	0.58	0.41	13
14	13.27	9.30	6.53	4.61	3.26	2.31	1.64	1.17	0.84	0.60	0.43	14
15	13.18	9.28	6.56	4.65	3.30	2.35	1.68	1.20	0.87	0.62	0.45	15
16	13.09	9.27	6.58	4.69	3.35	2.40	1.72	1.24	0.90	0.65	0.47	16
17	13.00	9.25	6.60	4.73	3.39	2.44	1.76	1.28	0.93	0.67	0.49	17
18	12.91	9.24	6.63	4.77	3.44	2.49	1.81	1.31	0.96	0.70	0.51	18
19	12.83	9.22	6.65	4.81	3.49	2.54	1.85	1.35	0.99	0.73	0.54	19
20	12.74	9.21	6.67	4.85	3.54	2.58	1.89	1.39	1.02	0.76	0.56	20
21	12.66	9.19	6.70	4.89	3.59	2.63	1.94	1.43	1.06	0.79	0.59	21
22	12.57	9.18	6.72	4.94	3.64	2.68	1.99	1.47	1.10	0.82	0.61	22
23	12.49	9.17	6.75	4.98	3.69	2.74	2.04	1.52	1.13	0.85	0.64	23
24	12.41	9.16	6.77	5.03	3.74	2.79	2.08	1.56	1.17	0.88	0.67	24
25	12.32	9.14	6.80	5.07	3.79	2.84	2.13	1.61	1.21	0.92	0.70	25
26	12.24	9.12	6.82	5.11	3.84	2.89	2.19	1.66	1.26	0.96	0.73	26
27	12.16	9.11	6.85	5.16	3.90	2.95	2.24	1.70	1.30	0.99	0.76	27
28	12.08	9.10	6.87	5.21	3.95	3.01	2.29	1.75	1.34	1.03	0.79	28
29	12.00	9.09	6.90	5.25	4.01	3.07	2.35	1.81	1.39	1.07	0.83	29
30	11.92	9.08	6.93	5.30	4.06	3.12	2.41	1.86	1.44	1.12	0.87	30
31	11.85	9.06	6.95	5.35	4.12	3.18	2.47	1.91	1.49	1.16	0.91	31
32	11.77	9.05	6.98	5.39	4.18	3.25	2.53	1.97	1.54	1.21	0.95	32
33	11.69	9.04	7.01	5.44	4.24	3.31	2.59	2.03	1.59	1.25	0.99	33
34	11.62	9.03	7.03	5.49	4.30	3.37	2.65	2.09	1.65	1.30	1.03	34
35	11.54	9.02	7.06	5.54	4.36	3.44	2.72	2.15	1.71	1.36	1.08	35

Age at date of trial	Multiplier calculated with allowance for projected mortality from the 2004-based population projections and rate of return of											Age at date of trial
36	11.46	9.00	7.09	5.59	4.42	3.50	2.78	2.21	1.76	1.41	1.13	36
37	11.39	8.99	7.11	5.64	4.48	3.57	2.85	2.28	1.83	1.47	1.18	37
38	11.32	8.98	7.14	5.69	4.55	3.64	2.92	2.35	1.89	1.52	1.23	38
39	11.25	8.97	7.17	5.74	4.61	3.71	2.99	2.42	1.96	1.59	1.29	39
40	11.18	8.96	7.20	5.80	4.68	3.78	3.06	2.49	2.02	1.65	1.35	40
41	11.11	8.95	7.23	5.85	4.75	3.86	3.14	2.56	2.09	1.72	1.41	41
42	11.04	8.94	7.26	5.91	4.81	3.93	3.22	2.64	2.17	1.78	1.47	42
43	10.97	8.94	7.29	5.96	4.89	4.01	3.30	2.72	2.24	1.86	1.54	43
44	10.91	8.93	7.33	6.02	4.96	4.09	3.38	2.80	2.32	1.93	1.61	44
45	10.85	8.93	7.36	6.08	5.03	4.17	3.47	2.89	2.41	2.01	1.68	45
46	10.79	8.93	7.40	6.14	5.11	4.26	3.56	2.97	2.49	2.09	1.76	46
47	10.74	8.93	7.44	6.21	5.19	4.35	3.65	3.07	2.58	2.18	1.84	47
48	10.69	8.93	7.48	6.27	5.27	4.44	3.74	3.16	2.68	2.27	1.93	48
49	10.64	8.94	7.53	6.35	5.36	4.54	3.84	3.26	2.78	2.36	2.02	49
50	10.60	8.95	7.57	6.42	5.45	4.64	3.95	3.37	2.88	2.47	2.11	50
51	10.57	8.97	7.63	6.50	5.54	4.74	4.06	3.48	2.99	2.57	2.22	51
52	10.54	8.99	7.69	6.58	5.64	4.85	4.17	3.60	3.10	2.68	2.32	52
53	10.52	9.02	7.75	6.67	5.75	4.96	4.29	3.72	3.22	2.80	2.44	53
54	10.49	9.04	7.81	6.75	5.85	5.08	4.41	3.84	3.35	2.92	2.56	54
55	10.47	9.07	7.87	6.84	5.96	5.20	4.54	3.97	3.48	3.05	2.68	55
56	10.44	9.09	7.93	6.93	6.07	5.32	4.67	4.10	3.61	3.19	2.81	56
57	10.41	9.11	7.99	7.02	6.18	5.44	4.80	4.24	3.75	3.33	2.95	57
58	10.39	9.14	8.06	7.11	6.29	5.57	4.94	4.39	3.90	3.47	3.10	58
59	10.37	9.17	8.13	7.21	6.41	5.70	5.08	4.54	4.05	3.63	3.25	59
60	10.36	9.21	8.20	7.32	6.53	5.84	5.23	4.70	4.22	3.79	3.41	60
61	10.36	9.26	8.29	7.43	6.67	6.00	5.40	4.87	4.39	3.97	3.59	61
62	10.37	9.32	8.39	7.56	6.82	6.16	5.57	5.05	4.58	4.16	3.78	62
63	10.40	9.39	8.49	7.69	6.98	6.34	5.76	5.24	4.78	4.36	3.99	63
64	10.43	9.47	8.61	7.84	7.15	6.52	5.96	5.45	5.00	4.58	4.21	64
65	10.48	9.56	8.74	8.00	7.33	6.72	6.17	5.68	5.23	4.82	4.44	65
66	10.53	9.66	8.87	8.16	7.52	6.93	6.40	5.91	5.47	5.07	4.70	66
67	10.59	9.77	9.02	8.33	7.71	7.15	6.63	6.16	5.73	5.33	4.97	67
68	10.65	9.87	9.16	8.51	7.92	7.38	6.88	6.42	6.00	5.61	5.25	68
69	10.72	9.99	9.32	8.70	8.14	7.62	7.14	6.70	6.29	5.91	5.56	69
70	10.80	10.11	9.48	8.90	8.36	7.87	7.41	6.99	6.60	6.23	5.89	70
71	10.88	10.25	9.66	9.11	8.61	8.14	7.71	7.30	6.93	6.58	6.25	71
72	10.99	10.41	9.86	9.35	8.88	8.44	8.03	7.65	7.29	6.96	6.65	72
73	11.14	10.60	10.09	9.63	9.19	8.78	8.40	8.04	7.70	7.39	7.09	73
74	11.33	10.83	10.37	9.94	9.54	9.16	8.81	8.48	8.16	7.87	7.59	74

Age at date of trial	Multiplier calculated with allowance for projected mortality from the 2004-based population projections and rate of return of											Age at date of trial
75	11.57	11.13	10.71	10.32	9.95	9.61	9.29	8.98	8.70	8.42	8.17	75

Table 26 Multipliers for loss of pension commencing age 75 (females)

Age at date of trial	Multiplier calculated with allowance for projected mortality from the 2004-based population projections and rate of return of											Age at date of trial
	0.0%	0.5%	1.0%	1.5%	2.0%	2.5%	3.0%	3.5%	4.0%	4.5%	5.0%	
0	17.05	11.07	7.22	4.72	3.10	2.04	1.35	0.90	0.60	0.40	0.27	0
1	17.03	11.12	7.29	4.79	3.16	2.10	1.39	0.93	0.62	0.42	0.28	1
2	16.94	11.12	7.33	4.84	3.21	2.14	1.43	0.96	0.64	0.43	0.29	2
3	16.85	11.12	7.36	4.89	3.26	2.18	1.47	0.99	0.67	0.45	0.31	3
4	16.76	11.12	7.40	4.94	3.31	2.23	1.50	1.02	0.69	0.47	0.32	4
5	16.67	11.11	7.44	4.99	3.36	2.27	1.54	1.05	0.72	0.49	0.34	5
6	16.58	11.11	7.47	5.04	3.41	2.32	1.58	1.08	0.74	0.51	0.35	6
7	16.49	11.11	7.51	5.09	3.47	2.37	1.62	1.11	0.77	0.53	0.37	7
8	16.40	11.11	7.55	5.15	3.52	2.42	1.66	1.15	0.79	0.55	0.38	8
9	16.31	11.10	7.58	5.20	3.57	2.46	1.70	1.18	0.82	0.57	0.40	9
10	16.22	11.10	7.62	5.25	3.63	2.51	1.75	1.22	0.85	0.60	0.42	10
11	16.14	11.10	7.66	5.30	3.68	2.57	1.79	1.26	0.88	0.62	0.44	11
12	16.05	11.09	7.70	5.35	3.74	2.62	1.84	1.29	0.91	0.65	0.46	12
13	15.96	11.09	7.73	5.41	3.79	2.67	1.88	1.33	0.95	0.67	0.48	13
14	15.87	11.09	7.77	5.46	3.85	2.72	1.93	1.37	0.98	0.70	0.50	14
15	15.78	11.08	7.81	5.52	3.91	2.78	1.98	1.42	1.02	0.73	0.53	15
16	15.70	11.08	7.84	5.57	3.97	2.84	2.03	1.46	1.05	0.76	0.55	16
17	15.61	11.08	7.88	5.63	4.03	2.89	2.08	1.50	1.09	0.79	0.58	17
18	15.53	11.07	7.92	5.68	4.09	2.95	2.14	1.55	1.13	0.82	0.60	18
19	15.44	11.07	7.96	5.74	4.15	3.01	2.19	1.60	1.17	0.86	0.63	19
20	15.36	11.07	8.00	5.80	4.22	3.07	2.25	1.65	1.21	0.89	0.66	20
21	15.27	11.06	8.04	5.86	4.28	3.14	2.30	1.70	1.25	0.93	0.69	21
22	15.19	11.06	8.08	5.91	4.34	3.20	2.36	1.75	1.30	0.97	0.72	22
23	15.10	11.06	8.12	5.97	4.41	3.26	2.42	1.80	1.34	1.00	0.75	23
24	15.02	11.05	8.15	6.03	4.48	3.33	2.48	1.86	1.39	1.05	0.79	24
25	14.94	11.05	8.19	6.09	4.54	3.40	2.55	1.91	1.44	1.09	0.82	25
26	14.85	11.04	8.23	6.15	4.61	3.47	2.61	1.97	1.49	1.13	0.86	26
27	14.77	11.04	8.27	6.21	4.68	3.54	2.68	2.03	1.55	1.18	0.90	27
28	14.69	11.04	8.31	6.28	4.75	3.61	2.74	2.09	1.60	1.23	0.94	28
29	14.61	11.03	8.35	6.34	4.82	3.68	2.81	2.16	1.66	1.28	0.99	29
30	14.53	11.03	8.39	6.40	4.90	3.75	2.89	2.22	1.72	1.33	1.03	30
31	14.45	11.02	8.43	6.46	4.97	3.83	2.96	2.29	1.78	1.38	1.08	31
32	14.37	11.02	8.47	6.53	5.04	3.91	3.03	2.36	1.84	1.44	1.13	32
33	14.29	11.01	8.51	6.59	5.12	3.99	3.11	2.43	1.91	1.50	1.18	33
34	14.21	11.01	8.55	6.66	5.20	4.07	3.19	2.51	1.97	1.56	1.23	34
35	14.13	11.01	8.59	6.73	5.28	4.15	3.27	2.58	2.04	1.62	1.29	35

Age at date of trial	Multiplier calculated with allowance for projected mortality from the 2004-based population projections and rate of return of										Age at date of trial
36	14.05	11.00	8.63	6.79	5.36	4.23	3.35	2.66	2.12	1.69	1.35	36
37	13.98	11.00	8.68	6.86	5.44	4.32	3.44	2.74	2.19	1.76	1.41	37
38	13.90	11.00	8.72	6.93	5.52	4.41	3.53	2.83	2.27	1.83	1.47	38
39	13.83	10.99	8.76	7.00	5.60	4.50	3.62	2.91	2.35	1.90	1.54	39
40	13.75	10.99	8.81	7.07	5.69	4.59	3.71	3.00	2.44	1.98	1.61	40
41	13.68	10.99	8.85	7.14	5.78	4.68	3.80	3.10	2.52	2.06	1.69	41
42	13.61	10.99	8.90	7.22	5.87	4.78	3.90	3.19	2.61	2.15	1.77	42
43	13.54	11.00	8.95	7.29	5.96	4.88	4.00	3.29	2.71	2.23	1.85	43
44	13.48	11.00	8.99	7.37	6.05	4.98	4.11	3.39	2.81	2.33	1.93	44
45	13.42	11.00	9.04	7.45	6.15	5.09	4.21	3.50	2.91	2.42	2.02	45
46	13.36	11.01	9.10	7.53	6.25	5.19	4.32	3.61	3.02	2.52	2.12	46
47	13.30	11.02	9.15	7.62	6.35	5.30	4.44	3.72	3.13	2.63	2.22	47
48	13.24	11.03	9.21	7.70	6.45	5.42	4.56	3.84	3.24	2.74	2.32	48
49	13.19	11.05	9.27	7.79	6.56	5.54	4.68	3.96	3.36	2.86	2.43	49
50	13.14	11.06	9.33	7.88	6.67	5.66	4.81	4.09	3.49	2.98	2.55	50
51	13.10	11.08	9.40	7.98	6.79	5.79	4.94	4.23	3.62	3.11	2.67	51
52	13.06	11.11	9.46	8.08	6.91	5.92	5.08	4.37	3.76	3.24	2.80	52
53	13.02	11.13	9.53	8.18	7.03	6.05	5.22	4.51	3.90	3.38	2.93	53
54	12.98	11.16	9.60	8.28	7.15	6.19	5.37	4.66	4.05	3.53	3.08	54
55	12.94	11.18	9.67	8.38	7.28	6.33	5.52	4.81	4.21	3.68	3.23	55
56	12.91	11.20	9.74	8.49	7.41	6.48	5.67	4.97	4.37	3.84	3.38	56
57	12.87	11.23	9.82	8.60	7.54	6.62	5.83	5.14	4.53	4.01	3.55	57
58	12.84	11.26	9.89	8.71	7.68	6.78	5.99	5.31	4.71	4.18	3.72	58
59	12.81	11.30	9.98	8.83	7.82	6.94	6.17	5.49	4.89	4.37	3.90	59
60	12.79	11.34	10.06	8.95	7.97	7.11	6.35	5.68	5.09	4.56	4.10	60
61	12.78	11.39	10.16	9.08	8.13	7.29	6.54	5.88	5.29	4.77	4.30	61
62	12.78	11.44	10.26	9.22	8.29	7.47	6.74	6.09	5.51	4.99	4.53	62
63	12.79	11.51	10.38	9.37	8.47	7.67	6.95	6.31	5.74	5.22	4.76	63
64	12.80	11.58	10.49	9.52	8.65	7.88	7.18	6.55	5.98	5.47	5.01	64
65	12.82	11.66	10.62	9.69	8.85	8.09	7.41	6.80	6.24	5.74	5.28	65
66	12.84	11.74	10.75	9.86	9.05	8.32	7.66	7.06	6.51	6.01	5.56	66
67	12.87	11.83	10.89	10.03	9.26	8.55	7.91	7.33	6.79	6.31	5.86	67
68	12.90	11.91	11.02	10.21	9.47	8.79	8.17	7.61	7.09	6.61	6.18	68
69	12.92	12.00	11.15	10.38	9.68	9.03	8.44	7.90	7.40	6.94	6.51	69
70	12.94	12.07	11.29	10.56	9.90	9.28	8.72	8.20	7.72	7.27	6.86	70
71	12.95	12.16	11.42	10.74	10.12	9.54	9.01	8.51	8.05	7.63	7.23	71
72	12.98	12.25	11.57	10.94	10.36	9.82	9.32	8.85	8.41	8.01	7.63	72
73	13.03	12.36	11.74	11.16	10.62	10.12	9.65	9.21	8.81	8.42	8.07	73
74	13.11	12.50	11.94	11.41	10.91	10.45	10.02	9.62	9.24	8.88	8.55	74

Age at date of trial	Multiplier calculated with allowance for projected mortality from the 2004-based population projections and rate of return of											Age at date of trial
75	13.24	12.69	12.18	11.71	11.26	10.84	10.45	10.08	9.73	9.40	9.10	75

Table 27 Discounting factors for term certain

Factor to discount value of multiplier for a period of deferment

Term	0.5%	1.0%	1.5%	2.0%	2.5%	3.0%	3.5%	4.0%	4.5%	5.0%	Term
1	0.9950	0.9901	0.9852	0.9804	0.9756	0.9709	0.9662	0.9615	0.9569	0.9524	1
2	0.9901	0.9803	0.9707	0.9612	0.9518	0.9426	0.9335	0.9246	0.9157	0.9070	2
3	0.9851	0.9706	0.9563	0.9423	0.9286	0.9151	0.9019	0.8890	0.8763	0.8638	3
4	0.9802	0.9610	0.9422	0.9238	0.9060	0.8885	0.8714	0.8548	0.8386	0.8227	4
5	0.9754	0.9515	0.9283	0.9057	0.8839	0.8626	0.8420	0.8219	0.8025	0.7835	5
6	0.9705	0.9420	0.9145	0.8880	0.8623	0.8375	0.8135	0.7903	0.7679	0.7462	6
7	0.9657	0.9327	0.9010	0.8706	0.8413	0.8131	0.7860	0.7599	0.7348	0.7107	7
8	0.9609	0.9235	0.8877	0.8535	0.8207	0.7894	0.7594	0.7307	0.7032	0.6768	8
9	0.9561	0.9143	0.8746	0.8368	0.8007	0.7664	0.7337	0.7026	0.6729	0.6446	9
10	0.9513	0.9053	0.8617	0.8203	0.7812	0.7441	0.7089	0.6756	0.6439	0.6139	10
11	0.9466	0.8963	0.8489	0.8043	0.7621	0.7224	0.6849	0.6496	0.6162	0.5847	11
12	0.9419	0.8874	0.8364	0.7885	0.7436	0.7014	0.6618	0.6246	0.5897	0.5568	12
13	0.9372	0.8787	0.8240	0.7730	0.7254	0.6810	0.6394	0.6006	0.5643	0.5303	13
14	0.9326	0.8700	0.8118	0.7579	0.7077	0.6611	0.6178	0.5775	0.5400	0.5051	14
15	0.9279	0.8613	0.7999	0.7430	0.6905	0.6419	0.5969	0.5553	0.5167	0.4810	15
16	0.9233	0.8528	0.7880	0.7284	0.6736	0.6232	0.5767	0.5339	0.4945	0.4581	16
17	0.9187	0.8444	0.7764	0.7142	0.6572	0.6050	0.5572	0.5134	0.4732	0.4363	17
18	0.9141	0.8360	0.7649	0.7002	0.6412	0.5874	0.5384	0.4936	0.4528	0.4155	18
19	0.9096	0.8277	0.7536	0.6864	0.6255	0.5703	0.5202	0.4746	0.4333	0.3957	19
20	0.9051	0.8195	0.7425	0.6730	0.6103	0.5537	0.5026	0.4564	0.4146	0.3769	20
21	0.9006	0.8114	0.7315	0.6598	0.5954	0.5375	0.4856	0.4388	0.3968	0.3589	21
22	0.8961	0.8034	0.7207	0.6468	0.5809	0.5219	0.4692	0.4220	0.3797	0.3418	22
23	0.8916	0.7954	0.7100	0.6342	0.5667	0.5067	0.4533	0.4057	0.3634	0.3256	23
24	0.8872	0.7876	0.6995	0.6217	0.5529	0.4919	0.4380	0.3901	0.3477	0.3101	24
25	0.8828	0.7798	0.6892	0.6095	0.5394	0.4776	0.4231	0.3751	0.3327	0.2953	25
26	0.8784	0.7720	0.6790	0.5976	0.5262	0.4637	0.4088	0.3607	0.3184	0.2812	26
27	0.8740	0.7644	0.6690	0.5859	0.5134	0.4502	0.3950	0.3468	0.3047	0.2678	27
28	0.8697	0.7568	0.6591	0.5744	0.5009	0.4371	0.3817	0.3335	0.2916	0.2551	28
29	0.8653	0.7493	0.6494	0.5631	0.4887	0.4243	0.3687	0.3207	0.2790	0.2429	29
30	0.8610	0.7419	0.6398	0.5521	0.4767	0.4120	0.3563	0.3083	0.2670	0.2314	30
31	0.8567	0.7346	0.6303	0.5412	0.4651	0.4000	0.3442	0.2965	0.2555	0.2204	31
32	0.8525	0.7273	0.6210	0.5306	0.4538	0.3883	0.3326	0.2851	0.2445	0.2099	32
33	0.8482	0.7201	0.6118	0.5202	0.4427	0.3770	0.3213	0.2741	0.2340	0.1999	33
34	0.8440	0.7130	0.6028	0.5100	0.4319	0.3660	0.3105	0.2636	0.2239	0.1904	34
35	0.8398	0.7059	0.5939	0.5000	0.4214	0.3554	0.3000	0.2534	0.2143	0.1813	35
36	0.8356	0.6989	0.5851	0.4902	0.4111	0.3450	0.2898	0.2437	0.2050	0.1727	36

APIL Guide to Damages

Factor to discount value of multiplier for a period of deferment

37	0.8315	0.6920	0.5764	0.4806	0.4011	0.3350	0.2800	0.2343	0.1962	0.1644	37
38	0.8274	0.6852	0.5679	0.4712	0.3913	0.3252	0.2706	0.2253	0.1878	0.1566	38
39	0.8232	0.6784	0.5595	0.4619	0.3817	0.3158	0.2614	0.2166	0.1797	0.1491	39
40	0.8191	0.6717	0.5513	0.4529	0.3724	0.3066	0.2526	0.2083	0.1719	0.1420	40
41	0.8151	0.6650	0.5431	0.4440	0.3633	0.2976	0.2440	0.2003	0.1645	0.1353	41
42	0.8110	0.6584	0.5351	0.4353	0.3545	0.2890	0.2358	0.1926	0.1574	0.1288	42
43	0.8070	0.6519	0.5272	0.4268	0.3458	0.2805	0.2278	0.1852	0.1507	0.1227	43
44	0.8030	0.6454	0.5194	0.4184	0.3374	0.2724	0.2201	0.1780	0.1442	0.1169	44
45	0.7990	0.6391	0.5117	0.4102	0.3292	0.2644	0.2127	0.1712	0.1380	0.1113	45
46	0.7950	0.6327	0.5042	0.4022	0.3211	0.2567	0.2055	0.1646	0.1320	0.1060	46
47	0.7910	0.6265	0.4967	0.3943	0.3133	0.2493	0.1985	0.1583	0.1263	0.1009	47
48	0.7871	0.6203	0.4894	0.3865	0.3057	0.2420	0.1918	0.1522	0.1209	0.0961	48
49	0.7832	0.6141	0.4821	0.3790	0.2982	0.2350	0.1853	0.1463	0.1157	0.0916	49
50	0.7793	0.6080	0.4750	0.3715	0.2909	0.2281	0.1791	0.1407	0.1107	0.0872	50
51	0.7754	0.6020	0.4680	0.3642	0.2838	0.2215	0.1730	0.1353	0.1059	0.0831	51
52	0.7716	0.5961	0.4611	0.3571	0.2769	0.2150	0.1671	0.1301	0.1014	0.0791	52
53	0.7677	0.5902	0.4543	0.3501	0.2702	0.2088	0.1615	0.1251	0.0970	0.0753	53
54	0.7639	0.5843	0.4475	0.3432	0.2636	0.2027	0.1560	0.1203	0.0928	0.0717	54
55	0.7601	0.5785	0.4409	0.3365	0.2572	0.1968	0.1508	0.1157	0.0888	0.0683	55
56	0.7563	0.5728	0.4344	0.3299	0.2509	0.1910	0.1457	0.1112	0.0850	0.0651	56
57	0.7525	0.5671	0.4280	0.3234	0.2448	0.1855	0.1407	0.1069	0.0814	0.0620	57
58	0.7488	0.5615	0.4217	0.3171	0.2388	0.1801	0.1360	0.1028	0.0778	0.0590	58
59	0.7451	0.5560	0.4154	0.3109	0.2330	0.1748	0.1314	0.0989	0.0745	0.0562	59
60	0.7414	0.5504	0.4093	0.3048	0.2273	0.1697	0.1269	0.0951	0.0713	0.0535	60
61	0.7377	0.5450	0.4032	0.2988	0.2217	0.1648	0.1226	0.0914	0.0682	0.0510	61
62	0.7340	0.5396	0.3973	0.2929	0.2163	0.1600	0.1185	0.0879	0.0653	0.0486	62
63	0.7304	0.5343	0.3914	0.2872	0.2111	0.1553	0.1145	0.0845	0.0625	0.0462	63
64	0.7267	0.5290	0.3856	0.2816	0.2059	0.1508	0.1106	0.0813	0.0598	0.0440	64
65	0.7231	0.5237	0.3799	0.2761	0.2009	0.1464	0.1069	0.0781	0.0572	0.0419	65
66	0.7195	0.5185	0.3743	0.2706	0.1960	0.1421	0.1033	0.0751	0.0547	0.0399	66
67	0.7159	0.5134	0.3688	0.2653	0.1912	0.1380	0.0998	0.0722	0.0524	0.0380	67
68	0.7124	0.5083	0.3633	0.2601	0.1865	0.1340	0.0964	0.0695	0.0501	0.0362	68
69	0.7088	0.5033	0.3580	0.2550	0.1820	0.1301	0.0931	0.0668	0.0480	0.0345	69
70	0.7053	0.4983	0.3527	0.2500	0.1776	0.1263	0.0900	0.0642	0.0459	0.0329	70
71	0.7018	0.4934	0.3475	0.2451	0.1732	0.1226	0.0869	0.0617	0.0439	0.0313	71
72	0.6983	0.4885	0.3423	0.2403	0.1690	0.1190	0.0840	0.0594	0.0420	0.0298	72
73	0.6948	0.4837	0.3373	0.2356	0.1649	0.1156	0.0812	0.0571	0.0402	0.0284	73
74	0.6914	0.4789	0.3323	0.2310	0.1609	0.1122	0.0784	0.0549	0.0385	0.0270	74
75	0.6879	0.4741	0.3274	0.2265	0.1569	0.1089	0.0758	0.0528	0.0368	0.0258	75
76	0.6845	0.4694	0.3225	0.2220	0.1531	0.1058	0.0732	0.0508	0.0353	0.0245	76

Factor to discount value of multiplier for a period of deferment

77	0.6811	0.4648	0.3178	0.2177	0.1494	0.1027	0.0707	0.0488	0.0337	0.0234	77
78	0.6777	0.4602	0.3131	0.2134	0.1457	0.0997	0.0683	0.0469	0.0323	0.0222	78
79	0.6743	0.4556	0.3084	0.2092	0.1422	0.0968	0.0660	0.0451	0.0309	0.0212	79
80	0.6710	0.4511	0.3039	0.2051	0.1387	0.0940	0.0638	0.0434	0.0296	0.0202	80

Table 28 Multipliers for pecuniary loss for term certain

Multiplier for regular frequent payments for a term certain at rate of return of

Term	0.5%	1.0%	1.5%	2.0%	2.5%	3.0%	3.5%	4.0%	4.5%	5.0%	Term
1	1.00	1.00	0.99	0.99	0.99	0.99	0.98	0.98	0.98	0.98	1
2	1.99	1.98	1.97	1.96	1.95	1.94	1.93	1.92	1.91	1.91	2
3	2.98	2.96	2.93	2.91	2.89	2.87	2.85	2.83	2.81	2.79	3
4	3.96	3.92	3.88	3.85	3.81	3.77	3.74	3.70	3.67	3.63	4
5	4.94	4.88	4.82	4.76	4.70	4.65	4.59	4.54	4.49	4.44	5
6	5.91	5.82	5.74	5.66	5.58	5.50	5.42	5.35	5.27	5.20	6
7	6.88	6.76	6.65	6.54	6.43	6.32	6.22	6.12	6.02	5.93	7
8	7.84	7.69	7.54	7.40	7.26	7.12	6.99	6.87	6.74	6.62	8
9	8.80	8.61	8.42	8.24	8.07	7.90	7.74	7.58	7.43	7.28	9
10	9.75	9.52	9.29	9.07	8.86	8.66	8.46	8.27	8.09	7.91	10
11	10.70	10.42	10.15	9.88	9.63	9.39	9.16	8.93	8.72	8.51	11
12	11.65	11.31	10.99	10.68	10.39	10.10	9.83	9.57	9.32	9.08	12
13	12.59	12.19	11.82	11.46	11.12	10.79	10.48	10.18	9.90	9.63	13
14	13.52	13.07	12.64	12.23	11.84	11.46	11.11	10.77	10.45	10.14	14
15	14.45	13.93	13.44	12.98	12.54	12.12	11.72	11.34	10.98	10.64	15
16	15.38	14.79	14.24	13.71	13.22	12.75	12.30	11.88	11.48	11.11	16
17	16.30	15.64	15.02	14.43	13.88	13.36	12.87	12.41	11.97	11.55	17
18	17.22	16.48	15.79	15.14	14.53	13.96	13.42	12.91	12.43	11.98	18
19	18.13	17.31	16.55	15.83	15.17	14.54	13.95	13.39	12.87	12.38	19
20	19.03	18.14	17.30	16.51	15.78	15.10	14.46	13.86	13.30	12.77	20
21	19.94	18.95	18.03	17.18	16.39	15.65	14.95	14.31	13.70	13.14	21
22	20.84	19.76	18.76	17.83	16.97	16.17	15.43	14.74	14.09	13.49	22
23	21.73	20.56	19.48	18.47	17.55	16.69	15.89	15.15	14.46	13.82	23
24	22.62	21.35	20.18	19.10	18.11	17.19	16.34	15.55	14.82	14.14	24
25	23.50	22.13	20.87	19.72	18.65	17.67	16.77	15.93	15.16	14.44	25
26	24.38	22.91	21.56	20.32	19.19	18.14	17.18	16.30	15.48	14.73	26
27	25.26	23.68	22.23	20.91	19.71	18.60	17.59	16.65	15.80	15.01	27
28	26.13	24.44	22.90	21.49	20.21	19.04	17.97	16.99	16.09	15.27	28
29	27.00	25.19	23.55	22.06	20.71	19.47	18.35	17.32	16.38	15.52	29
30	27.86	25.94	24.20	22.62	21.19	19.89	18.71	17.64	16.65	15.75	30
31	28.72	26.67	24.83	23.17	21.66	20.30	19.06	17.94	16.91	15.98	31
32	29.58	27.41	25.46	23.70	22.12	20.69	19.40	18.23	17.16	16.19	32
33	30.43	28.13	26.07	24.23	22.57	21.08	19.73	18.51	17.40	16.40	33
34	31.27	28.85	26.68	24.74	23.01	21.45	20.04	18.78	17.63	16.59	34
35	32.12	29.56	27.28	25.25	23.43	21.81	20.35	19.04	17.85	16.78	35
36	32.95	30.26	27.87	25.74	23.85	22.16	20.64	19.28	18.06	16.96	36

Multiplier for regular frequent payments for a term certain at rate of return of

37	33.79	30.95	28.45	26.23	24.26	22.50	20.93	19.52	18.26	17.13	37
38	34.62	31.64	29.02	26.70	24.65	22.83	21.20	19.75	18.45	17.29	38
39	35.44	32.32	29.58	27.17	25.04	23.15	21.47	19.97	18.64	17.44	39
40	36.26	33.00	30.14	27.63	25.42	23.46	21.73	20.19	18.81	17.58	40
41	37.08	33.67	30.69	28.08	25.78	23.76	21.97	20.39	18.98	17.72	41
42	37.89	34.33	31.23	28.52	26.14	24.06	22.21	20.59	19.14	17.86	42
43	38.70	34.98	31.76	28.95	26.49	24.34	22.45	20.78	19.30	17.98	43
44	39.51	35.63	32.28	29.37	26.83	24.62	22.67	20.96	19.44	18.10	44
45	40.31	36.27	32.80	29.78	27.17	24.88	22.89	21.13	19.58	18.21	45
46	41.10	36.91	33.30	30.19	27.49	25.15	23.10	21.30	19.72	18.32	46
47	41.90	37.54	33.80	30.59	27.81	25.40	23.30	21.46	19.85	18.43	47
48	42.69	38.16	34.30	30.98	28.12	25.64	23.49	21.62	19.97	18.53	48
49	43.47	38.78	34.78	31.36	28.42	25.88	23.68	21.77	20.09	18.62	49
50	44.25	39.39	35.26	31.74	28.72	26.11	23.86	21.91	20.20	18.71	50
51	45.03	40.00	35.73	32.10	29.00	26.34	24.04	22.05	20.31	18.79	51
52	45.80	40.60	36.20	32.47	29.28	26.56	24.21	22.18	20.42	18.87	52
53	46.57	41.19	36.66	32.82	29.56	26.77	24.37	22.31	20.51	18.95	53
54	47.34	41.78	37.11	33.17	29.82	26.97	24.53	22.43	20.61	19.03	54
55	48.10	42.36	37.55	33.51	30.08	27.17	24.69	22.55	20.70	19.10	55
56	48.86	42.93	37.99	33.84	30.34	27.37	24.83	22.66	20.79	19.16	56
57	49.61	43.50	38.42	34.17	30.59	27.56	24.98	22.77	20.87	19.23	57
58	50.36	44.07	38.84	34.49	30.83	27.74	25.12	22.88	20.95	19.29	58
59	51.11	44.63	39.26	34.80	31.06	27.92	25.25	22.98	21.03	19.34	59
60	51.85	45.18	39.67	35.11	31.29	28.09	25.38	23.07	21.10	19.40	60
61	52.59	45.73	40.08	35.41	31.52	28.26	25.50	23.17	21.17	19.45	61
62	53.33	46.27	40.48	35.70	31.74	28.42	25.62	23.26	21.24	19.50	62
63	54.06	46.81	40.88	36.00	31.95	28.58	25.74	23.34	21.30	19.55	63
64	54.79	47.34	41.26	36.28	32.16	28.73	25.85	23.42	21.36	19.59	64
65	55.52	47.86	41.65	36.56	32.36	28.88	25.96	23.50	21.42	19.64	65
66	56.24	48.39	42.02	36.83	32.56	29.02	26.07	23.58	21.47	19.68	66
67	56.95	48.90	42.40	37.10	32.75	29.16	26.17	23.65	21.53	19.72	67
68	57.67	49.41	42.76	37.36	32.94	29.30	26.27	23.73	21.58	19.75	68
69	58.38	49.92	43.12	37.62	33.13	29.43	26.36	23.79	21.63	19.79	69
70	59.09	50.42	43.48	37.87	33.31	29.56	26.45	23.86	21.68	19.82	70
71	59.79	50.91	43.83	38.12	33.48	29.68	26.54	23.92	21.72	19.85	71
72	60.49	51.41	44.17	38.36	33.65	29.80	26.63	23.98	21.76	19.88	72
73	61.19	51.89	44.51	38.60	33.82	29.92	26.71	24.04	21.80	19.91	73
74	61.88	52.37	44.85	38.83	33.98	30.03	26.79	24.10	21.84	19.94	74
75	62.57	52.85	45.18	39.06	34.14	30.15	26.87	24.15	21.88	19.97	75
76	63.26	53.32	45.50	39.29	34.30	30.25	26.94	24.20	21.92	19.99	76

Multiplier for regular frequent payments for a term certain at rate of return of

77	63.94	53.79	45.82	39.51	34.45	30.36	27.01	24.25	21.95	20.02	77
78	64.62	54.25	46.14	39.72	34.60	30.46	27.08	24.30	21.99	20.04	78
79	65.29	54.71	46.45	39.93	34.74	30.56	27.15	24.35	22.02	20.06	79
80	65.97	55.16	46.75	40.14	34.88	30.65	27.21	24.39	22.05	20.08	80

Actuarial Formulae and Basis

The functions tabulated are:

- Mortality assumptions for 2004-based official population projections for the United Kingdom.

- Loadings: none.

- Rate of return: as stated in the Tables.

Tables 1 and 2	$\bar{a}_x$
Tables 3 and 4	$\bar{a}_{x\,:\,\overline{50-x}}$
Tables 5 and 6	$\bar{a}_{x\,:\,\overline{55-x}}$
Tables 7 and 8	$\bar{a}_{x\,:\,\overline{60-x}}$
Tables 9 and 10	$\bar{a}_{x\,:\,\overline{65-x}}$
Tables 11 and 12	$\bar{a}_{x\,:\,\overline{70-x}}$
Tables 13 and 14	$\bar{a}_{x\,:\,\overline{75-x}}$
Tables 15 and 16	$_{(50-x)}\vert\,\bar{a}_x$
Tables 17 and 18	$_{(55-x)}\vert\,\bar{a}_x$
Tables 19 and 20	$_{(60-x)}\vert\,\bar{a}_x$
Tables 21 and 22	$_{(65-x)}\vert\,\bar{a}_x$
Tables 23 and 24	$_{(70-x)}\vert\,\bar{a}_x$
Tables 25 and 26	$_{(75-x)}\vert\,\bar{a}_x$
Table 27:	$1\,/\,(1+i)^n$
Table 28:	$\bar{a}_{\overline{n}\vert}$

INDEX

References are to paragraph numbers.